THE
VETERAN
NEXT DOOR

THE
VETERAN
NEXT DOOR

Stories from World War II - Vol. 1
1939 – 1946

A compelling collection of stories told and retold from the battlefronts of America's wars. Join Randall Baxter as he introduces us to veterans of our wars as they share their stories of loss, their lives, their heart aches, their victories, all up close, real life and personal encounters. You don't want to miss this. The Veteran Next Door, with host Randall Baxter.

Description by
Bob and Kim Thomas

RANDALL BAXTER

The Veteran Next Door

Printed in the United States of America
ISBN 978-1-967279-58-6 (sc)
ISBN 978-1-967279-59-3 (e)

2025.08.20

This book is printed on acid-free paper.

BlueInk Media Solutions
1111B S Governors Ave
STE 7582 Dover,
DE 19904

www.blueinkmediasolutions.com

ACKNOWLEDGEMENTS

The stories in this book are based on several interviews with veterans. In most cases, individuals provided the major source of information based on their personal experiences. The veterans and/or their family have had an opportunity to review the content and offer additional comments.

I would like to thank all the Veterans and their families, without them this book would not be possible.

Sonja DuBois for her work with "The Hidden Children

Eppie and Cathy Julian for their help with "A Servant, A Warrior, A Poet"

George and Linda Harper for their co-operation in "A Drifter Becomes a Marine"

Norm and Ozelle Bakley for "A Knife Cut, An Explosion, and A Bullet Hole"

Randy Speck, Mrs. Murl Conner (Pauline Wells Conner) for their help in:

"Audie Murphy Had Nothing On Murl Conner"

Dr. Robert Harvey for his contributions on:

"A Cotton Picker Joins The Red Ball Express"

John and Margie Shell for collaboration in: "Captured at the Battle of the Bulge"

Charles Beal and family for talking about his experience in WWII: "What Am I Going To Do?"

Harold Johnson for helping tells the story of: "The Germans have Jets?"

Clyde Beeler for relaying his experience in "The USS Pittsburg Has Just Lost Its Bow!"

Earl Henry Jr. for relating his Father's Story in, "A Son Remembers His Father He Never Met"

John Pirkle, Bob Thomas, WNOX for their help in: "The Battle of Athens"

Special thanks to Linda Marohn, my best friend and fiancé who without her support this book could not have happened.

I would also like to acknowledge the many people who have helped with their time and their ideas. A huge thank you goes to Tim Marohn for editing this book, and David Thompson for all his input in producing my Radio Program from which this book developed… Special thanks go to Joe Kiser for the artwork and the many sketches he provided for this book and to Michael Marohn for the computer support.

To Albert Styles, Charles and Lori McRae, Rosemary Carroll, John Koehler, Bethany Thompson,

Jerry Hatmaker, Tyler Haddock, Ray Wells, Doug Brown, and John Sutter for previewing chapters for readability.

To you for reading this book.

I NEVER WAS A SOLDIER

I never was a soldier,
but I played one as a child.
History was good to me,
I grew up free and wild.
No frozen feet, or jungle sweat,
Or bombs fell on my head.
There were always soldiers,
while I slept in my bed.
A fireman in a blown out hole,
Held a flag and cried a tear.
A soldier walked right up and said,
"I'll take that from here!"
And now, they find the mass graves,
of those who were not free.
Where were their soldiers,
like the ones who work for me?

By Randall Baxter
March 12th, 2002

INTRODUCTION

Hello, My Name is Randall Wallace Baxter. In this book I hope you will come to know me as Randy. I will be speaking to you as if I know you, throughout this book.

I want to open this book by saying to you in advance that I am not a United States Veteran.

I spent a lot of my career working as a Volunteer Veteran Advocate, dedicated to helping our Senior Veterans through the process of qualifying for benefits they earned and deserve from the Veterans Administration... I am not a part, nor am I an employee of the Veteran's Administration.

I am a Volunteer.

Several years after writing the poem you read a few minutes ago, I heard on the radio that WNOX 100.3 FM, (one of the oldest call letters in the United States of America) was forming a NEW Talk Format Radio Station and was interested in fresh programming. My high school friend, Bob Thomas, was one of the representatives, and also a host on the featured morning drive time show, Monday-Friday called the Ed and Bob Show.

I approached him about doing a program about the HISTORIC Events that led our citizens to become soldiers around the world.

I took Bob to lunch to talk about the possibilities, and he brought a co-worker with him, Harry Taylor. He listened to the conversation and at the end, Harry recommended that I call the show, THE VETERAN NEXT DOOR. I am so thankful I followed my new friend's advice.

The book you are about to read THE VETERAN NEXT DOOR STORIES FROM WORLD WAR II, VOL.1 is a selection of interviews I had with guests on my show.

America is such a large country, and there are so many communities, in each neighborhood, in our rush to get to work, and live our lives, we forget that many of our neighbors are VETERANS.

That elderly man walking his dog, or even lying in a hospital bed, or leading a Sunday School class could be a part of American history, and MAY talk with you about his experiences if you ask correctly, or show him/her that you have knowledge of events he may have been a part of, and that you would like to know more.

Literally, we possibly all have a neighbor who is: THE VETERAN NEXT DOOR!

I began these interviews in 2010, to date I have completed well over 600 conversations with Veterans from our wars from WWII to Operation Enduring Freedom. This first book is only a small part of the conversations I have had with men and women who fought in World War II, and in no way the last of the conversations I hope to have.

My college degree from the University of Tennessee in Knoxville qualified me to teach Social Studies up to the end of the Elementary Levels, and I am not certified to teach in today's educational environment. I taught in a small Business College called Knoxville Business College in the 1970's and had the opportunity to meet several Veterans on the GI Bill coming home from Vietnam. Some of these veterans became my friends, and my clients in my early days in the Insurance Industry at the New York Life Insurance Company.

I also need to confess to all you readers, that as a child, when the neighborhood was playing baseball and football, I could be found in my room, or outside playing with my toy soldiers, or in the woods playing soldier with some of my other friends. Many times I have told veterans in organizations I have been invited to speak to about my book and radio show, that while others were pretending to be Johnny Unitas or Mickey Mantle, I was pretending I was one of them.

My career in the Financial Services Industry made it possible to afford to attempt to do the radio program, this book is part of that story. I have attempted to tie the major events of World War II to these stories to be supplemental to the true efforts of this book, which is to share the personal experiences of some of the citizen soldiers. This book is not about world events, overall strategy or Generals or world leaders, It's about, people who were sucked into the events, and what happened to them, and what they have to teach us. I have attempted to place the stories in close chronological order to the major events in World War II. When I skip an event, it is not to minimize its importance. I am merely trying to set the stage for the next story.

I hope you enjoy this book as much as I have enjoyed the journey of gathering the information.

Randall Baxter

HOST of: THE VETERAN NEXT DOOR RADIO SHOW

AUTHOR of: THE VETERAN NEXT DOOR Stories from World War II Vol. 1

TABLE OF CONTENTS

PROLOGUE

When telling the stories of individual experiences of World War II, it seems best to know what events took place that leads us to each story. Volumes of history books by people more qualified than me, to report the chronological events taking us into World War II are available, and that is not the purpose of this book. There are some basic starting points that we need to establish before we enter the lives of the people who were pulled into this quagmire, at no fault of their own. What you are about to read, are partial reports of the facts that are being used to focus us into the individual stories.

Where do I start when it comes to saying what caused World War II? Was it the Sea Battle between Japan and Russia in the early years of the 20th Century? Was that when Japan starting tasting the fruits of Imperialism, and the benefits of subjugating populations to obtain their resources? During the 1930s and through World War II, the Japanese military controlled the government of Japan. Unlike Germany and Italy, Japan did not have a dictator, but an oligarchic and militaristic system ruling the country.

Was it the rise of Communism in World War 1? Communism was a distant political system compared to that of the fascists who started to gain power in Germany and Italy after World War I. The liberal democracies were caught in the middle. Both systems: Fascist and Communist became the breeding ground of Dictators who became bitter enemies. Benito Mussolini and Adolph Hitler found fertile ground for their Fascist goals, as did Joseph Stalin in Russia for his Marxist/Leninist Dictatorship.

Was it the failure of The League of Nations, an early attempt at today's United Nations, OR!!!

Maybe it was the terms of the German Treaty of Versailles ending World War I
The main terms of the Treaty of Versailles were:

1. **War Guilt Clause** - Germany should accept the blame for starting World War One
2. **Reparations** - Germany had to pay £6,600 million for the damage caused by the war.
3. **Disarmament** - Germany was only allowed to have a small army and six naval ships. No tanks, no air force and no submarines were allowed. The Rhineland area was to be de-militarized.
4. **Territorial Clauses** - Land was taken away from Germany and given to other countries. Anschluss (union with Austria) was forbidden.

The Humiliation of the German people, and the debt placed on their shoulders led them to follow Adolph Hitler. He seemed to be restoring their honor and self-esteem.

The Fascist Dictators seem to be relying on the fact that England was losing its world empire, and France was devastated by losses in World War I.

The Generals in these nations had fought the First World War by lining up their soldiers in Trenches and ordering them to stop the German Bullets with their chests.

The majority of a young healthy generation had been destroyed, and the memories of that pain were still prevalent maybe leading to the Appeasement offered by the English and French Governments!

Italy wanted to re-establish the Roman Empire; Germany wanted to restore its honor.

Japan was hungry for raw materials and saw the weakness in France as it was given control over French Indo China, and as they raped and pillaged in Nanking, China, there was no-one prepared to be strong enough to protect themselves from invasion.

Even the United States had dropped its guard enough to attract the Japanese to think they could knock us out of the Pacific by attacking Pearl Harbor, and the Appeasement of the Allies had set the stage for the fall of Denmark, and the Netherlands and. Poland's brave soldiers were no match for the Panzer Tanks, and the Blitzkriegs of the German Luftwaffe, or the fact that the Russians were attacking at the same time gobbling up what would be left of Poland after the Nazis "liberated" the Germans in Poland and cornered the Jews in the Ghettos.

Our first story begins with the aftermath of the capitulation of the Netherlands, and the Nazis were packing the Jews into trains to go to the death camps.

As I said in my poem, in the Introduction of this book:

And now they find the mass graves:

Of those who were not free
Where were their soldiers?
Like the ones who work for me.

In this book,

You will learn about how a 2 year old survived the Nazi onslaught against the Jews.

Learn how a black sailor used only as a servant before the war becomes a warrior poet.

How a drifter becomes a marine,

A scholar gets wounded three times in the Pacific Theater before becoming an engineer on the Space shuttle.

A black cotton picker becomes a driver for the Red Ball Express, then the President of his Alma Mater.

A farmer with more medals in Battle than Audie Murphy, comes home quietly. And eventually is awarded the Medal of Honor by President Donald Trump posthumously.

How after high school a boy becomes a man fighting across Europe in the 76th Infantry.

A B-17 pilot has a first encounter with the new German Jets.

A city builds and gives a B-17 to the Army Air corps, and sends it off to war never to return.

An East Tennessee Mountain boy joins the Navy and his ship breaks in half in a typhoon.

The son of a navy officer on the USS Indianapolis describes his relationship with a father he never met.

And some of our veterans come home to a corrupt government and use the second amendment to solve the problem.

I hope you enjoy learning about The Hidden Children and the 2 year old that starts this book; her plight was not the cause of World War II. Or, was it? The servants, depression era drifters, cotton pickers, students, mountain boys and dentists of The USA didn't know her, but their superhuman efforts helped stop a tyranny, that could not be stopped by people whose lost control of their governments, and had themselves lost their freedom.

CHAPTER ONE

THE HIDDEN CHILDREN

Before diving into the experiences of THE HIDDEN CHILDREN in World War II I have something I want you to read:. It came from an excerpt from a book I was looking through called THE GERMANS, written by: Gordon A. Craig, a German historian. I thought that you might need to read it. It actually helps set the stage for THE HIDDEN CHILDREN.

"What then, shall we Christians do with this damned, rejected race of Jews? Since they live among us, and we know about their lying and blasphemy and cursing. We cannot tolerate them. In this way, we cannot quench the inextinguishable fire of divine rage. And, we can't convert the Jews, we must preferably and reverently practice a merciful severity. Setting fire to their synagogues and schools and covering over what will not burn with earth, so that no man will ever see a stone or cinder of them again. Breaking and destroying their houses, so they have to live in stalls like gypsies and learn that they are not the lords of our land as they boast, and must live in misery and captivity. Depriving them of their holy books, silencing their teachers, forbidding them the right to travel, or to trade, and seizing their wealth on the grounds that everything they possess, they have robbed, and stolen from us by their usury."

Well, that sounds like a bunch of Nazis, doesn't it? Well, this quote was in the year 1543 by a man that we all learned about in our history books, and his name was Martin Luther.

The German invasion of The Netherlands, Concentrating on Holland

Germany invaded Holland, a province of the Netherlands on May 10, 1940. The invasion, based on blitzkrieg tactics, was swift and devastating. According to THE UNITED STATES HOLOCOST MEMORIAL MUSEUM, Blitzkrieg" (lightning war). Blitzkrieg tactics required the concentration of offensive weapons (such as tanks, planes, and artillery) along a narrow front. These forces would drive a breach in enemy defenses, permitting armored tank divisions to penetrate rapidly and roam freely behind enemy lines, causing shock and disorganization among the enemy defenses. German air power prevented the enemy from adequately resupplying or redeploying forces and thereby from sending reinforcements to seal breaches in the front. German forces could in turn encircle opposing troops and force surrender.

Germany successfully used the Blitzkrieg tactic against

- Poland (attacked in September 1939)
- Denmark (April 1940)
- Norway (April 1940)
- Belgium (May 1940)
- the Netherlands (May 1940)
- Luxembourg (May 1940)
- France (May 1940)
- Yugoslavia (April 1941)
- Greece (April 1941)

Holland, part of the Netherlands, surrendered in just six days as her military had been unable to cope with the speed of blitzkrieg. Fear was also great - Rotterdam had been severely damaged by bombing. Could the same happen to Amsterdam? The Hague?

Holland was an irritation in the great scheme of the attack on France. The sooner the Germans could take out Holland, the sooner they could concentrate all their resources on France. For this reason, they wanted to shock the politicians of Holland into surrendering. Rotterdam was to pay the price for this. The Germans decided to launch a ferocious attack on Rotterdam that would have such an impact, that the government of Holland would initiate a surrender.

On May 14th, the attack on Rotterdam started. The Germans used the excuse for such an attack that British troops had landed by the Maas River, thus endangering German troops based in the area. No such landing had taken place by the British. The attack started at 13.30 and within five hours, the Germans entered the center of Rotterdam. There were 30,000 civilian casualties.

Jewish Situation under the German Occupation of The Netherlands

"Few Jews survived in Holland, but those few were saved as a result of the most strenuous efforts, for Holland was the one territory of the occupied West in which the Jews did not have an even chance to live." (Hilberg)

Everything worked against the Jewish population in Nazi-occupied Holland. Geographically, the terrain is flat with no natural hiding places. With the open sea to the north and west, the German Reich to the east and occupied Belgium to the south, escape beyond the borders was difficult and dangerous. Before the occupation most Dutch Jews already lived in close proximity to one another in a few large urban centers, with over half in Amsterdam alone.

Far worse for the Jews than the geographic disadvantage was that the German-imposed government was civil rather than military, and was therefore concerned primarily with control of the civilian population rather than with military matters. The governing body was headed by Arthur Seyss-Inquart, an Austrian veteran of the Anschluss known for his severity and efficiency in **promulgating Hitler's idea of "racial purity."** He closely followed the pattern of economic and social anti-Jewish measures which had previously been carried out with success in Germany. Designed to gradually destroy Jewish culture and eventually eliminate all trace of the Jews themselves.

There were perhaps three key factors to the success of the anti-Jewish measures in Holland. First, the initial wave of public protest on the part of the Dutch population was immediately and ruthlessly suppressed with extremely severe reprisals. From that point on protest became a more private matter, conducted largely by small underground groups engaged in sabotage against the Germans, or in aiding Nazi victims, particularly Jews, to hide or escape. As public protest disappeared, the Germans were encouraged to proceed with their systematic plan to empty the Jews from Holland.

The second factor was the German device of setting up a Jewish Council, the Joodsche Raad, composed of a group of prominent middle-class Jewish leaders, for the purpose of conveying German commands efficiently to the Jewish population. The Jewish leaders reasoned among themselves, as they did in other occupied countries, that their role in keeping the channels of communication with their German oppressors open, and of maintaining law and order in the newly formed chaotic ghetto population of uprooted families, would help the bereft Jews more than harm them. In retrospect it is easy to see how wrong they were, as the Council quickly became the unwitting tool of the German destruction machinery, actually delivering the Jews directly to the German deportation trains.

The third factor was the gradual nature of the implementation of the anti-Jewish measures, which lulled Jew and non-Jew alike into believing that despite the difficulties and inconveniences, things weren't that bad, and the Germans' demands could be accommodated. The common feeling was that the Germans would certainly lose the war and it was just a matter of waiting out the interim as best as possible. With this in mind, a great many Dutch Jews willingly reported to the trains, which they believed would take them to work camps where they would labor for the Reich. Of the 140,000 people who registered themselves with the Germans as being Jewish, 107,000 were deported, of which only 5,500 came back. Approximately 24,000 went into hiding, of whom about 8,000 were caught.

The following chronology of events shows how the German occupation government imposed its will upon the Jewish population of Holland.

May 14, 1940: Holland surrenders to Germany. Dr. Arthur Seyss-Inquart appointed Reichkommissar, the highest governing authority.

October 1940: Every government official must sign an affidavit that neither he, his wife, fiance', parents, or grandparents are Jewish.

Jews are not to be promoted or appointed to government jobs.

All businesses owned or operated partly or fully by Jews, or in which Jews have a financial interest, must register with German authorities.

November 1940: Jews in the Dutch Civil Service are dismissed.

December 1940: Persons of German "blood" are not allowed to work in Jewish households.

January 1941: All Jews residing in Holland must register with German authorities. Failure to do so is punishable by 5 years in prison or confiscation of property, or both.

The Jewish Council, Joodsche Raad, is established, consisting of 20 members, including rabbis, lawyers and middle class business men.

February 1941: The Amsterdam ghetto is established following a series of incidents arising from an attack on the old Jewish quarter by groups of Dutch Nazi sympathizers. Several subsequent counterattacks by Jewish and

Dutch youths set off severe reprisals by the Germans. A resultant general strike lasting several days is ruthlessly suppressed. This is the last large scale public demonstration of civilian protest in Holland to Nazi policies.

March 1941: Germans begin to "Aryanize" Jewish property.

The Jewish Council is given authority over all Jewish organizations.

Jews can no longer travel without a special permit from The Jewish Council, cannot participate in the stock exchange, cannot hold cultural posts, or enter public parks.

April 1941: German identification cards issued to the Dutch population.

July 1941: Jews who registered have their I.D. cards stamped with a large "J.

August 1941: Jewish children are barred from public and vocational schools.

All Jewish assets, including bank deposits, cash, and securities, are blocked in order to be confiscated. A maximum of 250 guilders per month is made available to a Jewish owner of such assets, for his own use.

January 1942: Forced labor camps for Jews are established.

May 1942: Jews must wear a yellow star with the word "Jew" printed on it.

Jews must observe a curfew between 8 P.M. and 6 A.M.

Jews are allowed to shop only between 3 P.M. and 5 P.M.

Public transportation is forbidden for Jews.

Telephones are forbidden to Jews.

Jews are forbidden to enter the homes of non-Jews.

German government is authorized to confiscate all Jewish property except for wedding rings and gold teeth.

July 1942: Deportations of Jews out of Holland begin.

Two concentration camps are established in Holland, Westerbork and Vught, from which Jews are shipped to other camps, primarily Auschwitz.

September 1943: In the last major round-up, 5,000 Jews, including the Jewish Council leaders, are sent to Westerbork.

May 1945: Holland is liberated by the Canadian Army.

SOURCES CONSULTED INCLUDE:

RESCUE ATTEMPTS DURING THE HOLOCAUST, Proceedings of the Second Yad Vashem International Historical Conference, April 1974, Ktav Publishing House, Jerusalem,1974

A HISTORY OF THE HOLOCAUST, Yehuda Bauer, Franklin Watts, New York: 1982

So, as time has gone on, the Jewish people have been persecuted by different people all over Europe, all over the world, the Middle East—sometimes even in America—and our story today is about how that affected the life of a two-year-old girl.

Her name today is Sonja DuBois. In 1942, her parents called her Clara Van Thyn. She has an amazing story to tell.

SONJA: This is me after my parents had given me away and I was living with my foster parents, William and Elizabeth Van Der Kaden. When I was less than two-years-old, living in the Netherlands, my parents were deported to Westerbork at first, which was a holding camp for Jewish citizens. The year was 1942. My parents ended up in Auschwitz and became two of the six million that were killed. (Part of the Final Solution) a.k.a The Holocaust! You know, I used to say "lost," there's no such thing. They were killed. So were my aunts and uncles, my grandparents. And my cousins. I'm the only one left.

How I got away was a miracle. My parents, I'll never know if they thought about this for a long time, or made an on-the-spot decision to leave me behind. It was a friend of daddy's, who was also an artist who helped me get safely to my Foster parents. I didn't find out that connection until 1999, 2000, actually. They decided to leave me behind, which had to be the greatest sacrifice parents could make. They were put on a train in Rotterdam, heading for Auschwitz.

NOTE to Reader:

Did her parents have a choice?

What would you have done?

a) Would you have held on to your daughter because of your love for her and taken her with you to her death?

b) Would you have looked for a way to hand her off to safety?

The following information was taken from the Holocaust Encyclopedia

The Westerbork camp was situated in the northeastern part of the Netherlands in the Dutch province of Drenthe, near the towns of Westerbork and Assen. The Dutch government established a camp at Westerbork in October 1939 to intern Jewish refugees who had entered the Netherlands illegally. The camp continued to function after the German invasion of the Netherlands in May 1940. In 1941 it had a population of 1,100 Jewish refugees, mostly from Germany.

From 1942 to 1944 Westerbork served as a transit camp for Dutch Jews before they were deported to extermination camps in German-occupied Poland. In early 1942, the Germans enlarged the camp. In July 1942 the German Security Police, assisted by an SS company and Dutch military police, took control of Westerbork. Erich Deppner was appointed camp commandant and Westerbork's role as a transit camp for deportations to the east began, with deportation trains leaving every Tuesday. From July 1942 until September 3, 1944, the Germans deported 97,776 Jews from Westerbork: 54,930 to Auschwitz in 68 transports, 34,313 to Sobibor in 19 transports, 4,771 to the Theresienstadt ghetto in 7 transports, and 3,762 to the Bergen-Belsen concentration camp in 9 transports. Most of those deported to Auschwitz and Sobibor were killed upon arrival.

SONJA: While they were at the train station, they had the choice to hold on to me, or hand me off to safety... I don't know if it was, you know, smuggled, or what the situation was, except before they got to Westerbork, which then became their jail until they ended up in Auschwitz. It's at the northeast border, not far from Germany. From Westerbork, the philosophy was as I understand it now, they would gather as many people in one family, and then deport them altogether. What I know is that all of my relatives died except one in Auschwitz, and my paternal grandmother ended up in Sobibor, and that was a killing camp. Everybody knew that. In Westerbork, there was still an excuse to be in, Auschwitz, it was a concentration camp, so folks were chosen to go to the right or to the left. And I have been reading for years now about what happened in that camp, and it's hard to say, to understand, but I hoped for an early death for my parents.

YES, when they arrived at Auschwitz, my hopes are that they came, and were sent to the left, which meant they were going to the gas chambers... At Westerbork, —we found the train they went on. The Nazis kept unbelievable records. I have been told that all of the people on that whole train, none of those people lived.

Information below is dated March 2007,

Dr. Evers-Emden was born to a Jewish family in Amsterdam in 1926. In August 1944 she was seized by the Germans and sent to Auschwitz, which she survived. In 1973 she became a lecturer in psychology at the University of Amsterdam. Her research on Dutch Jewish children hidden during the war, and on their parents and "hiding-parents," has been published in four books. She was decorated by the queen of Holland as an officer of the Orde van Oranje-Nassau.

The Children and Their Parents

Parental decisions concerning about hiding their children was not an easy one for several reasons. First, as of July 1942 there was no organized underground network for hiding children. Second, Jews' identity cards carried a large black J that could not easily be removed (children aged six and younger did not need an identity card). Third, one needed a place where the children could hide. Finally, hiding children required at least a little money, sometimes a lot. Not every hiding family could handle the costs, and some demanded payment as compensation.

By the end of 1942 an underground network was more or less functioning, but by that time most of Dutch Jewry had already been murdered. The young people who belonged to the underground organizations tried to persuade remaining parents to send their children into hiding. These were difficult conversations because the idea of relinquishing their children distressed the parents. They did not know where they would be sent, whether they would be safe, whether the strangers would care for them well, or how much the children would suffer from the sudden total separation from their parents. Often the underground members were sent away empty-handed.

How did I wind up with foster parents? I was given to a good friend of daddy's. He was quite a well-known artist in Holland. His name was Dolf Henkes.

He was single, took me home to his sister and brother where he lived all his life. From there, he found an underground connection. I still don't know which agency I ended up in, but eventually, contacted my foster parents who today I call Mom and Pop. See, I have two sets of parents: Mother and Daddy, they're the ones that gave me up, and Mom and Pop, who risked their lives to keep me safe. I'm known as a hidden child, except I wasn't hidden in a closet. I was way out in the open all my life. During World War II I was one of THE HIDDEN CHILDREN.

When things got too hot, when people asked questions we couldn't or wouldn't answer, we just moved to the other end of town. Imagine that happening today. Here we are, east side of Knoxville, could you move to Karns (about 15 miles) and disappear? Not a chance, but the lack of communication—not everyone had telephones. Sonja began laughing, "Cell phones, of course, were not even dreamed of yet. So, that's what helped keep me safe. We moved three times in those three years.

Oh, the locals and the Nazi soldiers that we encountered would look at the color my hair and ask questions. I went to a preschool class where I'm sitting in the front row, my first school picture, the only brunette. People were asking questions everywhere I went.

ADDITIONAL INFORMATION: Sonja Dubois was one of the lucky children during this era. Below is a description of what some of the other children had to do just to survive.

This description was on YouTube, it is a description of a child's experience not as lucky as Sonja's.

> *"We went up to them, and it was a manhole, and they were taking their turns, and leaping in. There were no steps, it was deep down. We didn't hesitate for a fraction of a second—we knew this was a possibility of life, whereas what we were leaving behind was a certain death, certainly for me.*
>
> *In the hold was terrible, it was like being buried alive. I was in the hold for nine months.*
>
> *I was taken through those small tunnels that we have to crawl, and he took me to a place where I could see the light—the daylight.*
>
> *This adult was talking about a childhood of being forced to live in a sewer system, and that light was coming down the drain hole."*

Sonja Dubois's real name was Clara Van Thyn, sometimes spelled <Tijne>. She was born on October 19th, 1940, but she celebrated her birthday in August, because that was the day she became the child of William and Elizabeth Van Der Kaden. Sonja's mission in life, and also the mission of the Hidden Children Foundation is to educate all people of the consequences of bigotry and hatred, so never again will anyone suffer the atrocity, the injustice, and the agony of the Holocaust.

From 1939 to 1945, all Jewish children in Nazi occupied countries were hunted and threatened with death. To survive, they had to go into hiding, or keep their true identity secret. Many were left to fend for themselves, wandering in search of food and shelter. They hid in the convents, the orphanages, the barns, the woods, the basements, and yeah, just like you heard, they even lived in the sewers.

As Hidden Children we were a group of youngsters who had parents who had made the ultimate sacrifice, by giving their children away instead of keeping them with them, thinking that they could keep us safer by giving us up. In most cases to non-Jewish families? Yes, others gave their children to, orphanages, Catholic hiding places. I had a friend or two that survived that way. There were a lot of older children—older, I'm saying 8, 9, or 10 years old—who roamed the streets, who lived in sewers. There are terrible stories. That's why my life was glorious in comparison to them. I lived with one family the whole time. My parents didn't come back, they were killed, and the Van Der Kadens kept me as their own. I learned my true name when a relative who was married to a Christian and stayed safe, came to find me. All this information came out.

I was born October 19th, 1940. But, my birthday celebration during the war was in August because that's when I came to Mom and Pop, figuring it was a new life for them. They wanted a child very badly, and it was a new life for them, they didn't have any children of their own—never did—and it meant life for me. There was no way I was going to survive had I been taken to Auschwitz, and for a long time, I didn't consider myself as a survivor because life was good. I have a lot of emotional scars because my own foster parents decided to protect me by hiding my identity from me, even after the war.

I understand that now. During the war, It became a habit. Why would I want to know anything about my heritage? Why? Because, we all do. Not when we are six or seven years old. That was too dangerous for them to tell me who I was. It would have blown the whole mission and it would have hurt who I was as a child.

I don't blame anybody for that. It's just that it took me until 1999 to find out that yes, I do have a relative. For fifty-nine years I did not know who I was.

My distant cousin called, and here we have modern communication that made this happen. On an answering machine! Twice! She left a message. "I think we may be cousins." Well, she didn't leave a telephone number, which was fine—I knew she was going to return the call. There'd been so many hoaxes, anyhow. So, the third time, sure enough, we connected.

We talked, and after about five minutes I knew that, yes, she was.

She knew about an oddity. Daddy had a dis-figured ear shell, and I'd seen one picture of them only, ever, and that came just before we came to the states. We didn't talk about that yet. But, as a youngster, when I look at that picture, that's who I saw: This man with a strange ear, and these were my parents.

Yeah, which makes me hopeful in the fact that they were sent to the left, because he had a defect?

We talked about pictures, and I had only seen a picture of daddy at that time. And so, my cousin came to Knoxville, TN. I picked her up at the airport and we talked for the weekend. The following year, my husband and I went to see her family, and the amazing thing happened: I spoke to the only person ever that knew daddy as a person. You know, he's been a name on a piece of paper. I'm the only proof he existed.

Author's note: You know, listening to Sonja Dubois talk took me back to the start of this chapter when I told you about the way people were feeling in 1543, about the Jewish people. Then we went forward 400 years to find that the Nazis were persecuting the Jews and all their families. Killing these children and hunting them down because they were Jewish. Then we go another 70 years and we find that one of those children who had been persecuted in World War II finally runs into a relative, and makes a connection to the only person who knew her father. When they're talking on the phone, she hears in the background sounds of the recent bombing of Tel Aviv in December of 2012. This family has been persecuted because they were Jewish for over 500 years. Maybe more!

Can you imagine being given away to another set of parents when you were two-years-old, and not remembering anything about your original parents, or understanding why they would give you away? Knowing that, as a child, the very fact that if you saw men marching with black boots, would get you to a point where you would never want to wear black boots again? Later on in your life, after you're full grown, you learn the story, and have a phone call. Where somebody said, "Hey, I think I'm a relative of yours, and I think I have something that you're going to want to see." You make friends with them, and you see all the bonds, and then they show you a picture of your long lost parents?

Isn't it fantastic?

Sonya laughed as she explained, that's the first picture I had ever seen of my father. I keep it in my purse! I tell the students that I teach, or that I speak with, that they all know by the time they are 12-years-old who they look like. Grandparents pull out the pictures to show their friends, and their friends say, "Oh, he looks just like his mother, or his brother!" All my life, I wondered who I looked like, and when I first got the picture, I didn't see it. They are only twenty eight—this is before they are married. So, I had to look at pictures of myself when I was about 38-40, and that's when. I knew who I looked like.

I got it when I was 60... I'm 72 now. Yeah. (This was I 2010)

It was in a wedding movie. I took it from one of the frames. I carry it with me all the time—everywhere. I have a bigger one at home, and I have this little shrine in my living room—that's what we call it! It has this picture, it has a picture of my cousin and myself, it has another one that was found in Canada. A picture of all of us.

Author's note: So, here you go. A 60-year-old female living in the United States finds out that there is a movie, a film, of a wedding in the Netherlands in the late 1930's, and someone has gone through that film, frame by frame, and found a picture of Clara Van Thyn's a.k.a. Sonja Dubois's parents to give to her as a gift, and she had never seen a picture of her parents before.

WHAT A STORY!

Sonja's been through a lot, you know, and she's got a mission in life, and I think it's time we stop right now and learn about this mission.

SONJA: The Holocaust, the fact that it happened, is unknown to a lot of this generation.

Even denied. The reason that I'm really anxious to speak to as many students as possible is that time is marching on, and soon it will only be in history books maybe, and documentations and film. But you can't talk and get answers from those situations. I challenge the kids to ask me questions. This is a real person—I'm 72, there are a couple of folks in Knoxville who have numbers on their arms who are too old to go out and talk. Kids under six didn't have to have their arms tattooed in the concentration camps, because they hung out with their mothers, and the Nazis figured they'd get them one way or another.

Look at how we met, you just never know when there's an opportunity to share that racism is not dead.

Author's note: We met at a Senior Citizens Center where I had been invited to be a guest speaker on the KOREAN WAR.: Ms. DuBois travels around East Tennessee and wherever she can go, and especially into schools, mostly middle schools.

You know, lots of the children were hiding in the sewers, and Sonja was hiding out in the open, trying to pretend like she was a little Christian child. And eventually, the war came to an end. Let's listen to Sonja's story about that.

SONJA: And yes, I remember liberation in 1945.

I don't know why a 5-year-old is taken out in the pitch dark at night, with all these people, singing, making noise, flying their flags, you know, flags were confiscated with a lot of other things. People were robbed of radios, of course, no communication between people. This was May 5th, 1945, and it was after dark, and I had no idea why I was out there in Pop's arms. But they took me out, just like everybody else was out celebrating the liberation. We were liberated at first by Canadians, and the story I like to tell is how they drove with their huge tanks through the streets, and threw out goodies. Lucky Strikes, I'll never forget those little white packages with the red circle on it… Cigarettes for the guys, or women, who knows. Also, Hershey bars. My very favorite was Bazooka Bubble Gum.: I ate more Bazooka Bubble Gum than you want to know! Us little kids collected the comics, right, and because of that, the odor of bubble gum is despicable to me. Yeah! I had my fill. The grandchildren were very young, and they used that bubble gum for toothpaste. I was not happy.

But, you know, if it wasn't for those soldiers, who knows how many more than six million and there were millions more that weren't Jews.

My Pop was about forty at that time, on Liberation Day? They brought me to America. I lived with them all my life, Mom only died, in 2008. Johnson City, TN. And after Pop died, in 1996, we brought her closer. Pop was in his 90s when he died.

Author's note: Hearing Ms. DuBois tell her story about her parents makes me remember that not only are our veterans from World War II passing away at a phenomenal rate every day, so are the parents and the civilians and the people who were affected by all the things that happened in World War II. You know, and sometimes those things cause memories today.

SONJA: Memories have triggers. Mostly smells that bring me back to those events. Like, kerosene will give me instant headaches. When we did have food, it was prepared on a little kerosene stove. I was never hungry. Lots of people in Holland were very put-upon. They were hungry, they traded in their valuables to farmers to try to get food. But here again, underground connections that Pop had provided me with a hot meal every day. I went to an aunt and uncle. You know, everyone's aunt and uncle in Holland would not be mine but, whether it was a relation or not, just a form of being addressed, and I went to an aunt and uncle who fed me a hot meal every day. And when I came home, Pop had saved me my portion of soup from the soup kitchen, could you believe that?

The reason we had soup kitchens is that yes, there were food stamps, but there was no food to trade for. So, cities opened soup kitchens. People had nothing to eat. People ate tulip bulbs and died from the potential gas that's in there. They suffered horribly. I will never forget the first time that we had lovely, white bread. Today, I still think of that as being better than today's pancake. We still had our blackout curtains, so it had to be like, probably, right after the war. Packages fell from heaven—that's how you would see it as a kid, there were parachutes. The Swedes, it was Swedish white bread and butter. Amazingly good. You know, Sweden is the only country I know of who protected their Jews. There may have been others. How could this inhumanity to other human beings happened? You know, the lesson here I think, is that it didn't happen overnight.

Sweden protected their Jews, they did not bow to the Nazi occupation, and they sent packages of bread and butter. By plane, with little parachutes.

I was just a little girl, it didn't matter! It was the package that was important, not where it came from, but I remember that we still had to black out our curtains, and each person had half a loaf of bread and butter. I put so much butter on it! You could see your teeth sink into it! That was heavenly! I was going to say, I wasn't hungry, but I'm sure I didn't have treats, either.

Author's note: Holland was a small country, but why did they not stand up and defend themselves?

1. You had no geography/topography to stop tanks.
2. It would have been total destruction if you would have defended your selves.
3. The safest thing to do was to not defend yourself and set up an underground.
4. Plus, there were lots of German sympathizers in the Netherlands, not all but plenty.

First they came for the Socialists, and I did not speak out—

Because I was not a Socialist.

Then they came for the Trade Unionists, and I did not speak out—

Because I was not a Trade Unionist.

Then they came for the Jews, and I did not speak out—

Because I was not a Jew.

Then they came for me—and there was no one left to speak for me.

-Martin Niemöller

Lutheran pastor and anti-Nazi theologian

SONJA: There were many, many camps, as you probably know, having spoken to soldiers that were there. They were mere children, of course, they were young soldiers, but they liberated a lot of camps. I want to mention that in every country that the Nazis occupied, they did not work alone. Everywhere, they had collaborators, and the danger is that people didn't start out to be collaborators. Much like today, we are indifferent to what's happening around us, and the indifference turned to silent bystanders, and from there, they helped the enemy. And it was, you know, it was subtle initially. All laws were changed against Jews. I remember going to the beach after the war, that's where we used to vacation: In the Netherlands, at the beach?

SONJA: Yeah, and at the little steps going down, they had a sign that said "no dogs, no Jews."

Author's note: Let me tell you how lucky and how fortunate we are to have Sonja DuBois tell her story. When World War II began in September of 1939, there were approximately 1.6 million Jewish children living in the territories that the German armies, or their allies would occupy. When the war ended in May of 1945, more than 1 million, and perhaps as many as 1.5 million Jewish children were dead. Liberation from the Nazi tyranny brought no end to the suffering of the few Jewish children who survived. Many would face a future without parents, grandparents, or siblings. They spent their lives knowing that any moment, they could make a mistake that could cost them their life. They had to live through the hardships of starvation, and constant fear of being rejected by the community. They lived under false paperwork, and they were always looking for good hiding places, and new religions they could disguise themselves under.

You know, Sonja's story has made me think of lots of things I've learned since I started my radio program. It made me understand why a man whose dad called him a sissy would get in a wooden airplane and go fight the German soldiers. It made me realize why somebody from Jefferson City, or actually in Oak Ridge, TN and would wind up living in Jefferson City would ride down in one of those planes as an assault soldier, knowing that when he got out, the men who were killing those children, or representing the people killing those children were there to fight them. It made me realize that 19-year-old boys from East Tennessee were going to go into Europe and fight across the snow and watch their buddies get killed, knowing that their mission was to liberate these families and these children, and how some of the men would be captured at the Battle of the Bulge, and march through the snow in the cold. And how others would cross rivers in little canvas boats, using their gun butts as paddles, charging into German machine guns, just to get to the other side.

Some of these young men left their homes to sail the seven seas at great risk to themselves. Some flew dangerous skies over Europe.

It's always the children that get hurt the most in the wars, especially over time. It's been the Jewish children in Europe, and Sonja DuBois' story from the age of two to the time of being sixty years old and finally seeing the first pictures of her parents, and learning that there were still people alive who knew their parents as human beings, and not just a piece of paper, or a memory.

All this makes me feel the pleasure and honor of introducing these American Supermen who were called to service in the American military.

Soon you will discover why I consider them to be Supermen.

I hope you enjoy the next chapter, as much as I enjoyed introducing these people to you.

CHAPTER TWO

SUPERMEN

**"Stopping monsters who could not be
stopped by their own people."**

The AXIS Powers in World War II gained power over much of the world
through intimidation and force. When the Axis powers realized they
could bluff their way into some advantageous situations, and force people
weaker than them to obey, they moved swiftly to consolidate their gains.
Not wanting military conflict, many nations were willing to look the other
way as long as they were not directly involved, and their national interests
were not threatened.

This allowed them to do things all over the world similar to the persecution
of the Jews.

Children all over the world were hiding in some way or another.

My name is Randall Baxter and as I put this book together, I need you to
know. I never was a soldier, but I played one as a child. As I was growing
up in Knoxville, Tennessee in the mid 1950's and early 1960's you could
always find me somewhere near my plastic army men. If a war movie came

on TV, or at a local movie theater, my day would stop, or my weekend deemed incomplete if some way or another I could not get a viewing. It has been only in the past few years that I realized all of us non-veterans need to honor the American veteran who allowed our lives to be as wild and free as it has been. So before I go further, if you are a Veteran, please accept my gratitude and thanks for standing guard over me.

When I had a birthday coming up, I always asked for a new bag of plastic soldiers, I had a paper route so I could supply myself with the newest editions of DC Comics and Marvel Comics where I followed the exploits of Sgt, Rock of Easy Company, and Sgt. Fury. J.E.B. Stuart the Tank Commander, Beetle Bailey and SAD SACK., Overtime, I outgrew my toys, and when I graduated from the University of Tennessee, the Vietnam War had just about ended, and I became a teacher at a small school called Knoxville Business College. Primarily, it was a school that taught basic business skills to mostly young women. On opening day of the fall semester when I reported to class, I was surprised to see the makeup of the class had changed. It had tripled in size, and instead of mostly girls out of high school, the classes were populated by men in their early twenties to mid-thirties who had been released from our military, and most had served in Vietnam, and I first became aware of the GI BILL. These ex-soldiers became my friends, and many became my clients in my next chosen profession of FINANCIAL SERVICES. My experiences with these men, who were my age, and had gone to war, reawakened a need to learn more about our Veterans. It made me realize that there are a lot of SUPERMEN; around Knoxville, Tennessee, and all over the United States of America who actually lived the lives of my child hood heroes.

I do a lot of public speaking by invitation at churches, civic clubs, and seminars. One day I was telling some of the stories I have collected from our Veterans, and I wrapped it up this way. The group was a Veteran Group of about 50 men and women, retired MARINES and spouses, and widows of MARINES. I told them that when my Mom would send me out to play baseball or football with the boys in the neighborhood, I would go and do as I was told. While those boys were pretending to be Johnny Unitas, and Mickey Mantle, I knew that before the day was over, I was going to go pretend I was one of those soldiers. I have had the honor of meeting, not Johnny Unitas or Mickey Mantle, but heroes from Guadalcanal, Bougainville, Chosin Reservoir, and The TET Offensive. They were my heroes, my sports stars, my SUPERMEN.

These "SUPERMEN" you will read about in this book were born from about 1911 to 1925. Tom Brokaw called them the "greatest generation," and I am honored to be able to call many of these people my friends. Almost weekly I am notified of the passing of some wonderful person who chose to share their life and story with me. They have proven that SUPERMAN was not just in my comic books, or my imagination, but in the history my friends have shared with me. To do justice and to honor my friends. I want to present to you some of their stories. Stories of: THE VETERAN NEXT DOOR.

At the end of World War I, some of my SUPERMEN were teenagers. Some were not yet born, mainly poor folk, leading simple lives. In the Roaring Twenties, America was experiencing a time of great prosperity. Automobiles, telephones, motion pictures, industrial growth, and electricity were rapidly enriching our society at an unprecedented rate. Many Americans were building skyscrapers, working in automobile plants, and building railroads all over the USA. After the Wall Street Crash of 1929, many of them would be asking each other: "brother, could you spare a dime?"

In the 30's this generation was coming of age. The teenagers were mostly poor and saved their money to maybe go to the movies. They would see THE THREE STOOGES, a cowboy serial, and a feature film. I can only imagine the excitement of seeing these movies with your sweetheart, or your date, for the first time, to see *Gone with the Wind* or *The Wizard of Oz,* all in the same year?

We were stuck in an economic rut known as the Great Depression. Between 1929 and 1933, the United States gross domestic production had fallen 30%, and the stock market had lost almost 90% of its value. Almost 25% of our workforce was unemployed, and 34 million people belonged to families with no regular full-time wage earner. 11,000 of the US's banks had failed, and nine million saving accounts had been wiped out.

These were tough times for the Greatest Generation—and we had elected Franklin D. Roosevelt, a disabled man, to lead us out of our crippled economy and crippled mindset.

We were protected by two oceans, and the world around us, and the events seemed like they were so far away. We learned of these world events by reading the headlines of our newspapers, or hearing about things on our radios.

One way to start this story is with the headlines of those days:

JAPAN INVADES MANCHURIA 1931

JAPAN INVADES CHINA PROPER1937

JAPAN ATTACKS PEARL HARBOR DECEMBER 7, 1941
The Japanese knew what they were doing. They needed resources, and the United States of America and Western Europe were in the way.

ADOLF HITLER BECOMES CHANCELLOR OF GERMANY in 1933

NAZI PARTY EXECUTES COMPETITION IN "NIGHT OF THE LONG KNIVES" 1934

NEVILLE CHAMBERLAIN PROCLAIMS "PEACE IN OUR TIME" 1938

GERMANS INVADE CZECHOSLOVAKIA MARCH 1939
The Germans wanted to restore their honor, they had lost it in the First World War!

ITALY BECOMES A FACIST DICTATORSHIP 1925

ITALIANS ATTACK ETHIOPIA WITHOUT A DECLARATION OF
WAR OCT. 1935
The Italians? Well they seemed to think that being fascists was a good idea.

Benito Mussolini took over using brutality, posing as law and order.
I think in the end, it was Mussolini who betrayed the Italians!

SO, one day, we woke up, and the Japanese were in China, spreading
out, and then they sucker punched us at Pearl Harbor. The Germans had
become the big bullies in the neighborhood, and the Italians had brutalized
Ethiopia, Yugoslavia, and Lybia.

Were the Japanese really raping the women and bayoneting the babies? Yes!!

Were the Germans really systematically eliminating the Jews? Yes!!

Were the Italians seizing the opportunity to re-establish the Roman Empire?
Yes, they were!

The fear these tyrants projected had to be stopped. How did we do it?
We organized our schoolboys: farmers, mechanics, heavy equipment
operators, black cotton pickers, and many more who were dreaming of
better education in math, science, technology, and even drifters from job
to job. They took the energy, resources of a sleeping giant, and applied their
own discipline, tenacity, and implementation skills to stop the monsters
WHO COULD NOT BE STOPPED BY THEIR OWN PEOPLE? None
of these aggressor governments had "the Bill of Rights" and certainly not
"the Second Amendment."

These American men and women became the SUPERMEN of the stories
you are about to read.

I met John Shell as a referral, from a phone call from someone who listens
to my radio program.

The lead source told me I need to meet and interview a man in Seymour,
Tennessee before he died.

When the war started, John Shell of Knoxville, Tennessee had already enlisted, thinking the war was going to start, and that he wanted to be involved. I had the honor and privilege of interviewing him in his home, on his death bed. I asked him about his life before the military. He told me he worked for Knoxville Iron Company as a machine operator.

"I wasn't, but, Lord Mercy when I went to work, I was about, 13, 13-14 years old.

He was adamant about his next statement "I did not get drafted!! …. I was a volunteer".

Mr. Shell served time in the Army before World War II and even had the opportunity to come out of the Army for a little while because they needed copper miners out West. The federal government decided it was better to free up some of their soldiers to get the copper mined, and not have a shortage of workers, so he came out the Army, and then he had to go back in once the war started.

I never met Lt. Murl Conner. I received a contact one day from Randy Speck, who had listened to my show and wanted to share with me the experiences of one of his neighbors.

The story you will read in this book will show you there were other heroes in Europe besides Audie Murphy. Many years after I met Murl Conner's wife Pauline Wells Conner. President Trump awarded him the Medal of Honor by placing it around her neck.

Then there was Mr. George Harper, who was in Paducah, Kentucky when the Japanese bombed Pearl Harbor. His daughter listened to my program and called to tell me about her father. Mr. Harper told me: "Well, it was on a Sunday morning… I forget the time, I was sitting at my desk, and they announced the war broke out at Pearl Harbor."

He became a Marine. His travels took him to Bougainville, Guadalcanal and Guam.

More on this later...

Dr. Robert Harvey, a retired Professor of Mathematics and President Emeritus of Knoxville College had made the decision as a young man to leave Mississippi and go to school. He knew he did not want to be a cotton picker for the rest of his life—and he wanted to become an expert in math, and maybe a professor. Telling me about his life before World War II, Dr. Harvey, was a student at Knoxville College. He had just finished his junior year. "I came to Knoxville College from Camdem Academy in Alabama in December. I came to Camdem from Sumrall, Mississippi, where I was the son of a Baptist minister, and that my income and savings came from picking cotton." His education was stopped midstream by World War II, and he became a driver in what became known as "THE RED BALL EXPRESS".

Also during this time Harold Johnson was thinking about a career in the Army Air Corps, he would be flying B-17 Bombers, and had a brush with a new German Jet.

One day I was invited to a presentation by a retired farmer from Sweetwater, TN. His name was Clinton Riddle. A son of a farmer. He was a farmer too, but he didn't really like all the hard work, and his father had even gotten angry at him a couple of times and called him a "Sissy", and told him he had better join the army soon before the war got started, and get himself a good office job.

"Well", he explained, "I had graduated from high school. I had taken a course in department store management, and got two credits in high school for that, and I worked until Thanksgiving. I signed up to build airplanes in Nashville at Anderson Aircraft School, and they were not supposed to draft out of the school, but they did. So, I came home, was drafted, and I took my basic training down at Camp Wheeler in Georgia. I applied for clerk school, and I was gonna get me an office job, and not have to go in the battlefield. When they shipped me out to Fort Bragg, NC, the old sergeant came out, cursing, saying, "What'd they send a clerk up here for? What we need are machinegun and mortar men!" And there went my office job!"

He rode down to Normandy in a Wooden Glider, Co-piloted a Glider as a private first Class in the Market Garden operation, and fought in the Huertgen Forrest:

James Julian was already in the Navy when the war started, He lived on a Navy dorm ship, basically the ship was not seaworthy, but could be used as a dorm for the black sailors.

One lucky day I visited a family to do some TRUST work.

In real life, I do that a lot. I met Norm and Ozzie Bakley and they became my friends, and my clients. Norm Bakley was working on the West Coast when World War II began. He got stabbed, shot, and blown up in the Pacific.

Charles Beal was still in high school, and Clyde Beeler was thinking about joining the Navy. A life completely different from the one he knew on Clinch Mountain in Grainger County, Tennessee. Other people were doing other things. Some were worried about their brothers that might be going to war. One Tennessee citizen was trapped in Germany. He lived in Tennessee, but he was a German citizen, and he wound up in the German army.

But, in 1942, the strategy was that the Japanese had to be pushed back. They were after resources, and the Americans had to decide the best way to get to Tokyo to end the war on the Pacific side. To do that, they looked toward Australia. Two islands popped up on the radar and our military leaders decided, "Hey, we have to have those." One was called Guadalcanal, and the other one was called Bougainville. Soon I will take you there. The time will be 1942 to late 1943.

The following was a popular song in the early days of WWII:

You Can't Say No To a Soldier
Performed by Joan Merrill
Recorded July 1942
Written by Mack Gordon, Harry Warren
From the film, "Iceland"

Listen little lady, it's the order of the day
Issued by the highest of authority
Fellows in the service simply can't be turned away
You know that defense but get priority
So if you're patriotically inclined
Heed the call to arm and keep this thought in mind
You can't say no to a soldier, a sailor or a handsome marine
No, you can't say no if he wants to dance
If he's gonna fight he's got a right to romance

So, get out your lipstick and powder
Be beautiful and beautiful too
If he's not your type then it's still okay
You can always kiss him in a sisterly way
Oh, you can't say no, no you gotta give in
If you want him to win for you

You simply can't say no, no no no no no no
To a soldier or a handsome marine
Lady, what do you say, if he said, "let's dance"?
I'd say brother, you have got a right to romance, let's dance
So, get out your lipstick and powder
Be beautiful and beautiful too
If he says it's cold on those submarines
You can knit a sweater, but that's not what he means

Oh you can't say no, no no no no no no
Then [?]
Oh, you better give in
if you want him to win for you

John Shell, the heavy equipment operator, joined the Army.

George Harper, the itinerant worker in Kentucky, joined the Marines.

Norm Bakley, from the West Coast, arrived for battle in the Americal division, in the US Army.

A green soldier with higher rank than many of the Guadalcanal veterans he commanded.

Robert Harvey? —he went to Europe, and he was in the quartermaster division working for General George Patton, driving a truck. He was put there because of the color of his skin.

Charles Beal-right out of high school—became a member of the Army's 76th Infantry Division and fought across Germany before his 19th birthday.

Clyde Beeler, our Grainger County mountain boy became a sailor. And it was late 1943.

As I was saying earlier, one soldier knew there was a war blazing on both sides of the American Continent. His father called him a sissy. He wanted to be an office clerk, and wound up in the airborne? Fought in Africa, fought in Sicily and Italy, went to England for a little break, and somebody decided that because of his small stature, he would be a good person to ride in one of those airplanes that doesn't have a motor. He became a glider soldier. And on D-Day, he rode in on a glider. Well, he survived that. A couple weeks later, he went back to England, and somebody got the idea to send the gliders in again in a battle, or an operation called Operation Market Garden. It was a little bit of a problem—they didn't have many good glider pilots, so they trained our soldier to be a glider pilot. He was a Private; he was going to be the co-pilot. So he rode in, and his plane crashed. He didn't get to fight in Operation Market Garden; he was injured in a plane crash. He's still fighting for his Purple Heart, because they say it was an accident, and not part of the battle. That doesn't seem fair. He was told to get a little R&R, and they sent him to a little town called Bastogne. And there he was, right in the middle of the Battle of the Bulge. He fought through that and survived. Then found himself in a little place called the Hürtgen Forest.

In his words: "It was difficult in the forest there, because the artillery came in and hit the trees and made the trees burst. It was very dangerous to be in and under the trees when the shells came in".

I asked him "Of all the battles you fought in, which one you think was the most violent? He answered," Well, when I went into the Siegfried Line, because the morning of our attack, well, the night before, our company commander had gotten sick and went back to the hospital. They sent a new officer fresh from the States without any experience in combat to replace our officer. When he arrived he sent for me, and said, "Clinton, I understand you've been with the company for a long time, and I want you to help me." We were on patrol of the Siegfried Line that night, and the next morning, we attacked, and there were bunkers there that some of the Germans had been—some of them said had been there almost twenty years, and they couldn't be driven out. Well, they took three companies of us, A, B, and C Company. A went first, then B company, we were pinned down, C company was in reserve, and as they came up, we would rise up and join with them. To make a long story short, when the battle was over, out of my company, only three of us were on our feet. And they had killed that young officer that had just come to the company."

Even a sissy in his father's eyes had become a SUPERMAN in my eyes.

The SUPERMEN in this book did things they would never have dreamed of doing.

They sailed around the world, fought on Pacific Islands they had never heard of before.

Helped bridge the gap of racial tension in the military, delivered supplies and crying troops to the front line, wrote letters to children they would never live to meet. Saw their buddies explode, felt the cold steel of a knife cutting across their shoulders, or a grenade shaking their insides loose, a bullet ripping through their hip. They would bring gold teeth home as souvenirs, not for their children to play with, but they did not realizing what they were. They would feel the fear of their ships being torpedoed, or break in half in a typhoon, and float in the ocean while sharks drug their buddies under the water, They would experience the first German Jets attacking their B-17 formations, and when they came home they had to confront corrupt local governments that had taken over their counties while they were gone.

Author's note: Later, in early September, 1945, the Japanese surrendered.

[Victory Polka — The Andrew Sisters]

There's going to be a Hallelujah Day
When the boys have all come home to stay
And a million bands begin to play.
We'll be dancing "The Victory Polka."

And when we've lit the torch of liberty
In each blacked out land across the sea
When a man can proudly say 'I'm free'
We'll be dancing "The Victory Polka."

And we will give a mighty cheer
When the ration book is just a souvenir.
And we'll heave a mighty sigh
When each gal can kiss the boy she kissed good-bye.

And they'll come marching down Fifth Avenue
The United Nations in review
When this lovely dream has all come true.
We'll be dancing "The Victory Polka."

Dance, dance, dance "The Victory Polka."
Join, join the merry throng.
Sing, sing, sing "The Victory Polka."
Raise your voices loud and strong.

There's going to be a great Hallelujah Day
When the boys have all come home to stay
And a million bands begin to play.
We'll be dancing "The Victory Polka."

And when we've lit the torch of liberty
In each blacked out land across the sea.
When a man can proudly say 'I'm free'
We'll be dancing "The Victory Polka."

Chorus:
And we will give a mi-mi-mighty cheer
when the ration book is just a souvenir.
And we'll heave a mi-mi-mighty sigh
When each gal can kiss the boy she kissed good-bye.

And they'll come marching down Fifth Avenue
The United Nations in review
When this lovely dream has all come true.
We'll be dancing "The Victory Polka."
We'll be dancing "The Victory Polka."

The parade was in New York City. It was a ticker tape parade. Some sailor kissed a nurse. The monsters in Germany and Italy and Japan had been conquered, and our SUPERMEN had come home. Only three in this book came home walking. The others were malnourished and frostbitten, and hadn't eaten well for over 100 days. They were suffering from sword injuries across the back, and concussion injuries from grenades. They had to recover from chest wounds. They had post- traumatic stress, but we did not call it that we called it shell shock, and some had to suffer the emotional stress of standing on a ship one day, and watching a Japanese bomber drop two shells on an American aircraft carrier, and watch it burn with two thousand sailors onboard.

Life after the war was their goal. To become an antique dealer, a dairy farmer, an engineer, working on the space shuttle. One became a math professor of Knoxville College and served as President of Knoxville College more than once. They all became family men and worked until they retired and some have recently passed away.

These and many more in the chapters ahead are the men who conquered fascism, and these are all SUPERMEN who lived in and around my hometown, Knoxville, Tennessee. This book is about their lives and how World War II changed their worlds.

It's also about how ordinary men and women were called to fight the men of the AXIS powers who of their own volition decided they were superior to the rest of us, until they met our own SUPERMEN!

SUPERMEN I know as: THE VETERAN NEXT DOOR!

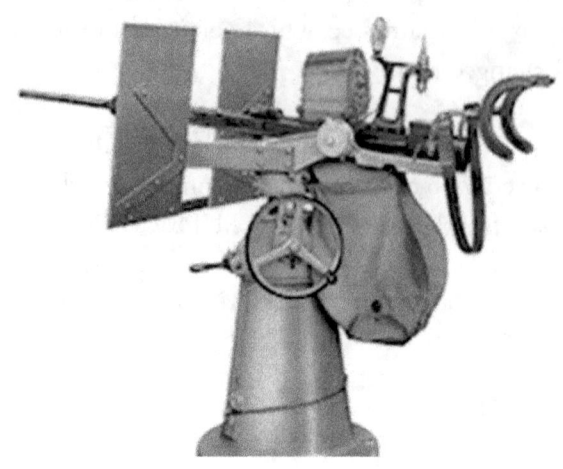

CHAPTER THREE

A SERVANT, A WARRIOR, A POET

A BLACK SAILOR's Experience in World War II
Waiting on Officers and shooting at Stukas,
Italian bombers and Kamikazis

When the Japanese bombed Pearl Harbor, James Julian was already in the Navy. He would up with a world tour. What did the black man before World War II have in common with Rodney Dangerfield? They didn't get no respect!

From its establishment, the United States has worked hard to close its racist past. Before World War II, African-Americans, or "negroes" as they were known back then, had little, if anything to do with the US Army, and the government in general. The USA was vaulted into World War II by the surprise attack on Pearl Harbor by Japan in December 1941. Once the US declared war, a group of prominent Negroes had petitioned to the war department to create a non-segregated Armed Forces unit, in order for Negroes to contribute their share in protecting the US. The US Government turned down their demands, but the Army allowed the training of Negro officers.

Reportedly, over 900,000 Negro Americans served in the Armed Forces during World War II. However, they were initially used as mess hall servants. After much agitation and protesting, the Army allowed Negroes to become front line staff.

The period between the world wars marked the nadir of the Navy's relations with black America. Although the exclusion of Negroes that began with a clause introduced in enlistment regulations in 1922 lasted but a decade, black participation in the Navy remained severely restricted during the rest of the interwar period. In June 1940 the Navy had 4,007 black personnel, 2.3 percent of its nearly 170,000-man total. All were enlisted men, and with the exception of six regular rated seamen, lone survivors of the exclusion clause, all were steward's mates, labeled by the black press "seagoing bellhops."

The Steward's Branch, composed entirely of enlisted Negroes and oriental aliens, mostly Filipinos, was organized outside the Navy's general service. Its members carried ratings up to chief petty officer, but wore distinctive uniforms and insignia. Even chief stewards never exercised authority over men rated in the general naval service. Stewards manned the officers' mess and maintained the officers' billets on board ship, and, in some instances, took care of the quarters of high officials in the shore establishment. Some were also engaged in mess management, menu planning, and the purchase of supplies. Despite the fact that their enlistment contracts restricted their training and duties, stewards, like everyone else aboard ship, were assigned battle stations, including positions at the guns and on the bridge. One of these stewards, Dorie (Doris) Miller, became a hero on the first day of the war when he manned a machine gun on the burning deck of the USS *Arizona* and destroyed two enemy planes.

By the end of December 1941 the number of Negroes in the Navy had increased by slightly more than a thousand men to 5,026, or 2.4 percent of the whole, but they continued to be excluded from all positions except that of steward. It was not surprising that civil rights organizations and

their supporters in Congress demanded a change in policy. MESSMEN
VOLUNTEER AS GUNNERS, *Pacific task force, July 1942.*

The Navy got the message. Armed with these instructions from the White
House, the General Board called on the bureaus and other agencies to
furnish lists of stations or assignments where Negroes could be used in
other than the Messman's Branch, adding that it was "unnecessary and
inadvisable" to emphasize further the undesirability of recruiting Negroes.
Freely interpreting the President's directive, the board decided that its
proposals had to provide for segregation in order to prevent the injection of
the race issue into the Navy. It rejected the idea of enlisting Negroes in such
selected ratings as musician and carpenters mate or designating a branch
for Negroes (the possibility of an all-black aviation department for a carrier
was discussed). Basing its decision on the plans quickly submitted by the
bureaus, the General Board recommended a course that it felt offered "least
disadvantages and the least difficulty of accomplishment as a war measure":
the formation of black units in the shore establishment' black crews for naval
district local defense craft and selected Coast Guard cutters, black regiments
in the Seabees, and composite battalion in the Marine Corps. The board
asked that the Navy Department be granted wide latitude in deciding the
number of Negroes to be accepted as well as their rate of enlistment and
the method of recruiting, training, and assignment. The President agreed
to the plan, but balked at the board's last request. "I think this is a matter,"
he told Secretary Knox, "to be determined by you and me."

The experience of the black men during World War II changed as time
went on. This is James Hall's version, I heard him do his song on YouTube:

Mr. Hall (a black soldier or sailor, I do not know which!) was entertaining
his friends when he recited this soliloquy.

> **HALL:** December the seven, forty-one
> That's when the Second World War had just begun.
> They tell me Mussolini was holding out his paw
> And trying to get the European countries under Hitler's law.

First have a little patience I'm gonna tell it to you
The first thing they done, they got rid of the Jews

But Great Britain got trouble in mind
She rushed the poor boys to the firing line

Better than that, the Germans bombed beautiful Paris late one night
They had to look to America for to get supplies

They loaded up the vessel and started across
But the news reached back that the vessel was lost.

Mr. Roosevelt didn't like that, he said "I just can't see
Why Adolf Hitler trying to rule the sea."

He sent him a message right straight from the phone
say, "Looka here Hitler, leave my vessel alone."

But ole Tojo looked back in the States
Him and Mussolini could not communicate
Old Japan went a hushing by
she wouldn't fight on either side.
She was a nation that wouldn't argue
But you know what she did, turned around and bombed Pearl Harbor
I don't know, but I was told
That's the way Pearl Harbor base got stole.

Said they bombed Pearl Harbor from belly to belly,
At the place, when they got there, there's Captain Kelly.
'course, he earned his medal, just before he died.

Captain Kelly was America's First World War II aviation Hero, killed soon
after Pearl Harbor

After a successful bombing mission.

Back to our Poem:

Well here's where we came in at.

Negro soldiers standing at attention
They were the poor boys in every dimension.
But I'm gonna to tell you about a colored man
December the seven, forty-one
That's when the Yanks started mighty manning the gun
He stepped on deck and he got dead aim
He brought a Japanese bomber down in flames
Some got wounded, some got killed
But naturally we know God's Holy Bible got to fulfill.

THIS VERSE IS ABOUT DORIS "DORIE" Miller, the first Negro sailor to be awarded the Navy Cross, he later died at sea with many of his crew members.

I found out later there was a ration on rubber, so was gasoline
I had to get my black head in the Philippines.
That's where I was, so help me God.

That's one Negro sailor's version of his own experience in World War II

THIS IS THE SAILOR I WANT TO TELL YOU ABOUT!
James and his wife Eppie

James and Eppie Julian of Alcoa, Tennessee, experienced World War II together, but had to separate during the war... Eppie was born on September 20th, 1919, and James was born on March 4th, 1920, and they were married on May 10th, 1941. They were both 21 years old, and James was in the Navy, and there was a war about to start.

The black men in America were just as patriotic as everybody else.

Allow me to introduce if I may:

Huddie William Ledbetter better known as stage name **Lead Belly** was an American folk and ... **Lead Belly's songs** covered a wide range of genres and topics including gospel music; blues about ... He also wrote **songs** about people in the news, such as Franklin D. Roosevelt, Adolf **Hitler**, Jean Harlow, and many more! You can hear the Hitler Song on Youtube.com

<Hitler Song —By: Leadbelly>

Hitler started out in 1932
Yeah, he started out in 1932
When he started out, takin' them homes from the Jews

That's one thing Mr. Hitler did do wrong
That's one thing Mr. Hitler did do wrong
When he started out drivin' them Jews from their homes

James Julian joined the Navy and stayed on a ship that was like a dormitory just for black men, and most of them were stewards for men that were officers in the United States Navy. He trained for a couple of years, and he wound up, when the war started, going to Greenland on his first mission.

We're gonna bring him to the ground
We're gonna bring him to the ground
We're gonna bring him to the ground someday

Instead of God in Heaven
He gonna rule the world, he said so

Instead of God in Heaven
He gonna rule the world
But we American people tell he will be shot down just like a squirrel

Not only was James Julian a steward on the ship, but he was also trained to be an anti-aircraft gunner on that ship, and after his trip to Greenland, he wound up in the Mediterranean Sea at the invasion of Sicily.

Mr. Hitler, we gonna tear your playhouse down
Mr. Hitler, we gonna tear your playhouse down
You been flying mighty high but you on your last go-round

We're gonna tear Hitler down
We're gonna tear Hitler down
We're gonna tear Hitler down today

We're gonna bring him to the ground
We're gonna bring him to the ground
We're gonna bring him to the ground someday

After the invasion of Sicily, we sailed into the Atlantic, turn left, head south, and around Africa, and back up to a country we know today as Yemen—but back then, it was called Oran, and Julian's ship picked up German prisoners of war from the Battle of Africa, and then turned back around and took them all the way to South Carolina, to the prisoner of war camps.

We're gonna tear Hitler down
We're gonna tear Hitler down
We're gonna tear Hitler down today

We're gonna bring him to the ground
We're gonna bring him to the ground
We're gonna bring him to the ground someday

After dropping off the prisoners of war, it was down to the Panama Canal, up to San Francisco, over to the Philippines, and up to, on Easter morning, the Battle of Okinawa in 1945. After that, it was Tokyo Bay for the end of the war.

Most soldiers in World War II, get to talk about their Pacific excursions or their European excursions, James Julian was all over the globe, serving the United States Navy.

Mr. Julian joined the US NAVY because of the economy.

What made him pick the Navy?

JAMES JULIAN: The cleanliness of it, the lack of trudging, having to be in difficult places and times, seemed to me like I picked the Navy over the Army to avoid the marching and going in mud holes and trenches. My wife Eppie followed me during the war, whenever she could.

EPPIE: I was in school. In high school, we were friends, classmates, we went to see the basketball games together, and we were in the glee club together. So, we knew each other pretty well, we started off right. We had been dating, most of that came through mail.

"Eppie provided us with some of his poems and letters."

We Sailors

We sailors are rough, we sailors are tough,
We've sailed the ocean wide
We've risked our necks we're salts of the decks
We've sailed against the tide.

Over the seas, we've rolled forty degrees
We've pitched to and fro.
During many a sails, we've weathered the gail
And proven our worthy to the core.

We've scurraged to our stations on the double
That we have man'd so well.
We've put battle to a test, at high success,
And given the enemy hell.

This war is hard, not a game of cards
You can take it from me.
We sailors are roughest and always the toughest,
Who'll fight to a victory.

We Sailors

by: James Julian

We Sailors are rough
We sailors are tough
We've sailed the ocean wide.
We've sailed against the tide

Over the seas we've rolled forty degrees
We've pitched to and fro.
During many a sails, we've weather the gale
And proven our worthy to the core.

We've scurraged to our stations on the double
That we have manned so well
We've put battles to a test, at high success
And given the enemy hell.

This war is hard, not a game of cards
You can take it from me,
We sailors are roughest and toughest,
Who'll fight to a victory?

JAMES: After my boot training in Norfolk, Virginia, I spent two years in Annapolis, Maryland. I was on the USS Cumberland, quartered on the USS Cumberland, on the same dock that the Reina Mercedes—a lot of people call it the Reina Mer-cuh-des—the bay ship. The midshipmen and officers, to get the nomenclatures on and the Naval Command was on the Reina Mercedes. The Cumberland was just a quarters for the black sailors that fed the midshipmen, three times a day.

Everyone on that ship, The USS Cumberland was black. Well, they were using it as quarters—for sleeping quarters.

It wasn't active. It was just one of the old ships, I imagine it was one of the old sail ships, and they just used it for our quarters. It didn't go out to sea, or anything like that?

I imagine it's still there.

Author's Note: *(The USS Cumberland was decommissioned on October 31st, 1946 and delivered to the war Shipping Administration for disposal on July 22nd, 1947) http://www.navsource.org/archives/09/46/46008.htm?*

According to Wikipedia:

The **Battle of Château-Thierry** was fought on May 31, 1918 and was one of the first actions of the American Expeditionary Forces (AEF) under General John J. "Black Jack" Pershing. ... American forces had linked up with their French allies at the Marne River on June 3, 1918 and had forced the Germans back across the river. Fresh American troops were demoralizing the German soldiers opposing them.

JAMES: I shipped out on the USS Chateau Thierry. That was a ship named for a World War I battle? The Chateau Thierry was used as a transport ship, but our duty was a mission to the North Pole in Greenland, across the Arctic Circle. We had to stay up there six months. We had an expedition up there, to do some spy work.

Greenland was a colony of Denmark during World War II, and the German government had taken over Denmark. Denmark's government was still in power, but it was heavily influenced and controlled by the German Army. So, Greenland was sitting out there, thinking, "Hey, what am I going to do? We're a country out here, but we don't have any leadership." The Germans were trying to take over the east coast of Greenland. The British and Canadians were wanting to take over Greenland and make Greenland a colony of Great Britain, but the United States stepped in and said, "NO". Greenland is going to be an individual state until the war is over, and then it's going back to Denmark." So, the Germans were trying to set up weather camps all over the east coast, and the Americans were trying to do the same thing. So, eventually, the Germans were run out and, the Americans, set up their weather stations on the east coast of Greenland, and those were the weather stations that they used to plan for the D-Day invasions.: There was a time the Germans were threatening our shoreline with U-boats, and they were getting a little closer to crossing the Atlantic, and the United States anticipated, and they set up a secret mission to find out some way to track them?

IN DARKNESS

Hovered in darkness and couldn't see
   Rolling and Listing with misery
Sailed a ship upon the sea.
   Nestling a crew back home.
All of a sudden the taut sirene
   Pierced a sound that came unseen
A ship was attacked by a submarine
   That seeked to stop her roam.

A perilous darkness no night could match
   As the torpedo devastated number four hatch
Then wide and far went a dispatch
   A ship was going down
As other sailors had abandoned ships
   With sadness and confusion written on their lips
These sailors dove to initiative dips
   Some to save, some to drown.

Bobbing in boats being tossed by the waves
All "sneed by darkness endured these waves
The seaward wind had begun its rave
   Of twisting twinkling plights
All that their human hearts could hold
   Of joy and happiness remains untold
The dense of darkness had begun to unfold
   When a vessel of refuge filled their sights

In Darkness
by James Julian

Hovered in darkness and couldn't see
Rolling and listing with misery
Sailed a ship upon the sea
Nestling a crew back home
All of a sudden the taut sirene
Pierced a sound that came unseen
A ship was attacked by a submarine
That seeked to stop her roam.

A perilous darkness no night could match
As the torpedo devastated number four hatch
Then wide and far went a dispatch
A ship was going down
As other sailors had abandoned ships
With sadness and confusion written on their lips
These sailors dove to initiative dips
Some to save, some to drown.

Bobbing in boats being tossed by the waves
All silenced by darkness endured by these knaves
The seaward wind had begun its rave
Of twisting twirling plights
All that their human hearts could hold
Of joy and happiness remains untold
The dense of darkness had begun to unfold
When a vessel of refuge filled their sights

The Invasion Of Sicily

As we neared the Sicilian coast,
We did not sing, we did not Boast,
We did not drink or tell a toast.
    An invasion was at hand.
The faces of yanks were hard and stern,
Browned by the sun of African born,
Versed on tactics and eager to learn,
    Of skilled preciseness in this new land.

The darkness was cut by a half moon,
Ships were spotted like moving lagoons,
The battle would begin and very soon,
    On the coast of Sicily.
As we zig-zagged and moved in slow,
Flares were dropped and shone aglow,
All the troops had to lay below,
    For the battle was about to be.

With plenty of power to exert,
All of the crew were on the alert,
For enemy plane which to avert,
    For their flares were all around.
Silenced and solemn with listening ears,
We approached our foes without any fear.
For a democratic cause in the future years
    To make safe and profound.

The Invasion of Sicily
by: James Julian

As we neared the Sicilian Coast,
We did not sing, we did not boast,
We did not drink or tell a toast.
An invasion was at hand.

The faces of yanks were hard and stern,
Browned by the sun of African born,
Versed on tactics and eager to learn,
Of skilled preciseness in this new land.

The darkness was out by a holy moon,
Ships were spilled like moving lagoons,
The battle would begin and very soon,
On the coast of Sicily.

As we zig zagged and moved in slow,
Flares were dropped and shone aglow,
All the troops had to lay below,
For the battle was about to be.

With plenty of power to exert,
All of the crew were on the alert,
For enemy plane which to avert,
For their flares were all around.

Silenced and solemn with listening ears,
We approached our foes without any fears,
For a democratic cause in the future years
To make safe and profound.

The gallant defenders were on their guards,
When our warships commenced to bombard,
And neitherside seemed to PETARD,
　Under heavy ARTILLERY.
Fires were started on the shore,
Tracers were flying more and more,
From each gun that yield a bore,
　To avert a catastrophe.

WE moved in with all precision
Manuevering slowly without a collision
Nothing but gunfire filled our vision,
　From batteries dead ahead.
Ack ack were bursting all about;
Anti-aircraft fire like water spouts,
For enemy aircraft on their scouts
　The sky was soaring Red.

Finally the ALARM of battlecry,
CALLED us all to the scene of sky,
That bent Coney Island on the fourth of July,
　This was war and no celebration.
The moon was sinking in the west,
The island appeared as a flaming coast,
As defenders fought with faithfulness
　Trying to save a nation.

The gallant defenders were on the guards,
When the warships commence to bombard,
And neither side seemed to retard,
Under heavy artillery.

Fires were started on the shore,
Tracers were flying more and more,
From each gun that yield a bore,
To avert a catastrophe.

We moved in with all precision
Maneuvering slowly without a collision
Nothing but gunfire filled our vision,
From batteries dead ahead.

Ack-ack were bursting all about
Anti-aircraft fire like water spouts,
For enemy aircraft on their scouts
The sky was soaring red.

Finally the alarm of battlecry,
Called us all the scene of the sky,
That beats Coney Island on the Fourth of July,
This was war and no celebration.

The moon was sinking in the west,
The island appeared as a flaming crest,
As defenders fought with faithful mess,
Trying to save a nation.

The water we sailed was littered with oil,
The smoke hung high in a twisting coil,
A long peace was broken by a scene of toil,
'Upon this Axis possession.
Bombs were bursting upon the sea,
From axis planes of hostility.
Our guns were angled to the proper degree,
'We manned our station without recession

The water we sailed was littered with oil,
The smoke hung high in a twisting coil,
A long peace was broken by a scene of toil
'Upon this Axis possession.

Bombs were bursting upon the sea,
From Axis planes of hostility.
Our guns were angled to the proper degree,
We manned our station without recession.

JAMES: My job was to take care of officers, and their ship.

Eppie, did not know what he was doing on his missions?

I was not allowed to tell her. In fact, we didn't know what we were doing up there either… We found out later what it was.

EPPIE: When James was gone, I mostly got paid to clean houses. And when I was out of school, I started working in a dental office as an assistant to a dentist off Pryor Street in Atlanta. When I left there, I went back to school for a semester. Later, I went to New York, so I could be near him when he came in at the port. Otherwise, he would have leave, and I couldn't get there, and he couldn't get home. So, I just decided to go to New York. And then, when I went to New York, I started working.

James: When we left Greenland, We came back to six ports in Boston, Newport, New Virginia, Newport, Rhode Island, and I was assigned to the USS W. A. Man AP112 transport. About 1943. We were in the invasion of Sicily That was July 10th, I believe it was '43.

JAMES: I was a gunner on the 20mm battery. I was in the invasion on the northwest side of Sicily? It was a troop carrier.

JAMES: Our ship had anti-aircraft guns. We fought enemy airplanes. Oh yes, German airplanes in Sicily. *chuckles* I don't know who hit what, but we had 85 rounds with tracers—you could follow your tracers. It was in the daytime. We had to fight our way in. I forgot how many men we lost, but we didn't lose men on our ship. Didn't lose a man.

EPPIE: I did not know he was in the invasion of Sicily, not until afterwards. I heard a part of it on the radio, and we had a PM paper in New York that had very good reporters. He would report news as I was coming home from work on the bus, and I heard somebody— had a radio on, and they were hollering, "duck, duck, the bombs are coming! There's shrapnel every place!" And I said, oh my God, I thought everything was blowing up over there. When I got home, I listened to it again, and I wasn't really sure where it was until the next morning, and they were talking about the invasion of Sicily.

JAMES: Well, one incident in the invasion of Sicily. My loader threw a magazine in crooked! And I pulled the trigger on the machinegun, and it bit those bullets half in two. Part of it was spilling into the bridge, it was hot! He got excited because a plane was coming at us. What do you call it? The German Stuka. He got excited and put that thing in, and it bit the bullet in two, and powder started coming down on that hot bridge, and I had to unbuckle myself and get out of there and grab the magazine and throw it over the boat. That was the closest we got.

Yeah. *laughs* Didn't want to get blown up.

We got what you called a second loader—he took the first Loader" place and stuck another magazine in there, and we started all over again after I got buckled up. That was the closest I'd ever been to…

They replaced that guy and put another guy in his place? We always had a second loader, just in case something like that happened.

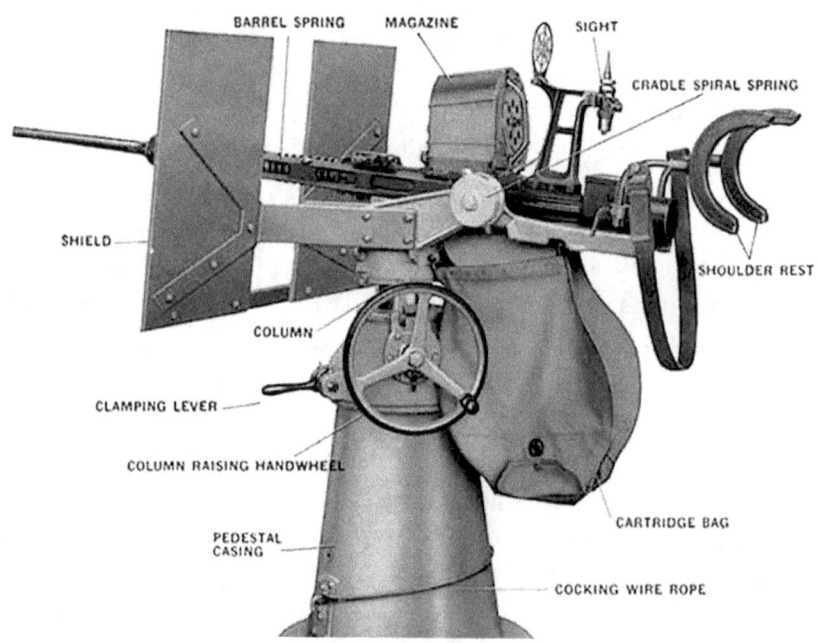

After SICILY: Mr. Julian had been fighting with his anti-aircraft gun against the German Stukas and the torpedo planes. When that was over, his ship was given orders to sail around Africa, all the way down to the southern end and all the way back up on the east side of Africa to a country called Oran. O-R-A-N. Today, we know it as Yemen. Inside Oran, there were several prisoner of war camps. The British and American soldiers had captured German soldiers in the Battle of Africa, and they had to be transported to prisoner of war camps to the United States. They loaded those prisoners of war and they took them back around Africa to the United States into South Carolina. The prisoners of war were farmed out in South Carolina and went all the way to Mississippi. Most prisoner of war camps were in the South, because the weather conditions made it cheaper to keep them in the South. You didn't have to heat the building so much and you could keep the prisoner of war outside and you could keep them working, and they were used for farm labor. A lot of our farmers had gone to war, so the German prisoner of war camps were used to pick cotton and to raise rice and do whatever needed to be done. And according to the Geneva Convention, the American people who used those German workers had to pay them. You will see in a later story the Germans were not so inclined to treat our POWs so well.

After that, Mr. Julian took a trip south through the Panama Canal, and went up to San Francisco, switched ships, and got on the USS Teton, and sailed into the Pacific.

JAMES: We invaded Okinawa in '45, I believe it was. We were in on Easter Sunday. I'll never forget that Easter Sunday. You know, there was a real famous prayer—I know you heard it—but in IWO JIMA on Easter Sunday, he was talking about the dead at IWO JIMA and at the same time, we were over there attacking Okinawa. It was the same day. It was a mess. That's about when Ernie Pyle got killed. He just popped his head out of a foxhole, and he was shot. We were right there. It was in eyesight of our ship, and he got killed. We got the word the next day. People were up on reading his articles and everything, it was like one in the family, lost.

Author's question: Do you remember when Ernie Pyle got killed, Eppie?

EPPIE: No, I had not heard it, and I don't really remember the day and all that.

Author's note: Ernie Pyle got his fame in Europe. When the war wound down in Europe, he went to the Pacific.

Okay, so, I'll tell you one story myself: my mother used to tell us her brother—he was in the Navy too, and his name was Frank Kinzalow, He would send my mom messages, and the message would say, "Juanita, what is the name of the church in Riceville on the right before you get to the highway?" And my mom would look at that and it would be the Oak Grove Baptist Church. So, my mom would go in and tell my grandmother that Uncle Frank was in Okinawa. Because they would send messages back and forth, and she could always interpret that.

The Battle of Okinawa was one of the hardest contested battles in the Pacific towards the end of World War II. Okinawa was part of the country of Japan, and when the Americans came to take it, the Japanese Army, and the Japanese citizens were told that if they did not stop the Americans, that the Americans would loot, and rob, and rape, and pillage the whole country, and that had to be stopped. The people of Okinawa were also given a direct order to jump off cliffs, and the soldiers were ordered to fight to the death, and if they couldn't fight anymore, to jump off the cliffs of Okinawa. So, there were about five hundred naval fighting vessels, and eleven hundred support vessels from the US Navy attacking Okinawa. The biggest part of the battle that most people remember are the boats of the US Navy fighting off the Japanese kamikaze. Thousands and thousands of Marines died, and about five thousand Navy sailors were killed during the Battle of Okinawa. They were coming in hard and fast were they not?

JAMES: In Sicily, we worried about the torpedo bombers. But, the kamikaze, you'd hit one, and damage him, and he's going to pick out a ship to try to take somebody else with him, you know. We never got hit, though. When you were in the invasion of Sicily, you were worried about torpedo planes? But when you got to Okinawa, you were worried about the kamikaze.: We were manning our battle station until the war was all over.

Months later we heard Truman dropped the bomb, so we left there and went to Yokohama. We were tied up beside the Battleship Missouri when the peace treaty was signed by all the dignitaries on the USS Missouri. We relayed the first message back that the war was over. We were the first communication ship to get word back to the United States, but I had enough points to get out, so I left my ship at Yokohama and came back to San Francisco. The American Military had a point system that placed soldiers and sailors in order when it came to receiving an Honorable Discharge. Since he was in the Navy before the war started, James Julian was given early priority to go home.

EPPIE: It was soon after the war was over, I think when he got to San Francisco.

When he found out he was leaving, he let me know he was coming home to me in New York by way of San Francisco.

JAMES: We had a point system, see, and I had did four years in service 'cause I went in 1939 and my time was up. So, instead of shipping over— shipping over means signing up for four more years—I extended for two, and my two years was up, so you can't get two extensions, so, I had to sign up for four more years, which would have made me have ten. So I was practically on hold in the point system, and I had enough points to get out, so I was among the first to be eligible for discharge. So, that's the reason I left my ship at Yokohama, Japan No, I came back on the ship, by the way of the Philippines. I landed in San Francisco, then I caught a train from San Francisco to New York Beach, New York. That's where I discharged.

EPPIE: Yes, I was waiting for him.

EPPIE to JAMES:" Tell him about the train trip".

JAMES: The train trip to New York was all tube train. Just by accident, Eppie's brother was a porter employee on the train.

EPPIE: Accident for him. *laughs*

JAMES: We had to pool to get home. I had to share a bunk with a white guy that was off of my ship, and he didn't want to bunk with a black man. And, so, the porter went back to the cattle car, and found a white boy, that said he needed to get out of that cattle car. He didn't care who he slept with! So, he slept in the bunk with me, and we had the best of eating, liquor drinking, all the way across! Five days!

So I was getting treated like a king because of Eppie's brother? That's good! That other guy deserved it, did they put him in the cattle car?

Author's note! Good! That first guy deserved no better than he had acted.

You have been learning about the exploits of James and Eppie Julian during World War II. They got married on May 10th, 1941. There were war clouds on the horizon, and they had to separate for a while, while James went off and fought World War II. Eppie started off in Atlanta, but wound up in New York, working, and she went to New York, because occasionally, James would come into port, and she wanted to be there when he got in.

For James, he started out in 1939 on a dorm ship, on a dorm ship of just black men. The United States Navy had a ship just for them, to keep them separate. The military was still segregated he worked as a steward like most black men in the Navy, Serving the Navy officers. He also trained to be an anti-aircraft gunner on the 20mm mounted guns. Eventually, he wound up on a ship going to Greenland, as his ship was involved in the task force trying to find a way to stop the German U-boats, and trying to stop the German invasions of Greenland as they too wanted to set up weather stations. The US ships were up there to stop that. Afterwards, he shipped out to the Mediterranean and fought in the invasion of Sicily, almost got killed when magazines jammed and threatened to explode. He had to throw the hot ammunition overboard. Then Uncle Sam's Navy took him on a tour of Africa, around both coasts to pick up prisoners of war. Taking them to South Carolina to be interred as Prisoners of War. Then, through the Panama Canal, up to San Francisco, over to Hawaii, into the Philippines, up to the Battle of Okinawa. When the Battle of Okinawa was over, he arrived in Tokyo Bay, on the USS Teton. That ship served as the communication ship of the Supreme Allied Commander, Douglas MacArthur. The USS Teton, relayed the very first message telling the free world that the Japanese had signed their surrender.

What did Mr. Julian get paid during this time? The US Navy paid stewards twenty-one dollars per month. Out of that, two dollars was taken out for insurance, and Mr. Julian had ten dollars a month sent home to his mother. He got paid every two weeks, so that meant the first week he had five dollars left over, and the second week, he had four. But after six years in the Navy, he had had promotions and pay rate increases, and at the end of the war, he was making thirty dollars a month.

During his tour in the Navy—money was so precious to everyone. Eppie had to visit him one day in the hospital, where a couple of American sailors had beaten him and robbed him, and his jaw was wired shut… Eppie went to the hospital to visit. As she was walking down the ward, she would say, "hello" to the wounded sailors. She didn't understand why none of them would respond, or why none of them would talk to her. By the time she got to the end of the line, she asked the nurse why everyone was so quiet. And the nurse's response was, "they're all deaf from injuries they had obtained in the war."

Eppie and James have children, grandchildren, and great grandchildren, most of whom live in Atlanta. They may not ever have existed, had James not been able to get that hot magazine thrown overboard at the Battle of Sicily. Or, if one of the German Stukas, who were dive bombing with torpedoes had hit his ship, or if one of the kamikazes at the Battle of Okinawa had hit his ship instead of one of the others.

He heard about the death of Ernie Pyle, and was nearby when it happened. His ship relayed the announcement of the end of World War II.

Eppie and James, I know your family surprised you with the celebration of your 70th wedding anniversary. James wrote Eppie a poem while at war.

To Evonne

To your heart I shall set afire
A flame of burning love
To kindle the spark to your each desire.
Of earthly things and Heaven's above.

To your voice I shall vow to hear
The words of inspiration
Their vibrance causes my heart to soar
With bright ideas of a new creation

To your smile that registers personality
With a blend of kindness and joy
An emotional sentimentality
All which are sweet, so shy and coy.

To your charm that is glory
Which devotional honor is due
And from my heart I'd write a story
To Evonne, my lovable you.

To Evonne "Eppie"

To your heart I shall set a fire
A flame of burning love
To kindle the spark to your each desire
Of Earthly things and heaven's above
To your voice I shall vow to hear
The words of inspiration
Their vibrance causes my heart to sear
With bright ideas of a new creation
To your smile that registers personality
With a blend of kindness and joy
An emotional sentimentality
All which are sweet, so shy and coy.
To your charm that is glory
Which devotional honor is due
And from my heart I'd write a story
To Evonne, my lovable you.

When I was second year high school a girl named Eppie Evonne West changed schools and fell right in my class when entered my school. All through high school I didn't have any intention of any affection ***** or petting her. I didn't seem to work to work up to her or take advantage of it. Exactly seven months after grad I joined the Navy. Eleven months later, I visited home and met her for the first time since graduation time. I asked he for her address and gave her mine. A three minute conversation and I was off again. I started corresponding through mail just friendly, and it grew into the bargaining of writing each other ever twenty four hours For a year and a half, this went on. Finally I got leave and went home. Three days after my arrival, she was Mrs. James William Julian. On the day of my arrival was the first time I had ever embraced her, or kissed. The glorious part and answer to love's extremities happen two days after marriage. Happening only twice in my 12 days at home, She is the sweetest person that exists, or will ever exist. My love for her is everlasting.

Mr. Julian passed away in 2012. He had become my friend.

Early in the war, American military strategists had to decide what islands were needed to push the Japanese back to their home islands and to defeat their powerful navy and army. The first land battles of the Pacific were Guadalcanal and Bougainville. On December 7th, 1941, a man moving from job to job was sitting at a desk in Paducah, Kentucky. His name was George Harper, and you are about to meet him.

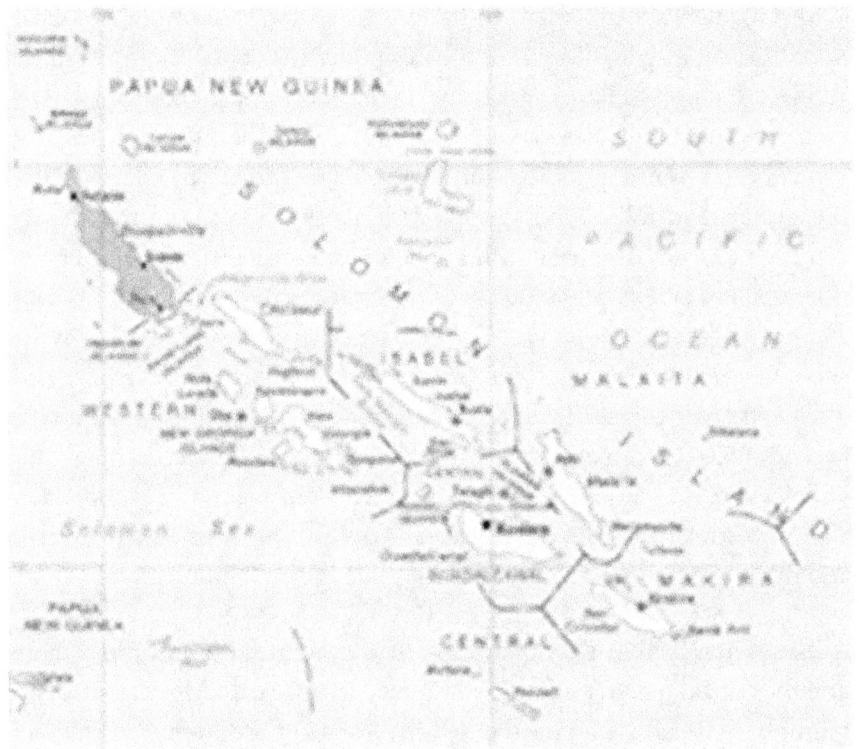

CHAPTER FOUR

THE ISLAND HOPPING BEGINS!

In August 1942, the United States mounted its first major amphibious landing in World War II at Guadalcanal, using innovative landing craft built by Higgins Industries in New Orleans. By seizing a strategic airfield site on the island, the United States halted Japanese efforts to disrupt supply routes to Australia and New Zealand. The invasion ignited a ferocious struggle marked by seven major naval battles, three major land battles, and almost continuous air combat as both sides sought to control Henderson Field, named after Loy Henderson, an aviator killed at the Battle of Midway. For six long months US forces fought to hold the island. In the end they prevailed, and the Allies took the first vital step in driving the Japanese back in the Pacific theater.

With Guadalcanal in American hands, Allied forces continued to close in on Rabaul in New Britain. As forces under the command of Admiral William F. "Bull" Halsey moved north through the Solomons, General Douglas MacArthur's troops pushed west along the northern coast of Papua New Guinea, grinding out a hard-fought victory by March 1943. But rather than follow this success with a risky invasion of the heavily defended Rabaul, American military planners hatched an ingenious plan: Allied planes and ships would isolate and neutralize Rabaul from the air and sea while the bulk of MacArthur's forces pushed westward to invade less-well-defended islands. This practice—skipping over heavily fortified islands in order to seize lightly defended locations that could support the next advance—became known as island hopping. As Japanese strongholds were isolated, defenders were left to weaken from starvation and disease. This new strategy turned the vast Pacific distances into an American ally, and the United States used it to leapfrog across the Pacific.

Author's note: All my life I have watched movies starring John Wayne and Steve McQueen, and many others, even Ricardo Montalban, and Humphrey Bogart, who tried to tell the stories of situations our soldiers have faced. I still watch those movies today when I have a chance.

As a child, I knew about a place called Guadalcanal, I had read a book called The Thin Red Line and later in my life saw a movie with the same name. I also remember a movie called Guadalcanal Diary starring Anthony Quinn.

Recently I read a poem by: Jerry McConnell who as an 18 year old experienced the battle, and who later wrote a poem called "The Grassy Knoll".

I think this poem does a really great job of describing the early events on Guadalcanal.

The Grassy Knoll

'Twas on August 7, back in '42
Weclimbed down the nets into boats
There was an air of sharp apprehension
We all had a lump in our throats.

The Captain had briefed us beforehand
On what was to be our goal -
A huge mound of earth near the airstrip
Insignificantly named, "Grassy Knoll."

"With this in our hands," it was offered
"Our aircraft can land on the strip."
But to many of those who listened,
It would be their very last trip.

The ocean spray lapped over the boat
Cooling faces now sweated with fear.
Not a word was heard from the bodies there
Crouched low from the weight of their gear.

A sudden thump announced our arrival
As the boat crunched the sand on the beach
The whine of the bullets were taking their toll
And more men were thrown into the breach.

Our target was seven miles distant
Which at the moment seemed mighty remote.
And we, who were going to be heroes
Were donning the horns of the goat.

The enemy had full intentions
Of stopping us dead in our tracks.
There was no way to go but forward
As the ocean was right at our backs.

The noise and the tumult were maddening
And the wounded were screaming with pain.
But it seemed that with each man who fell there
Our assault inched forward in gain.

At last we came into a clearing
That stretched out for several miles
The strain of the jungle was succored
And our faces were wreathed in smiles.

But our joy was soon turned to sadness
And we wished for the jungle again,
'Cause the heat of the sun was oppressive
And flesh-eating ant bites brought pain.

The canteens we carried were emptied
As men tried to slacken their thirst.
It looked like the heat would soon kill us
If the ants didn't do the job first.

The grass in the clearing was very tall
With blades like razor-edged knives
That cut and slashed our bodies and clothes
And further imperiled our lives.

Our pack straps cut deep in our shoulders
From the weight of the gear stowed inside.
But with bodies now aching and retching
We forged on, driven purely by pride.

We had made our landing at daybreak
Planning to arrive at our goal by noon.
It was now fast approaching nightfall
And we hoped for some light from the moon.

We moved on, to get out of the clearing
'Ere darkness obscured our view
And plodded on back into the jungle
Thankful the clearing was through.

The dense underbrush of the jungle
Which earlier had near spelled our end,
Embraced us with all-'round protection
And now became a good friend.

We fought back away from the beaches
Into jungle that steamed from the heat.
And now our troops were determined
That they weren't about to be beat.

The enemy men were soon routed
And our forces were gaining control.
But much to our later discomfort
They drew back to the big "Grassy Knoll."

We plodded our way through the jungle
Losing two steps for each one we'd gain.
Our bodies and clothing were sweat-drenched
As though we'd been soaked in the rain.

The effects of the day were now showing
That though tired, we were nervous with fear
And some men were firing at random
At each sound they happened to hear.

With this each man grew more cautious
And struggled to stay awake,
Lest he accidentally make noises
And get himself shot by mistake.

The night seemed long and endless
And we gratefully greeted the dawn.
But the sleepless night had taken its toll
And our bodies were tired and drawn

We ate up the last of our rations
Before we were forced to move on.
We felt like a legion of doomed men—
All our water and food were gone.

Our parched tongues were begging for water
And on nary a face was a smile,
And every man among us knew
We'd get none, for quite a while.

Each dew drop that perched on a plant leaf
Was greedily lapped up in thirst.
And thirst crazed men who once were friends
Battled to get to it first.

Our bodies and souls were so weakened
And the strain was breaking our backs.
When the order came to secure there
Every man fell down in his tracks.

The jungle so hot in the daytime
Became freezing cold at night,
And our weary and battered bodies
Were shaking from cold and fright.

A deathly silence prevailed there
Each man was deep in his thoughts.
When suddenly the quiet was broken
By the crackling of rifle shots.

The crack of a rifle then signaled
Our scouts had discovered the foe.
The advance was steady and cautious
All movements were careful and slow.

The noise of the fight was increasing
More rifles were joining the fray.
It was a time when men came close to God
And to themselves, they'd silently pray.

The full fury of war came in minutes
The cries of the wounded increased.
But for many a man who fell to the ground
The toil and suff'ring had ceased.

The enemy fire was deadly
Crisscrossing our lines at will.
Only one thing was on the enemy's mind
Line 'em up, squeeze 'em off, and kill!

It was difficult trying to move up
The cover-less grassy slopes.
But the withering fire of the enemy guns
Did little to dampen our hopes.

For we were determined to win there
And in spite of tremendous odds
We moved steadily onward and upward
While shell-fire tore up the earth in clods.

Discipline fast was fading
And tempers were getting hot.
Battle fatigue was fast setting in
We were a tattered and torn looking lot.

Then a rumble spread down thru the column
Sending chills clear down to the soul.
The dreaded time was approaching —-
We were nearing the big "Grassy Knoll."

The battered and weary Marines
With dirt, sweat and grime on their hide,
Quickly stopped all the grousing
And stiffened their backs with pride.

Hunger and thirst were forgotten
Men welded together as one.
Orders were quickly obeyed then —-
There was a big job to be done.

Apprehension once more called for caution.
We crept stealthily forward with care.
Not a man ever failed to take cover
Not a man would even dare.

At last we were nearing the summit
Return fire was beginning to thin.
The tide was completely reversed now
And we knew we were going to win.

The last handful of stragglers were captured
And the air was at last serene.
It was then we were able to survey
The bloody and grisly scene.

The dead and the wounded were littered
Most everywhere you could see.
There was sadness in spite of victory
For dead friends— and enemy.

It's hell when you stop to consider
The price that was dearly paid
For this lousy chunk of God's green earth
That on a lonely island laid.

Many a man paid the maximum price
He forfeited his life for the toll.
And all he got forevermore.
Was a plot on the big "Grassy Knoll."

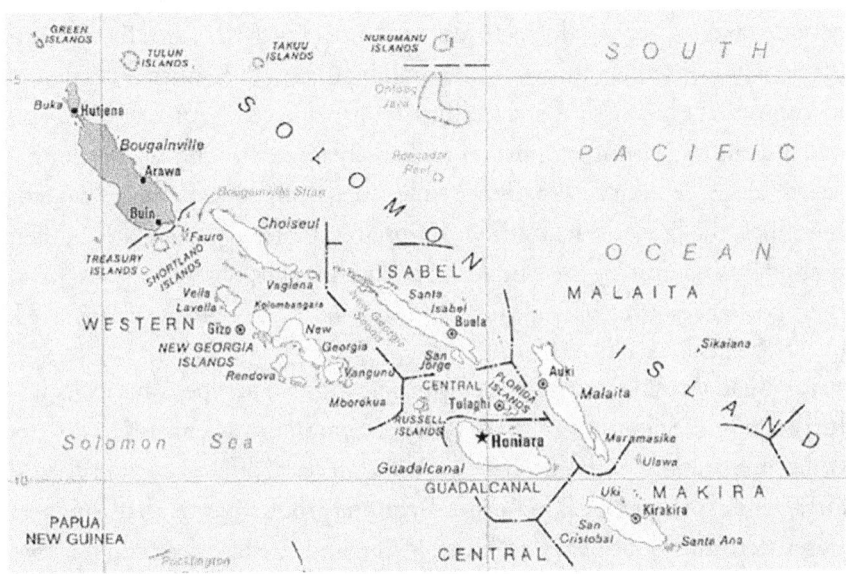

This map can help you understand the importance of Guadalcanal. The sound is bounded by Choiseul Island, Santa Isabel Island, and Florida Island to the north, and by Vella Lavella, Kolombangara, New Georgia, and the Russell Islands to the south. Bougainville Island of the Autonomous Region of Bougainville (Papua New Guinea) and Guadalcanal island, define northwestern and southeastern ends of the sound, respectively.

The islands protected shipping, and was known as THE SLOT. The south end, Guadalcanal had an airfield the Allies, (Mostly Americans) needed as an air base.

The Solomons Campaign

The Pacific War Online Encyclopedia © 2007-2008, 2010 by Kent G. Budge. Index

Against all expectations, the remote and economically unimportant Solomons became the focus of the decisive campaign of the Pacific War. The Japanese had seized Tulagi during the Battle of the Coral Sea, and after the battle they began building an airfield on nearby Guadalcanal from which they planned to project power into the Coral Sea. American code breakers discovered this threat to the sea lanes to Australia, and the Americans hurriedly improvised an amphibious assault against Guadalcanal to capture the airfield. The landings took place on 7 August 1942 and marked the beginning of a brutal and costly land, air, and sea battle that lasted until 9 February 1943. By the time Guadalcanal was finally secured by the Allies, the Japanese had suffered crippling attrition, particularly of their best pilots and destroyers. The Allies had suffered heavy losses as well, but their greater resource base meant that losses could more easily be replaced.

With Guadalcanal secured, the obvious next move for the Americans was further up the Solomons chain to Rabaul. Yamamoto attempted to disrupt Allied preparations with the *I-Go* operation, an aerial offensive against Allied airfields and shipping. This proved counterproductive in that Japanese losses were almost as heavy as Allied losses, and the Japanese could afford them less. In particular, carrier air groups were shifted to land bases to assist with *I-Go*, which was a gross misuse of the highly trained carrier pilots. The Americans had also used carrier groups from Henderson Field during the crisis at Guadalcanal, but only when their carriers were put out of action, and the groups were withdrawn once their carriers were repaired.

Allied forced occupied the Russell Islands on 21 February 1943, then moved against New Georgia (Operation TOENAILS) in January 1943. The New Georgia campaign proved long and costly, and thereafter the Allied commanders looked for opportunities to leapfrog around Japanese strongholds. Their efforts to do so were made easier by superb intelligence. Vella Lavella was seized against light opposition in August 1943, bypassing heavily defended Kolombangara. The Treasury Islands were seized on 27 October 1943 and Cape Torokina on 1 November 1943, bypassing the Japanese strongholds in the Shortland Islands and southern Bougainville. Thus, by 1944, the Solomons were firmly under Allied control and the stage was set for neutralizing Rabaul and breaking the Bismarcks Barrier.

Reference.

The Pacific War Online Encyclopedia © 2007-2008, 2010 by Kent G. Budge. Index

NOW IT IS TIME FOR OUR STORY!

It was only nine months since the Japanese had bombed Pearl Harbor, and our Marines were not very experienced even though they were well trained. It was only two months since the battle of Midway victory, and the stand at Wake Island was still on their minds.

These 18-25 year old men were approaching the beaches of Guadalcanal, anxious, and afraid.

The mission was an airstrip, near a "GRASSY KNOLL". Some distance from the landing spot,

When the landing crafts dropped them off, they had the ocean to their backs, no- where to retreat, and orders to move forward.

These Marines knew if we had the airstrip it would be like having an unsinkable aircraft carrier in the middle of the enemy's stronghold. They were virtually unopposed as they landed. Eventually the Japanese let our Marines know they were on the island. The cries of the wounded, the heat, and the jungle in front was their immediate foe.

Once through the jungle they were relieved to see the grassy plain. Soon, the shade of the jungle was gone and the trek in the grass got hotter and hotter, and I am not sure they were briefed about the biting ants. I did not know about the ants until I read the poem. And when I think of grass I do not think of a plant that would cut me if I brushed up against it. Nor did I know about the water shortages, and how that would be a factor that grew in urgency with every step forward.

They started with their backs to the ocean and pushed the Japanese back to where, soon, the Japanese would have their backs to the ocean. Before that could happen they had to cross that grassy knoll, and get back into the jungle each step confronting a weakening and more desperate Japanese Soldier whose creed was instilled that they were not to surrender.

This "second jungle" experience seemed almost a relief to be fighting in the hot shade. The confidence of the Marines began to grow. But they were also tired, and "jumpy".

Mistakes were made, "today we know it as "friendly fire", especially after it got dark.

It got cold at night.

The next day their rations and water were almost gone. The chance of resupply was not promising. Water was wanted, needed, and not expected.

With morning the fight renewed, the enemy had not slept, and set up criss crossing fire.

The fight went back to the "GRASSY KNOLL".

Tired, thirsty, and scared the marines moved up the hill. The Navy was helping with bombardments.

Since the Solomons lie in the Southern Pacific, the landings of 7 August 1942 on Guadalcanal were the responsibility of the South Pacific Fleet, led by Vice Admiral **Robert L. Ghormley** from his headquarters at Noumea, New Caledonia.[2] Adm. Ghormley's pessimism, inadequate staff work and unwillingness to visit the front led Adm. Nimitz to replace him with the much more aggressive and hands-on Vice Admiral **William F. Halsey** on 18 October 1942.[3]

Operational command of the invasion was assigned to Vice Admiral **Frank Jack Fletcher**. He also had direct command of the covering force, designated Task Force 61, where he flew his flag aboard fleet carrier *Saratoga*. The amphibious forces, Task Force 62, were led by Rear Admiral **Richmond Kelly Turner** aboard transport *McCawley*.

Bitter disputes between the two men arose during both the planning and execution of the invasion over how long Fletcher's aircraft carriers would stay in the vicinity of Guadalcanal to provide air cover for the Marines ashore. Fletcher decided the matter after multiple assaults on the Allied amphibious task force by bombers from the Japanese base at Rabaul on D-Day and D+1. These attacks convinced Fletcher that his crucial aircraft carriers could not be risked in the waters of the Solomons any longer and he ordered his carriers and Turner's still-half-full cargo ships out of the area on the night of 8 August. This decision resulted in much hard feeling among the Marines ashore, who felt that the Navy had abandoned them.

Research supplied by: wikipedia.org/wiki/Guadalcanal_naval_order_of_battle

After taking the hill the resistance weakened, and the enemy gave in, but the sweet victory was tempered with the bodies of the friends of these 18-25 year old men lying in their path.

THE GRASSY KNOLL" or read the book, THE THIN RED LINE or rent the movie.

This was a description of the first days at Guadalcanal, The battle was over in Feb 1943, what you just read was a synopsis of the first 48 hours. I was not there, I was not even born.

Henderson Field on Guadalcanal was captured on or about August 12, 1942.

This story is not about Guadalcanal, Iron Bottom Bay, or even the Battle of The Coral Sea, just about someone I know who happened to get there about the time this was all going on. I have had the honor of meeting of few of these men late in their lives and George Harper told me of his experiences on Guadalcanal and Bougainville. He was in the 3rd Marine Division, the story above was the First Marine division. George Harper arrived on Guadalcanal about June of 1943. He was there as an engineer, a squad leader.

The primary mission of the 3rd Marine Division was to execute amphibious assault operations and other such operations as may be directed. The Division is supported by Marine aviation, and force service support units and is prepared to be employed, in conjunction with a Marine aircraft wing, as an integral part of a Marine Expeditionary Force in amphibious operations.

The 3d Marine Division was activated on September 16, 1942 at Camp Elliott in San Diego, California. The Division was formed with cadre from the 2nd Marine Division and built around the 9th Marine Regiment. The first Commanding General of the Division was Major General Charles D. Barrett. By January of 1943 the 3rd Marine Division was moved by piecemeal, not as one unit, to Aukland, New Zealand. This movement was completed by March and in June the 3MarDiv deployed to Guadalcanal to train for the invasion of Bougainville, Island.

On November 1, 1943 the 3rd Marine Division landed at Empress Augusta Bay, on the west coast of Bougainville. For approximately two months the Division participated in the fight against stiff and heavy enemy resistance. On January 16, 1944, with the transfer of command in the area to the Army's XIV Corps, the last elements of the Division returned to Guadalcanal. During the course of the Battle of Bougainville the Division had approximately 400 Marines killed.

The Fighting Third returned to Guadalcanal in January, 1944 to rest, refit, and train. During the spring of 1944 the Division trained for several operations that were subsequently cancelled. The 3rd Marine Division was also held in reserve for the invasion of Saipan

George Harper was 90 years old when I met him. He lived in Paducah, Kentucky at the start of the war, and was living in Oliver Springs, Tennessee with his daughter, Linda Harper. Both participated in the interview.

We started: Let's start you off and tell us how you got in the Marines.

GEORGE: Well, it was on Sunday morning. I forget the time, but I was probably in Paducah, sitting at my desk. Actually I was a drifter. When they announced the war broke out at Pearl Harbor. After that, I wanted to get in the Marine Corps because I figured they were the best fighters in the world—which they are. As a civilian, I was working in an ice house catching ice? Catching big blocks of ice as they came down a chute. I was a little-bitty man. 155 pounds, and they'd come down as 300 pound blocks, and I'd take a set of hooks and catch one in each hand, and set it up on its end.

RANDY: You know, it's funny when you told me that, because I did that too at the Atlantic Ice Company in Knoxville, Tn. When I was going to college. I stood waiting on those 300 pound blocks—

GEORGE: Well, you're a bigger man, than I was—

RANDY: Well, I was a little bigger, but those blocks were the same size!

GEORGE: That's right! I lived in…… what was that little town?

LINDA: (George's daughter.) Herndon.

GEORGE: Herndon, Kentucky. Right next to Paducah.

I joined the Marines and went to boot camp, Parris Island, South Carolina.

laughs Nothing fun the whole 60 days there. You'd get up at 12 o'clock, clean the floors, and just to get it done, Serge would come and pour a bucket of sand right in the middle of it. Just for meanness.

Author's note: Did they ever talk to you about a phrase called "muscle memory?" I was reading a book while preparing for this interview. A marine wrote a story about when he was on Guadalcanal; it was dark, and a Japanese soldier stabbed him in the hand with a bayonet, and it crossed over onto his shoulder. He said with the training that he had on Parris Island, that he didn't mentally react, it was all muscle memory. When he got stabbed, he took the rifle away from the Japanese soldier and killed him with it. He said it was all muscle memory from the training he received on Parris Island, so that was pretty tough training, wasn't it?

GEORGE: It was real tough training. After boot camp, I got on a ship heading out to the Pacific. What happened between the time you left Parris Island and the time you got out to the first fight?

Author's note: I researched the 3rd Marines history and this is what I found: This is the time table of the Third Division at Parris Island, and then two months in North Carolina, where they still have services there now. They got through shooting at the rifle range, then went to California and stayed about two months, Headed out for the South Pacific, and stopped in New Zealand for four months, and then the next stop was Guadalcanal. The division transferred into Auckland, New Zealand between January and March 1943. In June of that year they moved onto Guadalcanal for additional training. 27 September 1943 saw the Marines land as part of the Battle of Bougainville and fight on the island until their last unit to arrive, the 21st Marine Regiment, embarked on 9 January 1944. During the course of the battles the Marines had approximately 400 killed.[3]

GEORGE: About April. We were in New Zealand for the first three months in 1943 for training. The conditions that were on Guadalcanal? Well, it was pouring rain conditions and they bombed us the first night we were there. I was making a trip with some truck drivers, and they bombed my ship while I was unloading the truck. First day I was there, they threw a bomb at me? First night, yeah. We went in after dark A plane dropped bombs. It hit the ship, it didn't hurt anything in particular. It burnt part of it, but it wasn't real serious: They made a dive, you know, and they all missed. I was already an engineer when I got there. They appointed engineers in North Carolina. Mostly built roads and back up for the infantry. The people before the war set out a lot of trees and we got to eat the coconuts off those trees. Green coconut, some of the boys had trouble getting the coconuts, but I was driving a dump truck, an all steel vehicle and I just backed it against the trees. *laughs* And the first tree I shook out, I shook out a monkey, and I was looking in the mirror and I jumped out and tried to grab him, and it was a good thing I didn't, 'cause he was scratching and wild. He came down with the coconuts.

I was the squad leader. I had sixteen, seventeen men under him, and I told them what to do. I mean, kind of relay things. A squad leader is responsible for the accomplishment of squad missions, but he's also responsible for the lives of a dozen other Marines. It's not like the war we have now. War settled here by hitting the ground, you left a year later, or whatever. You had to stay, you had no relief or anything.

Author's note: When the 3rd Marines landed on Guadalcanal, many were struck in awe about how serene the island appeared from the decks of the troop ships. The island looked like it was lush, green, mist covered hills, looked like pictures in a travelogue. But upon landing, they discovered a landscape so alien, it may as well have been on the moon. I asked George if he remembered the jungles or the grassy plains?—did you have a chance to go through the battle zone?

GEORGE: Not really. When we got there, we weren't around that, and we built roads above them, or whatever. And the Air Force was thirty miles away: I wasn't part of the initial battle, but I remember about it. And then after—I left Guadalcanal, AND then went to Bougainville?

Following the American success at Guadalcanal in February 1943, Allied forces advanced up the Solomon Island chain and in late 1943 commenced the Bougainville campaign as part of the larger Operation Cartwheel.[10] At the opening of the Allied offensives, estimates of Japanese strength on Bougainville varied widely, ranging between 45,000 to 65,000 Army, Navy, and labor personnel.[3]

The first phase of Allied operations to retake Bougainville (Operation Cherry Blossom)[11] from the Japanese 17th Army began with landings at Cape Toro kina by the U.S. Marine 3rd Division,

George: Well, we went into Bougainville, and the Japs was already bombing when we got there, but there was another time we stopped the ship and the ship got bombed before we got off of it. I didn't get hurt, but a piece of steel went right over my head. I was leaning back against an eight inch pipe running through the ship, and this shrapnel went over my head, and I heard it hit, and I looked down when it fell, and it was a piece of shrapnel. It would have cut my head off if it had been a little bit lower. 'course, we had orders to go low, but I didn't until actually that happened.

Author's note: Have you ever wondered why Guadalcanal was actually chosen as a battle site. Go back to the map I supplied. Guadalcanal was an island that the Japanese had taken over before the Americans got there. They did not staff it with crack troops, mostly with engineer battalions to build an airport. They were interested in the fruits and vegetables on the island to feed their Army. It became important after the Battle of Midway, because they had to make a decision. The Japanese Navy wanted to keep pushing the American troops, and to intimidate them, and the Japanese Army wanted to consolidate and defend what they had already conquered. So, there was a conflict in the Japanese military. The Americans wanted Guadalcanal because they could use it as a stationary air base like an unsinkable aircraft carrier. So, Guadalcanal became important for two different reasons, the Japanese army wanted to dig in and defend and stop the American advance and break the American feeling of success they had at Midway. The Americans wanted the island so they could open the door and send supplies to Australia and New Zealand and launch their attack to Japan.

Bougainville was a little different. The Generals and Admirals had agreed that they would take Bougainville and keep the airport and all the area around, but they didn't need the whole island. They had decided that it was a good idea to keep Japanese soldiers on the island of Bougainville because they couldn't be somewhere else. So, they didn't want to take the whole island of Bougainville, they just wanted to take the airport and keep the Japanese soldiers on the island so that we wouldn't have to fight them somewhere else.

So, anyway... Mr. Harper. You were at Bougainville, weren't you?

GEORGE: Yes, it was sad. Even after we captured the island and took it back, we ran out of food. Usually, the United States had the food there for you the day before. We were out of food, and we went throughout the complete island for three weeks. I was squad leader and had 16 men under me. That particular day, after it eased up a little bit, I was walking up a dirt road, and a truck had got sideways and PET milk slid off the truck. I could drink PET milk—I tasted it with a spoon, and I was by myself, and I reached out and took a can of that milk and took my knife and opened it, and drank the whole can of it.: That was the concentrated milk.

PET Dairy. We had Mayfield's Dairy in Kentucky.

Mayfield's was in Athens, Tennessee, and PET Dairy in Johnson City, Tennessee. I know PET Dairy well. Okay.

While I was in Bougainville, we had to go back and bail the Army out several different times. One particular time, we took Bougainville back four different times.

Author's note: Okay. So, the Marines and Army have always had a little bit of a conflict, because the Marines are the ones that you send in when you need to take something.

GEORGE: That's right.

Author's note: Alright, so in Bougainville, the Marines complained that they had to keep returning to the island, and they always gave the Army a hard time, saying, "we have to keep coming and bailing you guys out," and just in defense of the Army because I've got a friend who's about your age that was there, and I asked him about that, and he said, "Randy, they put us out there on such a thin line and told us to keep the Japanese pushed away, but they never gave us enough support. So when they broke through, we had to get support, and we would call the Navy and the Navy would bring the Marines in, and the Marines would come in and back us up." And he said that they were glad to have you there, but they knew that you all gave them a hard time, but you also need to remember you all were their help. You know, and it'd be nice to know, I tell my daughter LORI, not to go anywhere in the world that the US Navy can't get to in ten minutes, and it's good to know the Marines are that portable and can come and go on whatever island they want to and take it, or take it back.

GEORGE: That's right. So we left Bougainville in December of 1943 and turned it over to the Americal Division (see next Chapter), and then we went back to Guadalcanal. Stayed nine months. And that's when they were consolidating the island. They sent the Marines in there and they said, "Okay, we want the island cleaned up, no more Japanese on the island." And they sent us in to do that. One time while I was still there, after it had been settled for several months, I was eating lunch up there at the airport one day. Two Japanese came out of the mountains and got in the chow line. Got almost up there at the kitchen door, and somebody said, "well that's not our people, that's something else!" So they grabbed them out of the line, these two Japanese trying to steal food. They put us on duty right there on that island with no leave. I never had leave from the whole time I left the United States till I came back to America. Almost three years. You went out there until you either died or won the war.

Author's note: Guam. On July 21, 1944 the Americans landed on both sides of the Orote Peninsula on the western side of Guam, planning to cut off the airfield. The 3rd Marine Division, with George Harper in tow, landed near Agana to the north of Orote at 08:28,

GEORGE: Well, I was over there for ten days. I departed on my ship at 4 o'clock in the morning, and I was one of the first Marines on land. The landing craft infantry ship was supposed to lay plank down on the land, but there were so many reeds there, you had to stomp out a half-mile out in the ocean, and you'd jump out of the ship and the water was up to your chin most the time. You had to hold your gun over your head and your pack on your back and you were really overloaded before you jumped out. And then when we got close to land, I looked back to see what was going on, and at that time, the Japanese started bombing us. Hands and arms were going up in the air 1500 feet. That was the next ship behind me, the next landing craft carrier. I had orders to go on the land and pick out a place for my company to stop and get set up to start over the mountain road, and you stayed wherever you cleared till the rest of them showed up. That's what I did, and when sergeant came up with his platoon, he came up there and found my position, and fifteen minutes after he got there, they started firing. One of my buddies on my team, Cpl. Cassidy, I said, "let's get out of here, the next one will be right here." And sure enough, the next one dropped right where we stood. And Sgt. Cassidy got his right ear blew off his head, and another one—they taught us in school in the states how bad a shot the Japanese was, well, I picked up a helmet and a bullet went right between his eyes. I said, "Somebody's wrong, somewhere." Or else, They had a good ricochet shot!

"For three days there, the second day I was checking out the troops, and I got set out on a hill watching one of our American boys sighting a Japanese Soldier as he crawled one-legged, he'd already been shot in one leg, and he out-crawled him, so he got in that hole before he got shot. The next thing I knew, something hit me in the back, and I reached back with my thumb and finger and pulled out this bullet, The doctor said if it had been in much further, it would have ruined my life. All I did was pull it out with my thumb and finger, and a Navy man was about twenty feet from me, and he put iodine on it. He said, "you're gonna hurt real bad, but it's gonna be ok!"

Next day or two, 1st lieutenant comes in—I loved him, he was a good man. The 2nd lieutenants, they were crap, both ways up and down. But this lieutenant was a good one, his name was Lord, L-O-R-D, from Nashville, Tennessee. I've tried to find him since then, never did, but he's with me, so he said, "George, go with me, we've been pinned down three days, and all we've had happen is our staff sergeant got killed out front." He said, "If you go, I know you're an expert with a bazooka, and you could knock out that one machine gun. Then we'll be able to move." Well, I did just that. We both went out early—I didn't have a wristwatch or a pistol. Didn't have anything but an old M1 and a bazooka. I got in position, thought it was just right, and made a perfect shot. Those bazookas, they arced like that. I got my first round off and it went right in the place, it was perfect. In the meantime, I was rewinding to pull off the next shot. I was down on my hands and knees, and about fifty feet from me a Japanese came out of a hole—they could crawl in holes on that side, they could squat down in there. When he'd come out, they'd tap their hand grenades on their helmets to detonate them. When they tapped it, that got my attention, and I'd stop what I was doing. I saw them come out of a hole, and I said, "look out, Lieutenant!" because I knew they were hitting his position. The next thing I knew, that was early one morning, and late that afternoon, I woke up. When I got up, I stuck my hand down and every time my heart would beat, blood would squirt out of my hand. They said, "Harper, you're wounded, and you've gotta get out of here. You're wounded badly." Of course, I couldn't see what was going on in the dust and dirt, and I turned to what I thought was the right way to get back out, and it was, but I didn't know it. So, I ran about 60 yards, and I said, "That's funny, there's no firing or bullets or anything." So, I stopped and turned around and looked, and just as I looked, one of our American tanks had backed up and was firing at the same machine gun I'd already knocked out. But I guess there were more—they still had four machine guns in one hole.

Oh, I was bleeding all over. A fragment took my left big toe nail off, one fragment went right up through here and came out my mouth, and I had shrapnel up to this ear. I found out more about it when I had a car wreck years later, and. well, let's leave that off of here.

When I got up, I just left my old bazooka wadded up—of course, when the rocket went off, it ruined it anyway. I turned the way that I thought would head back to the beach, which it was, and when I saw the tank taking over, I started walking, and got maybe about a mile down and a Jeep came along and said, "hey, you want a ride?" I said, "I sure do." I got out to the beach, we were driving along the edge of the sand, and I looked up and saw the same boat that I'd been on—I forgot what it is now, but I knew what it was then. And he said, "It's heading my way, to the hospital." And he stopped the Jeep, I got out, went on the ship, they took good care of me. I didn't have orders or anything, I was just on my own.

Author's note: I had a second guest that day it's Linda Harper, she is the daughter of George Harper, United States Marines, 1940 vintage. Linda, tell us a little bit about being a daughter of a US Marine from World War II.

LINDA: Well, you were asking me earlier, when I first learned that dad was in the war, and when I was just a child of, say, three and four, I knew dad had some war artifacts. He had a whole sack of gold teeth that had been taken out of the dead Japanese, he had a Purple Heart, different items, and I used to go in—I knew where mom kept them, and I would just sometimes take an inkling to go in and play with them, and I did that all throughout my childhood. We never talked about the war, I never heard dad mention it until two years ago, when he was 88 and at that time, I had a friend from grade school who's a historian, and he was asking me about where my dad was in the war. I told him, because I did know Guam, Guadalcanal, and Bougainville, but when he found that out, he said, "my gosh, Linda, do you realize so many of the guys over there did not return? Do you realize where your dad was?" I said, "No, quite honestly Fred, I don't know anything about it." He said, "Do you mind if I have a conversation with your dad, will you arrange that?" I said, "Sure." So, two years ago, Fred got with dad, and asked him two hours' worth of questions, and it was during that time I learned some interesting aspects of it, and I learned it was also a miracle and that he had quite a will to survive, in order to return home and marry my mom and have a life and almost be 90. I learned stories such as when he landed in Guam, he was there ten days only, and on his third day, they were quite hungry, and they managed to get some canned food and they were so hungry, they were wanting to sit down and eat. They were looking for a place to eat, but there were so many Japanese bodies around, he just picked out a Japanese person whose belly was extremely swollen, and it could serve as a tabletop, and he just straddled that Japanese person and set his food on it and used it as his dinner table. I learned about when he was over there for three years, he had stayed in one foxhole for three months solid, just coming out and shooting. I learned he was a squad leader, and that he had sixteen guys, and he didn't lose anybody the entire time he was over there. And at the very end, he did get hurt, almost three years, and that's where he got the bazooka and the grenade—he had shrapnel all in his shoulders, and in his back, and in his legs. I remember a few years ago, a piece of shrapnel just working its way out of his legs.

About ten years ago, yeah. So, I just learned things like that with Fred talking with him. Until then, I never knew it. We never talked about it at home. As a child, we were reared as little Marines, quite honestly. I mean, it was like we were told one thing, one time, and we better not forget. Everything had to be clean and perfect, we were grade A dairy farmers, and because we were grade A dairy farmers, we were cleaning the farms, cleaning the pipelines, everything had to be clean and perfect. Of course, everything was run just like it was a military base. After being wounded in Guam, George Harper was in the hospital for four months. When he got well enough to travel he caught an Army ship back home, where he immediately married June Wilson. He worked in the oil wells for six years, and saved up enough money to buy a farm. He had three children, and went to school on the GI Bill. June recently passed away, and at that time, George Harper applied for his post-traumatic stress disorder benefits. He got 'em—June didn't want them. She didn't feel like it was right to accept that type of benefit.

The American Marine—his life was complicated many times by the lands that he visited. That they survived and accomplished their missions time and time again, often at the price of their own health, was a testament to their will and fortitude. In the end, they did their jobs. Not for fame or glory, but for each other, and because that is what Marines do.

I received a letter a few years later:

"Randall, I want to let you know that Dad, George Harper, passed away Sept. 28, 2012. Thank you for all of your kindness, your interest, and your positive impact on Dad during his last 20 months of existence on this Earth plane.

Linda Harper

George Harper's Daughter"

And now it is time to hear the Americal Version on Bougainville!

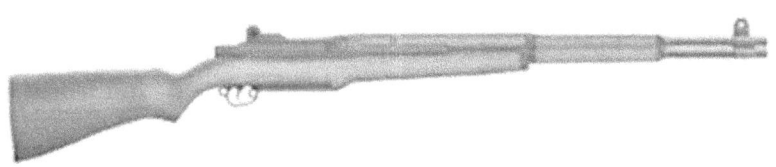

CHAPTER FIVE

A KNIFE CUT, AN EXPLOSION, AND A BULLET HOLE AND MY TRUSTY M-1

Introduction to the Invasion of Bougainville Island

After New Georgia, the next major operation was an invasion of the island of Bougainville, which was approached by landings at Mono and Stirling in the Treasury Islands on October 25-27, 1943. A Marine division landed on the west coast of Bougainville at Empress Augusta Bay on November 1, 1943. The Marines were followed within the month by an Army division and replaced in the next month by another Army division.

It was late November before the beachhead at Empress Augusta Bay was secure. This beachhead was all that was needed, and no attempt was made to capture the entire island. Allied planes neutralized enemy airfields in the northern part of the island, and the Allied command made use of its naval and air superiority to contain the Japanese garrison on Bougainville and cut its supply line to Rabaul by occupying the Green Islands (February 14, 1944).

Despite these measures, the Japanese maintained pressure against the beachhead, mounting an especially heavy but unsuccessful counterattack as late as March 1944. Success at Bougainville isolated all Japanese forces left in the Solomons. The Japanese sustained comparatively heavy air and naval losses during the campaign, which further crippled the Japanese Combined Fleet and had a vital effect on the balance of naval power in the Central Pacific.

By 1937, Japan had invaded China. Something was going on that historically became known as the Rape of Nanking. Part of that atrocity was performed by the Japanese Imperial Army, They were not alone. There were reports of Japanese officers competing to see how many they could kill, like a sports competition. In Bougainville, the Japanese soldiers were not killing unarmed civilians. They were facing the US Marines and the Americal Division of the United States Army.

DOESN'T THAT MAKE YOU FEEL PROUD OF OUR SOLDIERS!

Success at Bougainville isolated all Japanese forces left in the Solomon Islands, and heavy air and naval losses further crippled the Japanese Combined Fleet. The skirmishes at Bougainville ended land combat in the South Pacific.

General MacArthur had his orders, and his own plans for the South Pacific. He was the commander of the Army in Asia. He wanted to cut a path from the Solomons, New Britain, and to the Philippines. This would cut off the raw material supplies of Southeast Asia to Japan. The powerful Japanese military and naval bases of Rabaul were in the way. Air bases were needed—air bases on Guadalcanal and Bougainville. General MacArthur and Admiral Nimitz agreed that they did not need the whole island of Bougainville, just the airbase and the bay, about six square miles, or two or three percent of Bougainville. Not taking the whole island would bleed the Japanese Army—the Japanese would have to attack. Someone would need to be there to fight them, just to keep them busy.

The Americal Division was formed in 1942, consisted of orphaned National Guard units from North Dakota, Boston, and Illinois, and helped defend Henderson Field at Guadalcanal. In December of 1943, they at first filled in as replacements to relieve the 1st Marine Division in Bougainville. Eventually replacing the Marines, but not until learning what they needed to know about combat with the Japanese. This attributed to less attrition to the Americal Division as might have been expected. In March of 1944, the Americal Division participated in the offensive to drive the Japanese further away from the airbase in Bougainville. Bougainville was originally controlled by twenty-five to forty thousand Japanese Army soldiers. The Japanese Army felt humiliated by their defeat at Guadalcanal. There was more to come. Bougainville is a long, 250 square mile island, mountainous in the north and populated primarily in the south and east of the island. In the middle of the island, on the west coast, was a bay, and an airfield built by the Japanese. The bay and the airport had a mountain that could control the countryside—the bay and the airport—with artillery. It had to be taken and defended to protect the airfields.

Norm Bakley of Knoxville, TN fought in the American Division in 1943 and 1944. Norman Bakley was 87 years old at the time of our interview, he married Ozell Bakley. They have three children, four grandchildren, four great grandchildren, and one great-great grandchild. *Both have since passed away.*

The First Marine Division's commander, Major General A. A. Vandegrift, was so impressed by the soldiers' stand that he issued a unit commendation to the regiment for having demonstrated "an overwhelming superiority over the enemy." In addition, General Vandegrift took the unusual step of awarding Lt. Colonel Robert Hall, commander of the 3rd Battalion, 164th, with the Navy Cross for his role in these battles. The 164th was then occasionally referred to as the '164th Marines' due to their special relationship with the Marines on Guadalcanal.

In November the 164th took part in the offensive across the Matanikau River. Other elements of the division arrived piecemeal in the last few weeks of 1942.

In January 1943, the 132nd Infantry Regiment of the division took Hill 27 and 31 of the Mount Austen complex. The division later participated in offensives to sweep Guadalcanal of remaining Japanese resistance. After the last Japanese defenders were killed, captured, or evacuated from the island, the division was relieved on 9 February 1943.

*** Special thanks to Doug Brown of Landrum, South Carolina for his help in researching this information and advising me how important this information was to the story you are about to read.

NORM: I was in training in California at the time, the Americal had come back from Guadalcanal, and I had not been a part of that, of course. I missed Guadalcanal, and I had joined on New Caledonia where they were sent to get replacements and get reorganized to get ready for their next conflict. So, I joined in mid-1943.

New Caledonia was a Free French possession. The Americans did not consult with or ask much permission to move to new Caledonia. The Americans did put a higher ranking officer in charge, in order to deal with the Free French government.

I took my basic training in Second Armored Corp. We were actually being prepared to go over to Africa, to the World War over on the other side, but they decided they needed infantry more than they needed Army heavy equipment operators at that time, so, they said, "well, we're done with the armor requirement, we need more infantry guys. So, you, you, and you, go to that division, and you-you, go to that division." And that's how I ended up in the Americal Division.

Norm Bakley-Bougainville

The Americal Division had taken heavy losses, and quite a beating in the American Guadalcanal victory. They took about 62% casualties on Guadalcanal, so they needed a lot of replacements. These numbers are ambiguous but, reportedly: The Japanese lost a total of 24,000 men killed in the Battle of **Guadalcanal**, while the **Americans** sustained 1,600 killed, 4,200 wounded, and several thousand dead from malaria and other tropical diseases. I believe this to be combined Marines and Americal.

Information above taken from Wikipedia, there are other more accurate resources available.

NORM: They went over there in a National Guard unit. They were a task force of three different National Guard outfits that eventually became a division after they returned to Guadalcanal for organization and replacements. They got their name while they were at Caledonia. I felt like a replacement. I felt a little out of place, because I went overseas as a Sergeant, and they put me in charge of the weapons platoon with a bunch of soldiers who had been in conflict already, and were already veterans of Guadalcanal. I was in charge of them. I felt a little embarrassed, I felt a little inadequate, but they accepted me well, and it worked out well.

I was in the "light weapons" platoon. I had the small mortars and light machine guns, so I was what was known as a "squad leader" of the weapons platoon.

They designated the amount of equipment. I had three machine gun squads, and three motor squads, so I had six weapons, and that was predetermined. I would take the men out on patrols. On Bougainville, after they established the perimeter to protect the warehouses and the docks and the airport, my company was assigned to be a reserve company. They had reserves to fill hotspots if the main perimeter was attacked, and they'd call up reserve companies. While we were on reserve, they also used us to do patrols behind the enemy lines to try to harass them, cut of their supplies and try to find out where their concentrations were. Mainly to cut off their supplies of ammunition and food to get into the front lines.

Author's note: Okay, and I mentioned earlier that General MacArthur and Admiral Nimitz had already decided that they didn't want the whole island of Bougainville—they only wanted the bay and airport and whatever land they needed to protect that. So, when you say the word "perimeter," what were the guidelines for "perimeter?" Why would they say, go out so far, what was the deal there?

NORM: The primary deal for the perimeter to be established would be to be far enough out so the enemy could not have artillery that could reach the bay. As long as the perimeter was out there far enough that the artillery had to be kept behind their lines, and in that case, at the beginning, that was like nine miles. It was six to nine, depending on the shape of the perimeter, but at any rate, the primary principle was to keep that area protected so the planes could operate and all of our ships could come in and out. We had no intention of taking the island, that wasn't needed.: So, it's kind of like holding somebody—you've seen sometimes things where somebody would come in and hold somebody to where they could swing, but they couldn't hit you?: The Japanese artillery had to stay far enough away, and that's all they wanted—they didn't want the rest of the island?: They never did. Yeah, we didn't understand that at first, that we were only going to be there to hold that one small percentage of the island. We thought that we would move forward and take the island. Being young, energetic soldiers, kind of gung-ho, we wanted to get it done. But we never were asked to go any further than that perimeter.

They sent us in small patrols, primarily to determine where their routes were, where they were getting their supplies, their ammunition, and where they were getting their food brought up to the pillboxes for the fighting area at the frontline. The intent was to cut off those ammunition supplies and that food supply. We had some pretty well established trails you could pick out the trails in the jungle pretty easily, and we would go in and patrol those areas and set up overnight and try to discourage the enemy from trying to get any further, if you know what I mean.

Bougainville was probably one of the worst environments for combat, because it was almost 100% covered in jungle—and it was wet jungle. I don't know what the rainfall was in Bougainville, but it seemed like you were always in water at a certain depth. The east coast was pretty dry, but it was terrible, terrible terrain. Not a lot of high mountains, they were knolls and hills, they called them hills—some of them were knobs or knolls—but everything was covered in very, very dense jungle. It was really terrible conditions for warfare. The hills were numbered by their elevation? Hill 501 was probably 501 feet above sea level, Hill 700 was 700 feet above sea level. I think the smallest we were asked to keep control of was Hill 260, so they ranged from there up to… I think one of them was 1500. The way the battle progressed on Bougainville was that the airport was taken, and the bay was taken, and that was in November-December of '43? s. And until the end of March, 1st of April, I guess because we had taken some prisoners, they'd found that they were bringing in heavier artillery that might reach the airbase. So, they asked us on Easter Sunday to push back the area from the Toro Kina River to the Jaba River to expand the perimeter by about four or five miles. And, so that was a pretty dramatic push that particular week to expand it.: About three or four weeks before that push that you were talking about on Easter Sunday, on March 8th, the Japanese attacked the Hill 700, and overran the main hill defending the main airbase. They—the Japanese had gotten under the American artillery up close to the defenders, and it was foggy, and raining, and dark. Those were the general conditions we found most of the time.: It was always damp, nasty. It was a lot like the Olympic Peninsula in Washington, it was kind of rainy all the time, and it was not a comfortable situation: It was one of those dark, rainy nights, I found myself in a tight predicament. I was out on patrol.

On that patrol we were ordered to go out and see if we could cut off supplies on a particular trail that we had spotted before. We went out and set up overnight, I believe there was just eight of us, and I set six of them up in two different spots on one side of the trail, and one of the BAR operators and myself were on the other side of the trail. And it had rained all night as usual. And the next morning, I was wiping off my M1 rifle and drying it off, and one of the groups of three on the other side were sitting there, one of the guy's watches had gotten full of water, and the other three on the other side were eating breakfast. So, we were kind of not watching it.

We were letting ourselves get in a bad situation. That was what we were doing, with all of us being preoccupied.

Suddenly I looked up, and there was a Japanese patrol between my position and the positions I had set up on the other side of the trail. It was unbelievable. And it looked like there were six or seven Japanese. As I went to open fire on the first one that I saw, having wiped off my M1 that night, I pressed the clip release, not knowing it, and I fired one shot. The clip jumped halfway out, and jammed my rifle. Took me a few seconds to get it loose, but in the meantime, I looked around to see why I wasn't getting my BAR fire. And I looked down at the little gentleman we called Blackout. A little Italian boy we had from New York, and he was down there, with his BAR laying across his leg, and he had his rosaries out and was saying his prayers. As far as he was concerned, the war was ending for him in a hurry, and he was concerned about being right with the Lord before he did any shooting. He never did get his BAR going. I had to use my M1, my ol' trusty M1. *chuckles*

We got between the setup I had, the guys had crossed away from us, I got them alerted that something was going on and between us, we shot four of 'em, as I recall. Two of them kept going down the trail, and we didn't want that because they could go in and report where we'd been, and it was a good ambush spot that we had set up before, and we would use 'em quite often. We didn't want them knowing the area. So, one of the riflemen that I had across the trail from me, and I pursued the two that got away. We had to get rid of them because we didn't want them to go back and tell where we'd been. We took care of that problem at that time.

Author's note: Okay. One special footnote: when the Japanese were corralled, they would mass an attack what they thought was the weakest point. The defending Americans would eventually run out of ammunition, and the overwhelmed lived or died where they stood. Fighting had raged on Hill 700, and the Japanese were beginning to give up their captured ground, but still held some positions on the top of the hill. It was time for the final push.

When the order came to take the top, the commanding officer was hit in the chest. So, Lt. Sam Hendrix, a University of Tennessee football player, led the charge over the top. GO VOLS! So, Norm, what was your mission on patrol?

NORM: Our mission was primarily to cut off the supplies, and to thoroughly understand where the enemy were positioned. There were dug-in pillboxes all over the area, and we had to know where they were just so that the perimeter people would be advised as to where the strong points were, and the weak points.

Pill box, the Japanese were experts at building pill boxes. They would dig down in the earth, probably four or five feet, and then they would build a dome type top with sandbags—anything that was available, timber, logs, and cover it with earth so there was no way even artillery would affect them. You could fire artillery, and fire it, and fire it, and you'd tear up the timber around them and you'd tear a lot of stuff up, but you weren't killing anybody. They were dug in tremendously well, and they had tunnels between these pillboxes so they could get back and forth, and it strengthened one spot if they needed it, and weakened another spot. It was scientific, the way they had put it together, and all I can say is that it was engineered. Those pillboxes were well engineered. They were strong, they were trustworthy, and they had places to sleep and rest out of the environment.

General MacArthur and Admiral Nimitz didn't include us on their battle plans, but I understand there was some grumbling in the ranks about the tactics that were being used on Bougainville? We wondered why we weren't being asked to progress and do what we had been sent over to do, and that's get the war over with. We wondered why we were just sitting there, so to speak. We spent 13 months there, and to us, it seemed like that was 13 months that wasn't needed. We could have cleaned the island off and laughed and went to the next campaign, but that's not what the generals wanted. That was not the plan.

What the generals wanted, in some of the writings that I've read, is that they knew that all they really wanted was the airbase, all they really wanted was the bay. It was to be used as a launch pad to clear out Rabaul and move out into New Britain, and cut off the supplies by going straight to the Philippines and cutting off the supplies to Japan. But they didn't tell us that. The only thing we were ever asked was that one time on Easter, when they asked to make the perimeter bigger, was to be sure that the artillery could not reach the airbase, because that was all we were doing was keeping the airbase safe, and our supply areas where the docks were and the ships would come in. And Easter Sunday happened to be the day they picked for us to expand the perimeter.

While looking for photos in a drawer in his office, Norm pulled out a box of old photos, that seemed precious to him, and he told me about a lot of them, it reminded me of this Song/poem.

Carbon Leaf:" The War Was In Color

Songwriters: CARTER GRAVATT, TERRELL H. CLARK, SCOTT
ANDREW MILSTEAD, BARRY THOMAS PRIVETT

I see you've found a box of my things—
Infantries, tanks and smoldering airplane wings.
These old pictures are cool. Tell me some stories
Was it like the old war movies?
Sit down son. Let me fill you in

Where to begin? Let's start with the end
This black and white photo don't capture the skin
From the flash of a gun to a soldier who's done
Trust me grandson
The war was in color

From shipyard to sea, From factory to sky
From rivet to rifle, from boot camp to battle cry
I wore the mask up high on a daylight run
That held my face in its clammy hand
Crawled over coconut logs and corpses in the coral sand

Where to begin? Let's start with the end
This black and white photo don't capture the skin
From the shock of a shell or the memory of smell
If red is for Hell
The war was in color

I held the canvas bag over the railing
The dead released, with the ship still sailing,
Out of our hands and into the swallowing sea
I felt the crossfire stitching up soldiers
Into a blanket of dead, and as the night grows colder
In a window back home, a Blue Star is traded for Gold.

Where to begin? Let's start with the end
This black and white photo don't capture the skin
When metal is churned. And bodies are burned
Victory earned
The War was in color

Now I lay in my grave at age 21
Long before you were born
Before I bore a son
What good did it do?
Well hopefully for you
A world without war
A life full of color

Where to begin? Let's start with the end
This black and white photo never captured my skin
Once it was torn from an enemy thorn
Straight through the core
The war was in color

The Fiji Island Fighters

NORM: Fijians were tremendous natives. They were strong, well thought of, and they were close to Australia. When the war started, the Australian government decided they were going to train some of them to be soldiers. They had, actually, right until the time of the war, they had headhunter troops there in the islands, so they were pretty vicious fighters. They trained them to be soldiers, and the techniques they used were so different from ours, because they were used to the jungle, for one thing, and they were used to using knives, machetes. Silent warfare, if you will, versus the kind of warfare we were familiar with. And they were well-trained, they were dedicated, and they assigned a battalion of Fijian soldiers to the America division, and we kept probably what would be considered a squad with us on Bougainville in a reserve with us, as a matter as fact. And then when we'd go on patrol, many times, they'd go with us and assist us, and it turned out that we were probably more of the assistants than they were.

They were so well-versed in jungle fighting, that we looked like amateurs compared to them. They were tremendous.

Sometimes, when there was a Japanese sniper, that we would send the Fiji warriors to go find them? On one patrol in particular I remember, we ran into a very heavy concentration and getting sniper fire from more than one direction, and we sent those guys in there to try to make it safe for us to enter it. And again, as I mentioned a while ago, *silent.* You didn't hear anything, but all of a sudden, the area would be cleared. They would climb up those trees, get up in those trees, and actually kill these Japanese with knives or machetes before they even knew they were there. I never saw anybody that was so quiet and so well-trained in how to do it. And they would clear an area out in short order, in 20-30 minutes they could clear an area out of snipers, and we could move forward.

There was concern that the Japanese would invade at the very beginning of the war, and there were facilities built on Fiji to protect Fiji in case there was an attack, but it became apparent that they weren't interested. We moved on to other islands. The Fiji island warriors used knives and more silent weapons.

Talking about the weapons I had to use. If I had to pick only one weapon right now that was my weapon of choice during World War II, the M1 was that weapon?

It was just reliable. It had tremendous firepower, and it was your buddy. As a squad leader, and as a platoon leader, we didn't normally carry a rifle. We carried carbines or pistols, because we had to be agile and move around with our troops, who were assigned M1s, but I never went on patrol without it. They're just such a trustworthy weapon that I wouldn't be caught without one.

The machinegun crew was one of the reasons I wasn't assigned an M1— why I wasn't—why we also didn't carry them was because we also had weapons to carry. You had—in the machinegun squad, for example—you had the gunners, and they would normally carry the machinegun, or parts of it. We'd break it down so more than one person could carry it, and then you'd have ammunition carriers assigned to them. So, you'd have a gunner, an assistant gunner, and maybe three ammo carriers in a squad, and that would make up a squad. Same way with the mortars, you'd break it down so two guys could carry the mortars, and then three guys carry the ammunition, and that's kind of the way, at least, I organized my troops. The guys carrying ammunition would also carry an M1.

They would sling it and carry it, but the platoon leaders or squad leaders normally had a carbine or just used the .45s.

NORM: We were told, I believe it was in December or January, we'd been there about 13 months so I think it'd be about January. We were told that we were going to go to the Philippines…

January '45, yes. And all we were told was that we were going to the Philippines to assist in the retaking of the Philippines, but we didn't know any more than that when we left. Leyte Island in the Philippines. The southern part of the Philippines, mostly. Open country. What a relief! You had farmlands, you had orchards, some timber, but it was timber—it wasn't jungle. It was much like it was in the United States. It was much like it is in Tennessee, but we didn't have any mountains there to speak of, you had hills and so forth. But it was a pleasure to have some open country where you could see what you were doing instead of the mud and sludge and darkness that you find in a jungle. The fighting was altogether different. The only thing we had to be concerned about in the Philippines was you weren't sure if you had some Filipinos who were sympathetic to Japan, and you might have civilians that would be carrying hand grenades, or become dangerous—become an enemy, so to speak, even though you didn't suspect it.: Then we left Leyte, and went to an island called Cebu Island? A beautiful island. Cebu Island was a university island, I believe there were seven colleges and universities on Cebu, and they had a lot of high Spanish people, and it was a metropolitan island, so to speak. It was really an educational island. It was probably the leadership of the education in the Philippines.

First, I was fighting in the jungle, then fighting on farmland and plantations, and then fighting in the city, but I didn't get much chance to fight in Cebu Island.

We made a beachhead just outside of Cebu City, and when we landed on the beach, one of my gunners stepped on a landmine and lost his leg, but I was standing close enough to him that I got some concussion from the inside, where it loosened up some of the organs in my stomach, and I was immediately evacuated out back to Leyte. I did not take a part in capturing Cebu City, which was the next day—they captured the city, but I was not a part of it. Yeah, I just got out of there quick. I did return, I wasn't out of it very long.: How long? About: Three week. I had had had a little experience where a Japanese soldier tried to kill me with a knife? That was earlier, that was over on Bougainville.: When we were asked to expand the perimeter from the Torokina River to the Jaba River, we had bypassed some of the Japanese in the pillboxes, and one of them decided he was going to see how many Americans he was going to get before he got killed, and I happened to be the handiest one. And one of my gunners hollered at me when he approached me from the back, and I ducked. When I did, instead of cutting my throat, he hit me in the shoulder. I was sent back to the field hospital for treatment for the stab wound to the shoulder. The guy that hollered at me killed him.

Two weeks before the war ended on Cebu Island, I was shot through the hip on patrol.

We were just mopping up, and we'd run into a hot spot, and I happened to be in the wrong place at the wrong time. But I was fortunate in a way, because the shell that I got hit with, or the bullet I got hit with, was a steel jacketed shell. Many of the shells they used over there were. Very soft, some of them were even wood, and they'd hit you and they'd splatter. They'd do a lot of damage. The one I was hit with a steel jacketed shell and went through, and didn't tear me up as bad as it would have if it were a soft shell.

We had field hospitals established on Leyte, and they had them also in the Merida area. But a field hospital was something that was set up quick, it was something that was set up to take emergency cases, take care of them, and send them back to a different hospital if they needed it. New Guinea had been set up as a very—I would guess, the best hospitals they had on the island were on New Guinea, and I was sent to New Guinea after my wound I received on Cebu, and I was evacuated off New Guinea back to the states. They had beautiful hospitals there—they were tents, but they were well-equipped, and they had wood floors and wood walls up part way and tents over them, but they had real nice hospitals on New Guinea. They let us know the bomb was dropped while I was at Barnes General Hospital in Washington State.

War was different then. It's altogether different. For one thing, we were in the war because our nation, our homeland, was in danger of being taken over, and we knew how important it was to fight the war, and win the war: to save our nation. Today, for one thing, they fight wars for different reasons, and I would think it would be very frustrating to be a soldier today, fighting in a land that the citizens weren't necessarily our enemy. It's just so different, and warfare itself is so different. We were out in the open most of the time, or we knew what was going on. Over there, in the islands, or in the area they fight in now, you don't know where the enemy is. I mean, it's a hunt and flush situation, and much more dangerous than warfare we were on, because we were open to do what was in front of us, most of the time.

Author's note: Later on you will hear a story about Charles Beal, and he carried an M1 across Europe. SGT. Norm Bakley, carried an M1 in the South Pacific, and I want you to read a little poem about the M1. A lot of the other soldiers in this book carried the same weapon.

M-1
By: R.A. GANNON

Do you wonder why that rifle
Is hanging in my den?
You know I rarely take it down
But I touch it now and then.

It's rather slow and heavy
By standards of today
But not too many years ago
It swept the rest away.

It's held its own in battles
Through snow, or rain, or sun
And I had one just like it,
This treasured old M-1.

It went ashore at Bougainville
In Nineteen Forty-Three.
It stormed the beach at Tarawa
Through a bullet-riddled sea.

Saipan knew its strident bark,
Kwajalein, its sting.
The rocky caves of Peleliu
Resounded with its ring.

It climbed the hill on Iwo
With men who wouldn't stop
And left our nation's banner
Flying on the top.

It poked its nose in Pusan,
Screamed an angry roar
And took the First Division
From Chosin Reservoir.

Well, time moves on
And things improve
With rifles and with men,
And that is why the two of us
Are sitting in my den.

But sometimes on a winter night,
While thinking of my Corps,
I know that if the bugle blew
We'd be a team once more.

In 1937, the Japanese Imperial Army never thought about running into young American boys at Bougainville. They never considered the fact that the will of American soldiers to survive the war and go home was more powerful than the pep talks given to the Japanese soldiers to restore their honor taken at Guadalcanal. The mud, the rain, the darkness, the fear, the fact that young men had to encourage their buddies to be brave, and to be calm enough to let a Japanese patrol go by before rising up and killing them all close-up. The tense feeling that you have been constantly behind enemy lines, searching for a soldier who was also searching for you. To see and feel the shock of a mine explosion that literally ripped and loosened your body organs from whatever keeps it in place. To escape death from a surprise knife attack, to be shot in the hips after you return from the knife injury, then come home to successful career, and 67 years later, share the black and white photos of friends who lived, and friends who died on Bougainville, Leyte, and Cebu Island.

Remember the poem? The War was in Color! You can hear it on YouTube. Just type in the song title.

It was about a grandfather singing to a grandson he never got to meet. He had been killed in the war, but as his son was looking through those black and white photos, the grandfather was singing, "SON, THE WAR WAS IN COLOR!"

That successful career of Norm Bakley included working on projects like the Apollo missions, and the space shuttle. If you're involved with Mr. Bakley at all, if you were in his church, or in his family, you may not have known his exploits. You may not have known to honor him with the respect deserving of this kind and gentle man, who went to church and unconditionally loved his family. I am proud to call him my friend, and I'm lucky to know his story and sacrifice for our country. Thank you, Norm Bakley.

One Holiday season I was asked by a high school friend, to speak to a group at a center called KARM. It is a Christian help center for the homeless. There were about 200 people at the dinner.

I told them about Norm's story. How he had been injured three times. Once by a Japanese suicide attempt with a large knife. Once by an explosion and once by a bullet. After the presentation, a man walked up to me, I knew who he was, and I had seen his picture and knew his struggle with alcoholism.

He looked at me and said, Mr. Baxter, Norm Bakley was my father. Thank you for telling his story. I knew he had scars, I saw them when he mowed the yard. I never knew the stories of what happened.

I never knew how he got that scar on his shoulder.

Norm passed away in 2012. He was my friend, and I will miss him. Let's go to the other side of the world and check on Murl Conner!

Lt. Conner is a man who should have received the "Medal of Honor", but his commanding officer was too busy fighting the war to write up the recommendation. President Trump fixed that recently.

CHAPTER SIX

AUDIE MURPHY HAD NOTHING ON MURL CONNER

In 1942, 22,000 young American in the 3rd Division got a ticket to go on a cruise. *A History of the 3rd Infantry Division not to be confused with the 3rd marines discussed earlier.*

A new war is coming!

After enjoying a peaceful break after World War I, the 3rd Infantry Division was mobilized in early 1941 after the President declared a state of emergency. The 3rd Division began the process of filling its ranks and prepared for war. In July 1942, the Division received its orders; prepare for the invasion of North Africa.

Operation Torch

The mission of Operation Torch was to secure French North Africa for the Allied forces in order to conduct operations on the European continent. One significant problem was that most of the landing areas were defended by French troops who had declared loyalty to Germany after France fell. This meant that the Americans, British, and Free-French forces would have to fight their former allies. The invasion was scheduled for November 1942 and would take place in three places, 1st would be Casablanca, an Atlantic port city on Morocco, followed by the capture of the Algerian port cities of Oran and Algiers.

The 3rd Division, under the command of Maj. Gen. Lucian Truscott, was given the task of capturing Casablanca. The 3rd Division embarked aboard transport ships and sailed directly from America to Morocco in what would become the longest sea voyage preceding an amphibious landing.

On November 8, 1942, the 3rd Infantry Division stormed ashore at Casablanca supported by 400 ships and 1,000 aircraft. The invasion was a complete surprise and the 3rd Division quickly established their beachhead but the French forces fought back bitterly. For three days, the Americans fought the French forces until finally, the French agreed to a cease fire and joined the Allied forces. With Casablanca secured, the Allies could now move men and materiel into the Mediterranean Sea without fear of the Straights of Gibraltar being sealed off.

North Africa
MURL CONNER FOUGHT FOR SIX MONTHS IN NORTH AFRICA
11/08/1942 TO 5/10/1943

After the success at Casablanca, the 3rd Division was ordered to move East in support of the British forces attacking Tunisia. The British had launched their attacks from two directions; westward from Egypt and eastward from Algeria. The German and Italian forces occupied abandoned French fortifications along the southern border of Tunisia called the Marth line. Realizing they did not have enough forces to drive the Germans and Italians from their positions, the Allies established defensive positions in the Tunisian mountains until reinforcements could be brought in to renew the attack. In February, 1943 the Germans fought back and defeated an American armored force at the Kasserine Pass and broke through the Allied lines. The German drive quickly stalled after reinforcements could not be brought forward and the Axis forces turned for a shallower envelopment than they planned.

The Allies were prepared for this and the Germans quickly encountered a British blocking force which stopped the German drive. After a brutal force march, American Artillery was brought forward and began to pound the German forces. Fearing that a large attack was imminent on the Mareth line, the Germans withdrew to their positions. On March 17, the 3rd Division, now part of the US II Corps, launched a diversionary attack to the rear of the Mareth line while the British Eighth Army assaulted the line in force. Two weeks later, the American and British forces linked up and by the end of April had captured the port cities of Bizerte and Tunis. On May 10, the last of the German and Italian forces surrendered and the Allies controlled all of North Africa. The 3rd Division got little rest as they were ordered to prepare for another amphibious assault.

Sicily
MURL FOUGHT FOR 2 MONTHS IN SICILY
07/09/1943 TO 09/09/1943

At the same time the black sailor you already met; James Julian was out in the Mediterranean Sea fighting Italian and German war planes!

The 3rd Infantry Division, reinforced by a Ranger Battalion and Combat Command A of the 2nd Armored Division, was tasked with landing at Licata on the left flank of the Allied invasion. On the night of July 9, 1943, the invasion force set sail. Sea conditions were horrible and the 45 mph gale force winds were dubbed "Mussolini Wind" by the seasick soldiers. Early on the morning of the 10th, the Allies hit the beach.

The landing was complicated by soft sand and shifting sandbars. Numerous landing craft became stranded and the soldiers were forced to wade ashore. The 3rd Division met only light resistance on their beaches, which was quickly defeated. With their beachhead secure, the 3rd Division moved inland and captured their first objectives within hours. After the American 7th Army had captured its objectives, they were ordered to stop at a key highway and relinquish it to the British 8th Army who was given priority for capturing the city of Messina. The commander of the 7th Army, Lt. Gen. George Patton, who did not like being relegated to protecting the British flanks, convinced the operation commander to authorize a "Reconnaissance in force" to the west and the city of Agriento. By July 15, Agriento had been captured by the 3rd Division and Patton was authorized to continue west and capture Palermo.

Patton organized the 2nd Armored, 82nd Airborne and the 3rd Infantry Division into a provisional Corps and sent them on a 100 mile drive to Palermo, the capital of Sicily. After three days of house-to-house fighting, Palermo fell to the Americans and 53,000 Italian soldiers were captured. With this stunning victory, the Allies controlled half of Sicily.

The 7th Army now received orders to advance on Messina. They would attack from the West along the north of Sicily while the British attacked north along the east coast. Messina was heavily defended by 4 German Divisions and was surrounded by rugged terrain and the Caronie Mountains. The 7th Army advanced along Highway 113 with the 1st Infantry and the 45th Infantry Divisions in the lead and the 3rd Division in support. After the 45th Division captured "Bloody Ridge" outside of Santo Stafano, the 3rd Division was brought forward and took over the advance. The Americans continued to attack the German positions and each objective was taken only after fierce battles. The 3rd Division faced it greatest opposition when it attacked San Fratello. The German forces, the 29th Panzer Grenadier Division, was deeply entrenched along a steep ridgeline and could not be driven out. On August 3, the 3rd Division began a series of attacks against San Fratello but none were successful. General Patton ordered an amphibious landing to flank the German position.

On August 8, the 2nd Battalion 30th Infantry, reinforced with two batteries of artillery and a platoon of tanks, landed at Saint Agata, 3 miles behind San Fratello. The landing caught the Germans by surprise and they were completely cut off from escape. Unfortunately the bulk of the German forces had already withdrawn the previous night but the 3rd Division captured over 1,000 POWs. Gen Patton desperately wanted to trap and destroy the 29th Panzer Division and on August 11th, he sent the 30th Infantry on another amphibious end-around. The second landing worked and the 29th was completely surrounded. The 30th Infantry was too light a force however to keep them bottled up and by the time the rest of the 3rd Division lined up, the 29th had escaped again. The 7th Army continued its advance on Messina and encountered dozens of blown bridges and heavy minefields. The Army Engineers worked feverishly to clear the way but the Americans could not catch the evacuating German forces. On August 17, the 7th Infantry of the 3rd Division entered Messina just 2 hours after the last German transport ships had left for Italy. Sicily was secured, in large part due to the 3 amphibious landings of the 3rd Division.

The 3rd Division was given a brief rest and re-supply while they prepared for the next invasion. Sicily was always meant to be a stepping stone to Italy so it was no surprise when the 3rd Division received its orders. They were going to take Naples.

The Invasion of Italy
MURL CONNER FOUGHT FOR 9-10 MONTHS IN ITALY 9/09/1943 to 06/44 maybe through July44.

On September 9, the Allies launched the invasion of Italy by sending their forces ashore at Salerno. After securing the initial beachheads, the remaining forces were brought ashore. The 3rd Division disembarked from their transports in the port and began their advance on Naples with the 82nd Airborne and the British 7th Armored Divisions. Naples fell to the Allies in early October. When they entered the city, they found it almost completely destroyed by the retreating Germans. Almost every building had been destroyed and ships in the harbor had been sunk. The Engineers went to work and within 2 weeks, the port was reopened and supplied began flowing in. The 3rd Division was transferred to VI Corps and pulled out for their next, their fifth, Amphibious landing of the war.

Anzio
He was at Anzio in January of 44

On the morning of January 22, 1944, the US 5th Army assaulted the beaches at Anzio. The landings were so successful, the invading Americans had captured their initial objectives by noon and had begun to push inland. The 3rd Division, on the southern flank, met only a single company of German infantry on their beach and made significant advances inland. The Division moved towards Cisterna but encountered stiff resistance and was forced to halt and consolidate their forces. The next day, Maj. Gen. Truscott ordered his Division forward and came within 3 miles of Cisterna when he was ordered by 5th Army command to hold in place as part of a general reorganization and consolidation of the beachhead forces.

For the next week, the Allies brought in supplies and troops but made no advances. This delay allowed the Germans to transfer thousands of troops to the Anzio area. The Americans, under the command of Maj. Gen John Lucas, did not know that the roads from Anzio to Rome were virtually undefended and a bold strike inland might have allowed the capture of Rome with few casualties. Gen Lucas erred on the side of caution and held his forces back while the Germans reinforced their units with 8 Divisions with 5 more on the way and waited.

On January 30 the 3rd Division, reinforced by 3 Battalions of Rangers, launched their assault on Cisterna. The Rangers were within 800 yards of Cisterna when they were ambushed by an entire German Motorized Infantry Division. The 15th Infantry Regiment was sent to try and rescue the Rangers. They were not in time as the Rangers were driven out into the open by a German Armored Division. The Rangers had no anti-tank weapons and were quickly cut down. Out of 767 men, only 6 Rangers survived. The 7th and 15th Infantry continued the assault on Cisterna against heavy opposition. The Germans were deeply entrenched and after 16 hours of fighting, the 3rd Division was still a mile away. After learning that more reinforcements were on the way, the 3rd Division was again ordered to hold in place and dig in.

On February 23, Maj. Gen Truscott replaced Maj. Gen Lucas as the VI Corps commander. On February 29, the Germans launched an offensive against the 3rd Division in the Cisterna sector of the beachhead with 2 infantry and 2 armored divisions. Truscott had prepared for this by reinforcing the 3rd Division's positions with massed artillery. The German attacks were quickly stopped by the artillery and mortar raining down on them and the entrenched 3rd Division troops. Despite repeated attacks, the Germans could not penetrate the American line. The German attacks continued along the 3rd Division's lines and the 7th and 15th Infantry suffered heavy casualties but by March 4, the Germans could not mass enough forces to attack. In the final assault on March 4, the Germans lost over 3,500 men and several dozen tanks.

Breakout

For the next three months, a lull settled over Anzio. Both sides were exhausted and could not conduct major operations. On May 5, Gen Truscott ordered VI Corps to prepare for their breakout offensive and on May 23, the 1st Armored Division with the 3rd Division in support, broke through the main German line. VI Corps quickly encircled Cisterna and attacked the trapped German forces. Fighting was heavy in the town but on May 25, German resistance ended and the Allies controlled Cisterna.

The price for Cisterna was heavy. The 1st Armored Division lost 100 tanks in the first day. VI Corps suffered over 4,000 casualties. With Cisterna secured, the 3rd Division was ordered to link up with the 1st Special Service Force and advance on Valmontone where they would attempt to destroy the German 10th Army. Valmontone was captured by the 3rd Division but the 10th Army escaped north. VI Corps rejoined the 5th Army and was ordered to advance on Rome. The 3rd Division, along with the 85th and 88th Infantry Divisions, reached the outskirts of Rome on June 4, 1944 encountering only light resistance. On June 5, the 5th Army entered Rome and was met by throngs of jubilant Italians. The 5th Army remained in Rome only a few days, then continued north after the retreating Germans.

Southern France

In August of 1944, the 3rd Division was ordered to execute an amphibious landing in Southern France. On August 15, the 3rd Division, with an Airborne task force and French Commandoes and two additional Infantry Divisions, stormed ashore and quickly eliminated the German defenses. The next day, the port cities of Toulon and Marseilles were captured. The 3rd Division, under the command of the 7th Army, began their drive north into France. The Germans were in full retreat and on September 11, the 7th Army linked up with Gen. Patton's 3rd Army.

The 7th Army continued its drive into France and then turned for its next objective, the Rhine River. The 7th Army and the 1st French Army drove east and reached the Rhine at Alsace. Because of logistical problems, the 7th Army was ordered to hold their positions and dig in. The next month, the Germans launched their Ardennes Offensive. The 7th Army was ordered to remain in place to ensure that the German units facing them at the Rhine could not be pulled out to reinforce the German offensive. For four months, the 3rd Division and the rest of the 7th Army conducted patrols and numerous raids along their front at the Rhine River.

The 3rd Division enters Germany

Finally, at the end of March 1945, the 3rd Division crossed the Rhine and broke through the German lines. After the breakthrough, the 7th Army was assigned to the 6th Army Group and ordered into the southeast areas of Germany. Retreating Germans were planning on staging a final defense in the Alps of Southern Germany and Austria. The 3rd Division got there first and the retreating German forces were eliminated. By the end of April, the 3rd Division was capturing town after town after German units surrendered wholesale. Finally on May 8, 1945, Germany surrendered.

The 3rd Division remained in Germany for several months serving occupation duty. They were relieved at the end of 1945 and in early 1946, returned to the United States. During World War II, 36 soldiers of the 3rd Infantry Division were awarded the Medal of Honor and 71 the Distinguished Service Cross.

Originally, of the 22,000 soldiers that started in 1942, there were only two that were still with this unit when the war was over.

The Third Division lost more soldiers in World War II than any other around the world. They are third in all-time-high, behind only the Second Division in Korea, and the First Cavalry in Vietnam. Soldiers in Iraq and Afghanistan wear the blue and white patch, and even recently have had soldiers awarded the Medal of Honor.

Our story is told by Randy Speck from Kentucky. He had heard my radio program and called to tell me about Lt. Murl Conner.

He has a wonderful story about the exploits of Lt. Murl Conner during World War II.

Mr. Speck: "I began writing short stories years ago, I was not in the military, but I grew up around Murl Conner and his family here in Clinton County, Kentucky… So, I've been well acquainted with his family all my life. Basically, Lt. Conner just grew up on a farm in a farming family in a farming community, and that was his life. He was the third person drafted from his community of Aaron, Kentucky. There used to be a post office there in Aaron, it's no longer there, but he was the third person from the Aaron Community who was drafted in World War II. Aaron, Kentucky is probably about ten to fifteen miles or so from Wolf Creek Dam, which is about 150 miles northwest of Nashville, Tn. He was probably 20 or 21 years old when he was drafted? And he had no idea where he was going or what was ahead of him, he just got drafted and turned himself in and took off! He was born in 1919—so, not having done the math—he didn't have any clue, but at the end of his time, he was one of only two people who stood with the Third Division the entire time.

Do I know much about his African experience? No, I really don't, it was the beginning of his time in the war, period, shipped off to Africa. Actually, he was shipped off to Africa on November the 8th, 1942, and Africa is where he entered his first combat with the troops of the Third Division.

The leadership was green, the infantry was green. They were not into an infantry battle, although the infantry was there and they fought hard, it was mostly tanks and artillery and the lines were really fluid. The battle lines could change 30 miles in a given day. That's the kind of life they lived, it was hot and dry. Conquering half of Morocco and then after that eight or nine months later, they wound up attacking Sicily. Then in Italy, and of course went on to France and finally, Germany. But he was in Italy, of course, and Anzio? I think that's how you pronounce that?

He was there in Anzio, and one of his fellow soldiers in the Third Division was a man by the name of Gordon Roberts, whose nephew is Richard Chilton, who many, many years later, would lead to the project of trying to get the Medal of Honor for Murl Conner.

Mr. Roberts was killed during the fighting there in Anzio, Italy. So, a man whose uncle was killed at Anzio started doing research to find information about his uncle, and that's where he learned about Murl Conner?

SPECK: Yeah. It was probably around 1996, or 1997, when Richard Chilton, who lived in Lake Geneva, Wisconsin, who was with the 11th Airborne Division in Korea, with the Israeli Paratroopers during Desert Storm—he was researching war records on his uncle, Gordon Roberts, who I've said was killed shortly after landing in Anzio, Italy—and one name, as he researched his uncle, one name kept coming up, and that name was Murl Conner. So, as Richard Chilton interviewed over 300 veterans of the Seventh Infantry regiment, and Murl Conner's fellow soldiers repeatedly spoke of his heroics efforts, and this led to Mr. Chilton actually coming to Albany, Kentucky to meet Mr. Murl Conner to begin his campaign to get the Medal of Honor for Murl Conner.

Author's note: Just to get you caught up on the Anzio beachhead: on that beachhead—there were 32,000 Allied soldiers that landed on Anzio. They thought for a while that it wasn't going to be contested, but it turned out to be a German trap full of tanks and artillery and soldiers. There were 70,000 German soldiers waiting on them at Anzio, and before we get too much deeper into this story, I want you to read a poem about the experiences of some of the British troops in Anzio.

[Pink Floyd - When the Tigers Broke Free]

It was just before dawn
one miserable morning in black 'forty four.
When the forward commander
Was told to sit tight
When he asked that his men be withdrawn.
And the Generals gave thanks
As the other ranks held back
The enemy tanks for a while.
And the Anzio bridgehead
Was held for the price
Of a few hundred ordinary lives.

And kind old King George
Sent Mother a note
When he heard that father was gone.
It was, I recall,
In the form of a scroll,
With gold leaf and all.
And I found it one day
In a drawer of old photographs, hidden away.
And my eyes still grow damp to remember
His Majesty signed
With his own rubber stamp.

It was dark all around.
There was frost in the ground
When the tigers broke free.
And no one survived
From the Royal Fusiliers Company Z.
They were all left behind,
Most of them dead,
The rest of them dying.
And that's how the High Command
Took my daddy from me.

I played that poem for Mr. Speck, on a YouTube video you can find at: http://www.youtube.com/watch?v=TH2LoYnQeog

Fold this page or write this down and go listen to a song you probably did not know was about the father of the author of the poem and song sung by Pink Floyd.

As you just read, that was about a British division that was at Anzio. They were given the order to hold when the German tanks broke through, and the end result was the whole company got wiped out.

SPECK: That was a very moving piece of music,

RANDY: Yes. There was also a poem though, written by one of the soldiers in the American 3rd Division. He wrote lots of poems about his experiences in World War II. Mr. Conner lasted longer than this soldier, this one got wounded, was sent home and received the "Medal of Honor".

[Audie L. Murphy — The Crosses Grow on Anzio]
THE CROSSES GROW ON ANZIO

Oh, gather 'round me, comrades; and
listen while I speak
Of a war, a war, a war where hell is
six feet deep.

Along the shore, the cannons roar. Oh
how can a soldier sleep?
The goings slow on Anzio. And hell is
six feet deep.

Praise be to God for this captured sod that
rich with blood does seep.
With yours and mine, like butchered
swine's; and hell is six feet deep.

That death awaits there's no debate;
no triumph will we reap.
The crosses grow on Anzio, where hell is
six feet deep.
. . . Audie Murphy, 1948

You can find this poem on the Internet, just type in the title.

We left you at Anzio with the Third Division, and the Third Division had gone on after they broke through at Anzio, they went into Rome and fought into Italy.

The American Advance into Rome was kind of hidden or downplayed by the press and on the radio stations, because there was another little event going on—we called it D-Day! D-DAY overshadowed what was going on with the Third Division in Italy Southern France,

Audie Murphy's fame would come soon, but not at the moment. The mission of landings in Southern France was to take some of the pressure off the soldiers in Normandy. The Germans didn't really have a lot of strength, and all they tried to do in Southern France was block the American advances. They did that with landmines. Snipers and delay tactics, but it was a very orderly retreat. It was a military retreat, but there were times that the Allies had a hard time keeping up with the Nazis, they were retreating so fast. The Germans were destroying bridges, and highways, and railroad cars, and railroad tracks all along the way. But, eventually, the southern forces in France joined up with the forces in Northern Europe the ones that came in on D-Day and the reinforcements that arrived later in the year.

But they reached a spot on a map on the borders of France and Germany. A little area that was always fought over by Germany and France called Alsace-Lorraine. It had changed hands several times over the past hundred years, the folks in Alsace-Lorraine during this time before the war started, were citizens of France, but most spoke German. When the German soldiers got to Alsace-Lorraine, they realized that now, they weren't invaders anymore. They were defenders—they were defending their home soil, so now the Germans turned into tougher fighters, and they weren't going to give any more ground like they gave up in France.

This was winter time, and one of the areas that the American soldiers reached was a place called the Colmar Pocket. The soldiers couldn't dig foxholes in the Colmar Pocket—the ground was frozen, and they ran into a determined German defense.

The Colmar Region of France was one of the last regions in France that German Forces occupied. This "pocket" of German troops was attacked by elements of the U.S. Seventh Army in January & February 1945.

To elaborate some on the answer already given.

The "Colmar pocket" was formed by the Rhine, since the German troops concentrated around Colmar-Munster-Mulhouse formed sort of a half circle, with the flat side to their rear which was the Rhine. The Rhine could only be crossed at certain points (the Germans had only three quality crossings). In that sense, the Germans were caught in a "pocket", but it was of course also a pocket of resistance.

The Germans were soundly beaten, but able to score an unexpected success by the evacuation of 50 000 troops from the pocket along with much important materiel.

Mr. Speck, can you tell us a little bit about what Murl Conner did in the Colmar Pocket?

SPECK: No, just that he was with his unit there while they went through that area. He picked up several of his decorations through those times—you know, going through Africa, Italy, France, and into Germany.

c) Distinguished Service Cross

Awarded for actions during the World War II

(Citation Needed) - SYNOPSIS: First Lieutenant (Infantry) Garlin Murl Conner, United States Army, was awarded the Distinguished Service Cross for extraordinary heroism in connection with military operations against an armed enemy while serving with the 3d Battalion, 7th Infantry Regiment, 3d Infantry Division, in action against enemy forces on 24 January 1945, in the vicinity of Houssen, France. First Lieutenant Conner's intrepid actions, personal bravery and zealous devotion to duty exemplify the highest traditions of the military forces of the United States and reflect great credit upon himself, the 3d Infantry Division, and the United States Army.

General Orders: Headquarters, Seventh U.S. Army,
General Orders No. 47 (1945)
Action Date: 24-Jan-45
Service: Army
Rank: First Lieutenant
Battalion: 3d Battalion
Regiment: 7th Infantry Regiment
Division: 3d Infantry Division

SPECK: Wounded a couple times, he received the awards for that—actually, he was wounded a total of seven times, he only received four awards for those, and he turned the other three down, actually. And then one day, -he found himself 2 days before Audie Murphy made his heroic stand that earned him the Medal of Honor, into the same Colmar Pocket offensive with some telephone wire and a problem? Yeah, the date was January 24th, 1945; I think it was like 0800 hours. He had already served 27 months in a combat unit, and had received a wound to his hip, and they tried to get him a flight back home, but he turned them down. His hip would be replaced when he returned home, but instead of going home as he was able to do, Lt. Murl Conner went AWOL from the hospital and ran back to his unit.

Just as he made it back to camp, he overheard an announcement that Lt. Colonel Ramsey was asking for volunteers to run a spool of telephone wire, some 400 yards. The only thing was the volunteers would be running directly into the enemy. Well, Murl Conner goes into Lt. Colonel Ramsey's tent and says, "I'm here to run the wire," and without any further hesitation, and with a bad hip, in near zero-degree weather, he grabbed the spool of wire and ran straight into an intense German tank, artillery, and infantry assault by 600 fanatical German infantrymen, which was assaulting in full fury the spearhead position held by Conner's battalion. He disregarded shells, which exploded 25 yards from him. He reached his destination, and for three hours, he lay in a shallow ditch after wave after wave of German infantry surged towards him—at times, as close as 5 yards from his position. His commanding officer later wrote as the last all-out German assault took forward, he ordered his artillery to concentrate on his very own position, resolved to die if necessary to halt the enemy, and, you know, friendly shells exploded within 5 yards of Murl Conner, blanketing his position. But, Lt. Conner continued to direct artillery fire on the assault elements swarming around him until the German attack was shattered, and of course, broken. Audie Murphy did no better in my opinion, and this is not long after he had his hip injury?

And actually, it was 48 hours before Audie Murphy did what he did to have his Medal of Honor awarded.

On that day, January 24th, 1945, at 0800 hours, Lt. Murl Conner was individually credited with stopping more than 150 Germans, destroying all the tanks, completely disintegrating the powerful enemy assault force, and preventing heavy loss of life in his own outfit. He almost single-handedly turned back the enemy advance and prevented heavy casualties in his own battalion. And the whole time, the ground was too frozen to dig a hole.

Officers asked for volunteers, and he ran into the tent, his commanding officer says, "Where are the others?" and he says, "I'm it."

Author's Note: So, let's go over to Richard Chilton just a little bit. You know, I read somewhere this morning, when I was doing research on this, that a lot of people who should have been awarded the Medal of Honor all through time, the only spectator or the only survivor was God.: So, in this situation, Robert Chilton—we talked about him earlier—he was doing the research on his uncle, and everywhere he went, people kept mentioning Murl Conner's name?

SPECK: Yes. Everywhere he went, he interviewed over 300 of Lt. Murl Conner's fellow soldiers, and each one of them talked about the efforts of Murl Conner and the things he would do, you know, so that got him to thinking that he needed to meet Mr. Conner, which he did.

RANDY: Okay, and what came of that? What happened?

SPECK: Mr. Chilton, of course, came to Albany, interviewed Murl Conner, who, by the way, passed away in 1998. He was 79 years old when he died of heart and kidney complications, and he just set out—first off, I think he went to his own unit, his former unit, got their support. One thing lead to another, he visited a few states, actually, Kentucky, Tennessee, Alabama, Illinois, and Rhode Island have all passed legislation authorizing the precedent to award a Medal of Honor posthumously to Lt. Conner.

RANDY: Okay. And you knew Lt. Conner after the war, can you describe his demeanor?

SPECK: Lt. Conner—I mean, Murl Conner—was extremely quiet.

Author's note: (I learned from another military officer, Lt. Col. Arthur Boyd of the Korean conflict that it is appropriate to call a retired veteran by his Rank).

Very, very quiet. He didn't speak a lot, you know, he was really, really a quiet person, and—it's kind of funny—ten miles to the south of Albany, across the Tennessee state line, in a place called Pall Mall, Tennessee, lived a man named Alvin C. York, who had the same demeanor. Quiet, country boy, you know, stayed close to the family, close to the farm, and Murl Conner actually lived the same way Alvin C. York lived. You know, I'm not sure if he was inspired by Alvin C. York's heroic efforts in World War I. Not sure why Lt. Murl Conner did what he did, except for of course, naturally, he loved his country. But, in his war efforts in World War II, Lt. Murl Conner was a hero.

Author's note: Lt. Murl Conner was from a little town called Albany, Kentucky. His community was called Aaron, Kentucky. He is Kentucky's most decorated war hero. He served on the front lines for several months, eight major campaigns. WOUNDED SEVEN TIMES! And it seems like this man was left out when they were awarding the Medals of Honor during World War II, and just to remind you of all the things we've talked about: he showed up in 1942, fought across Africa, fought in Sicily, Anzio, came through Southern France and fought in the Colmar Pocket, he fought across the Siegfried Line and across Germany, wound up in house-to-house fighting in Nuremberg. Of the 22,000 people who started out, there were only two of the original soldiers from 1942 that were still there in 1945, and Lt. Murl Conner was one of them. And in the meantime, he got to see over 4,000 of his compatriots die. Mr. Speck, told me about why he thinks Lt. Murl Conner should be awarded the Medal of Honor.

SPECK: Well, he came back to Albany after the war, and had a parade. Lt. Murl Conner, never bragged about his efforts, never talked about his efforts, most people had no clue what he had actually done until many, many years later.

Most of the following information was taken from THE WATCH ON THE RHINE newspaper of the 3rd Infantry Division submitted by: Lynn Ball Vol.94 No. 2.

In the heat of the battle, you know, where Murl Conner—by the way, online and in other works, you may see his name written as Garlin Conner, but it is actually Lt. Garlin Murl Conner, he was known as Murl—where he ran 400 yards unreeling the spool of wire, through the impact area of an intense concentration of enemy artillery fire in order to direct friendly artillery into a force of six Mark VI tanks and tank destroyers followed by 600 fanatical German infantrymen all attacking the position held by his battalion. He manned this post for 3 hours under fire. HE EVEN CALLED A STRIKE ON HIS OWN POSITION! He was individually credited with stopping more than 150 Germans. Destroying all the tanks, and disintegrating the powerful enemy assault forces preventing heavy losses for his battalion. His commanding officer, you know, did not have the time to stop and do the necessary paperwork needed for Conner to receive the Medal of Honor. He would later write to his son describing Conner's efforts, but as I said, after the war, came home, put the war behind him, began farming, raised a family, and many of his battle records were lost.

But the records that do exist officially document that Lt. Murl Conner repeatedly risked his life under enemy fire to capture and disable numerous enemy positions. Lt. Murl Conner was drafted to war in February of 1941. On November 8th, 1942, was shipped to Africa, where he entered his first combat with the troops of the Third Infantry Division, which travelled as we said, through the African campaigns, onto Italy, France, finally Germany. It was during the many months of trial and combat that Lt. Conner received a Battlefield Commission, and his many decorations for his gallantry in action, enduring seven campaigns, 28 months of combat action, Lt. Murl Conner received the Bronze Star with three oak leaf clusters, Silver Star with three oak leaf clusters, and the Distinguished Service Cross. He was wounded at least seven times during 29 months of nearly continuous combat service, but he refused to accept Purple Hearts for at least three of his wounds. He was given a Battle Commission to 2nd Lieutenant after only three months of fighting—many of his fellow infantrymen often said they watched in amazement as Lt. Murl Conner repeatedly risked his life to save others. It was said that LT Conner frequently volunteered to take the point on the most dangerous patrols. He stepped up, answered the call, did what he had to do, and came home.

RANDY: Okay. In your blog,

You're known on the internet as the Notorious Meddler. Just go to a search engine and type in The Notorious Meddler.

SPECK: Right.

RANDY: And you had written an article on June 23rd, 2010 to honor a hero. And inside that article, you talked about an American officer who had written a letter home to his son. Do you remember that?

SPECK: I sure do that.

RANDY: Can you tell us a little about that?

SPECK: The gentleman's name was Lt. Colonel Lloyd B. Ramsey of Arlington, Virginia. I think he's in an assisted care facility now—he was commander of the Third Division, Seventh Infantry, Seventh Army, and later achieved the rank of Major General—and by the way, retired Major General Ramsey, of who we're speaking was instrumental in getting a monument known as the Third Infantry Division Memorial, and that's placed in Arlington National Cemetery today. He wrote a letter to his father, whose name was W. H. Ramsey, and he admitted that during the heat of the battle, he didn't have the time to document, or to do the necessary paperwork that needed to be done in order for Lt. Murl Conner to receive the Medal of Honor, but he did deserve it. He just didn't have the time to do it, you know, and he spoke about all the awards that Murl Conner had received. He opens up the letter saying he's really proud of Lt. Conner, he will probably call you, and if he does, he will not sound like a soldier. He sounds like a good ol' country boy, but to my way of seeing, he's one of the outstanding soldiers of World War II. If not THE outstanding soldier. He was a Sergeant until July of 1944. Now is 1st Lieutenant. With the

Distinguished Service Cross, a cluster to a Silver Star and a Bronze Star, and he says he had never seen a man with as much courage and ability as Lt. Conner had displayed. This compliment from a man who normally doesn't brag much on his officers, but this is one officer nobody could brag enough about, and nobody could do him justice. He is a real soldier.

RANDY: And you think the reason he didn't get the Medal of Honor was because an officer didn't do the necessary paperwork?

SPECK: Yes. And I think it was a thing where it was strictly the heat of the battle with everything happening there all at once, and he didn't have time to stop and do the paperwork. And then, I don't know, it was something that was forgotten. Lt. Murl Conner came home, and didn't ask for it, didn't do anything to try to get his honor. He thought he had done his service; he was ready to go on with his life.

RANDY: Okay. When you compare him to Audie Murphy—I was looking at my records here, and Audie Murphy had two Silver Stars, and Lt. Conner had a Silver Star with three oak leaf clusters.

SPECK: Right. Lt. Conner served in the same Third Infantry Division as Audie Murphy, they were in the same division—of course, Audie Murphy, everyone knows, has always been recognized as America's most decorated hero of all wars, and you know, I mean, the honor should have gone to Conner. Technically, Murphy earned one less Silver Star for gallantry than Lt. Conner's four. The Medal of Honor would have given Conner more award than Murphy, thus making him at least tied with Audie Murphy as America's most decorated hero of all wars. But, as we know, it is yet to be awarded.

Even if I had never known Lt. Murl Conner, I would still be pushing for the nation's highest honor to be awarded to him, and I will gladly write and rewrite his story for however long it takes, because—well, because it's the right thing to do. To me, his story will never grow old, we do not have the option to give up as long as someone will read or someone will listen, awarding Lt. Garland Murl Conner the Medal of Honor is just something that has to be done—it needs to be done. His selfless acts of bravery should place him in the company of Sgt. Alvin York, who lived just down the road in Pall Mall, and of course, Audie Murphy—after all, Murl Conner was one of the greatest heroes of World War II.

RANDY: To add to this, Mr. Richard Chilton, a former Green Beret fought so hard to have the Medal of Honor awarded to Lt. Murl Conner because it is the right thing to do.

We want to thank Randy Speck for bringing us the story of Lt. Murl Conner, a young man from Kentucky who went off to fight a war. He fought in the same division as Audie Murphy. Audie Murphy had two Silver Stars. Murl Conner had a Silver Star with three oak leaf clusters.

Audie Murphy had two Bronze Stars. Murl Conner had a Bronze Star with three oak leaf clusters.

Audie Murphy was wounded four times. Lt. Murl Conner was wounded seven times.

Each received the Distinguished Service Cross.

Audie Murphy got the Medal of Honor.

No one wants to take anything away from Audie Murphy—he earned all those, he was a hero. No one even knew what Lt. Murl Conner did until Richard Chilton of Lake Geneva, Wisconsin began researching the story of his uncle, Gordon Roberts, who was a member of Murl Conner's platoon. One-by-one, each of the over 300 veterans of the Seventh Infantry Regiment spoke of Lt. Conner's heroic efforts.

Audie Murphy had one less Silver Star.

No report was written the day Lt. Conner ran 400 yards into the artillery fire, and stayed there for three hours calling the shells in on himself, destroying the same number of tanks Audie Murphy destroyed, ending the lives of over 150 of the German soldiers, after escaping from the hospital with a hip wound.

His commanding officer was just too busy to write up the report. That doesn't mean he didn't do it.

Recommendation Process for: "THE MEDAL OF HONOR"

Receiving the Medal of Honor is the highest honor bestowed by the American Military and personally presented by the President of the United States. Because of the need for accuracy the recommendation process can take in excess of 18 months with intense scrutiny every step of the way. The following charts demonstrate this process.

The following organizations and individuals play key roles in the Army Medal of Honor recommendation process:

CHAIN OF COMMAND

Submits award recommendation that meets the two year submission time limit to Department of the Army Personnel Command

MEMBER OF CONGRESS

Submits award recommendation that is outside the two year limit for submission to Department of the Army Personnel Command or the Secretary of the Army who forwards request to Personnel Command.

DEPT. OF THE ARMY PERSONNEL COMMAND

Army Decoration Board - Merit Review, can disprove based on criteria (Cdr, HRC can overrule)

Senior Army Decorations Board - Recommends approval, disapproval, or downgrade.

MANPOWER AND RESERVE AFFAIRS

Concurs or nonconcurs with Board recommendation

CHIEF OF STAFF OF THE ARMY

Concurs or nonconcurs with Board recommendation

SECRETARY OF THE ARMY

Recommends approval or can disapprove. Also forwards packet to Chairman, Joint Chiefs of Staff for comment.

SECRETARY OF DEFENSE

Recommends approval or can disapprove.

PRESIDENT

Approves or disapproves.

While completing this book, I had the opportunity to go to Albany, Kentucky to interview another World War II veteran who knew Lt. Murl Conner. His name was Mr. Spears, and he sang two wonderful World War II songs for me, in his wheel chair. He fought in the 78th Infantry the 309th Division and was frostbitten very bad. His son and daughter –in-law Happy and Sharon knew Lt. Murl Conner's wife and I invited her to have lunch, anywhere she wanted, in any restaurant she chose. "I just love Turkey sandwich's at Subway! she said. So we met at the local SUBWAY. She told me, as Paul Harvey would say, "the rest of the story."

Her parents took her to Albany, Kentucky for a parade to honor a war hero named Lt. Murl Conner. They hooked up the horses, and loaded up in the wagon to go to the parade.

She kept asking her mother to point out this war hero, she expected him to be 8 feet tall and made of steel. He was a small framed man when she finally got to see him. After two weeks, they met again at a revival. "That is the only place we had to go to court," said Pauline Wells, soon to be Mrs. Murl Conner. "He was older than me, and my mother told me to break it off, after the final revival meeting on Friday. When I told him, he said that just won't do, so they eloped to Georgia and got married.

They have a son, Garlin Paul Conner, who still works the farm, and four grandchildren.

Mrs. Conner still helps veterans as did Lt. Murl Conner make the connections they need to obtain their military benefits. In her 80's she was still works every day at an insurance farm bureau. If you want to contact her, to give her your support, just send me an email at support@randallbaxter.com and I will get the information to you.

It was such an honor to meet this lady, and her family deserves the recognition Lt. Murl Conner earned in World War II.

While Lt. Murl Conner was leading his men across southern France, Robert Harvey, soon to be Dr. Robert Harvey had arrived in France transporting a magazine in his trucks called THE STARS AND STRIPES.

His story is next.

Isn't it interesting that his story and history sound so much alike?

It has always been that way. THE BATTLE
Operation Grandslam | Jan. 24, 1945 | Houssen, France

3RD INFANTRY DIVISION
Read Unit History

On the morning of Jan. 24, 1945, 1st Lt. Garlin M. Conner was serving as an intelligence staff officer with the 3rd Battalion, 7th Infantry, 3rd Infantry Division, near the town of Houssen, France, when German formations converged on 3rd Battalion's position.

With his battalion at risk of being overrun, Conner volunteered to run straight into the heart of the enemy assault in order to get to a position from which he could direct friendly artillery on the advancing enemy forces.

With complete disregard for his own safety, Conner maneuvered 400 yards through enemy artillery fire that destroyed trees in his path and rained shrapnel all around him, while unrolling telephone wire needed to communicate with the battalion command post. Upon reaching the battalion's front line, he continued to move forward under the withering enemy assault to a position 30 yards in front of the defending U.S. forces. He plunged into a shallow ditch that provided little protection from the advancing enemy's heavy machine gun and small-arms fire.

> **"The fight in Southern France wasn't very bad until we got to the foothills of the Vosges Mountains. There, the Germans tried to make a stand and with the weather against us, made it more difficult. The enemy defended one river with snipers and altogether, they caused very heavy casualties among our troops."**

1st Lt. Garlin M. Conner's speech at the Clinton County Court House for a parade in his honor

With rounds impacting all around him, Conner calmly directed multiple fire missions on to the force of 600 German infantry troops, six Mark VI tanks and tank destroyers, adjusting round after round of artillery from his prone position until the enemy was forced to halt their advance.

For three hours, he remained in this prone position, enduring the repeated onslaught of German infantry which, at one point, advanced to within five yards of his position. When the Germans mounted an all-out attack to overrun the American lines and his location, Conner ordered his artillery to concentrate on his own position, resolved to die if necessary to halt the enemy.

Ignoring the friendly artillery shells blanketing his position and exploding within mere feet, Conner continued to direct artillery fire on the enemy assault swarming around him until the German attack was finally shattered and broken. By his incredible heroism and disregard for his own life, Conner stopped the enemy advance. The artillery he expertly directed while under constant enemy fire killed approximately 50 German soldiers and wounded at least 100 more,

We pay tribute to this Kentucky farm boy who stared down evil with the strength of a warrior and the heart of a true hero."

PRESIDENT DONALD J. TRUMP
White House Ceremony, June 26, 2018

Thus preventing heavy casualties in his battalion.

I was sitting at home and flipping through channels when I saw a news broadcast of the event. I heard the name, Murl Conner, and saw the president hanging the Medal of Honor around a sweet elderly lady's neck! I hope she celebrated with a Turkey Sandwich.

CHAPTER SEVEN

THE RED BALL EXPRESS AND ONE OF ITS DRIVERS

We're going to take a ride on the Red Ball Express!

June 6th, D-Day. Everybody knows that story! And after the victory and the conquering of the beaches, the United States and Great Britain came in and built a harbor, and they called it the Mulberry Harbour. The Mulberry Harbour was a huge complex where you could load trucks straight from ships and trucks could go right on the road, and everything would go fast. But then, on June 19th, about ten days after they got the harbor built, a large storm came in and destroyed Mulberry Harbour.

A few weeks later, Life Magazine posted a photo showing how it took 12 tons of supplies to equip one American soldiers. As Germany retreated, they destroyed the railroads. The supply lines grew longer and longer. There were 28 Allied Divisions operating using 20,000 tons of supplies every day. Makes me think about that song about logistics.

On August 25th, the Allies reached Paris. On that same day, the Red Ball Express plan went into action. It was the answer for a logistics problem the Allied Command had not anticipated. At its peak, there were almost 6,000 trucks being used. 75% of the Quartermaster units driving the trucks were African-Americans. They delivered supplies to the front lines. Most of the time, it was cold, and sometimes the rain would turn the roads into quagmires of mud. Not all the trucks made it. Most of the time, they were protected from German airstrikes by hauling their own anti-aircraft weapons. If the German bomb or bullet had hit a truck, they were usually carrying gasoline, or ammunition, sometimes food, sometimes blood, sometimes replacements. The truck could just explode.

The roads were sometimes bulldozed through the rubble. They heated their food, their c-rations, on the manifold of their trucks. And they faced theft by civilians, Americans soldiers, and German soldiers along the way. They had constant sniper fire, they were always stressed out about what might happen next. The Red Ball Express had been replaced by railroad systems by December of 1944. The Red Ball Express and the Pony Express had both gone the same way—they were temporary phenomenon.

So, what happened during those three months of World War II, during the time the Red Ball Express had hauled enough supplies to resist the Germans during the Battle of the Bulge? The Red Ball Express had established the procedures needed for efficient truck transport. This group of soldiers and their trucks were used to transport troops, to resist the Germans in the Battle of the Bulge.

What was the Red Ball Express, and who are the men that made it happen?

Dr. Robert Harvey was a retired interim president of Knoxville College, twice. When Knoxville College needed a man of integrity and leadership to guide them through troubled waters, they sought him out to lead them. I've known Dr. Harvey for years, mostly of him, I knew one of his children. Her Name was Dr. Denise Harvey, she was my friend. When I went to his home, I entered his living room and I saw twenty, or maybe twenty-five awards, and plaques of excellence and congratulations, I saw books, and many reviews of his accomplishments. I've even seen an article on him in the Congressional Record, read by East Tennessee District 2 Congressman

John Duncan. And the whole time, I saw few references concerning his World War II career, and all they said, "He later ventured to Knoxville College, where he received a bachelor's degree in mathematics in 1946, after serving in the US Army." Well, there's more to it than that.

Author's Note: I wanted to know about the young black man who was Robert Harvey. Before he was Dr. Robert Harvey?

HARVEY: I was a student at Knoxville College, I had just finished my junior year. I came to Knoxville College from Camden Academy in Alabama in December. I came to Camden from Sumrall, Mississippi, where I was the son of a Baptist minister, and income came from picking cotton. Picking cotton: I had an aptitude in mathematics, and that's how my Aunt recommended that I come and live with them near Camden, and that's how I got to Knoxville College.

I had enlisted in the Reserves, and I decided to go and volunteer after my junior year, and in the Reserves you'd be called up. So, rather than wait till I was called up, I joined. And so, I actually volunteered for the service, but I was subject to draft.

The Army had a program that trained you to participate in various sciences. What I was interested in was meteorology, and I thought that I'd go in the service as a meteorologist. And I'd be trained, I'd be perhaps, 1st, 2nd Lieutenant to begin with, and then at the end of the service I would have my education paid for by the Federal government—I have to serve in the service so many years. Well, when I volunteered, the Reserve part went out the window, because I was just another draftee! I enlisted in the service, and was trained in the infantry, and did basic training in infantry. It didn't work out the way I hoped. In another way, it worked out better because at the end of my service, I had enough credits in the GI Bill to get all of my graduate training at the University of Rochester, and I got my Master's, and at Kumaun University, got my Doctorate. I did my training in Camp Croft, South Carolina. Then to Camp Cleveland in Louisiana. That's where I met my wife. She had come to Knoxville College as a freshman in my junior year. That would have been1 942. I went in the service in

1943, now its 1944, and the war for me is imminent. I'm not sure it had begun—it had not begun when we got married, because we got married early in June. I think the next two or three days, the war started. So, I knew that I'm going to be involved in military services overseas. Dr. Harvey was married just a few days before D-day June 6, 1944.

Edwina came down one day, and we got married the next morning. I remember now, I'm confined to base, so I don't have time for honeymoons and all that. And the witnesses for our wedding were the minister's wife and himself, and I think one of his daughters. And I go back to base—I was off-base only overnight, and early morning—but I go back to base, and my wife came back to Knoxville. She left before we shipped out, and I didn't see her again. That's 1944 in June. I didn't see her again until August of 1945: After 13 months. One day to be married, then I saw her a year and a half later?

She stayed in college, I came back, re-entered Knoxville College and finished in 1946, and then I went off to graduate school. I actually taught a year in high school, then I went off to graduate school. From there, after I finished my residence, which means I spent at least a year at Columbia, I took a job at Knoxville College as an assistant professor of mathematics. That's how we returned to Knoxville, and we've never left!

I was shipped to England in the Quartermaster and truck transportation company, and our assignments were to haul supplies from various places down to the English Channel, for shipment over to France, where the war was going on.

D-Day, we were in Louisiana.

We took a train to New York, and then the Queen Elizabeth across the ocean to Scotland, then another train down to England, and we stayed in England until about September of that year. Then, we were shipped over to France.

When I went over to France, I was given the order to help move the Stars and Stripes?

History of Stars and Stripes

Creation

On November 9, 1861, during the American Civil War, soldiers of the 11th, 18th, and 29th Illinois Regiments set up camp in Bloomfield, Missouri. Finding the local newspaper's office empty, they decided to print a newspaper about their activities. They called it the *Stars and Stripes*. Today, the Stars & Stripes Museum/Library Association is located in Bloomfield.[3]

World War I

During World War I, the staff's roving reporters, and illustrators of the *Stars and Stripes* were veteran reporter or young soldiers who would later become such in the post-war years. Harold Ross, editor of the *Stars and Stripes*, returned home to found *The New Yorker* magazine. Cyrus Baldridge, its art director and principal illustrator, became a major illustrator of books and magazines, as well as a writer, print maker and stage designer. Sports page editor Grantland Rice had a long career in journalism and founded a motion picture studio called Grantland Rice Sportlight.[4] Drama critic Alexander Woollcott's essays for *Stars and Stripes* were collected in his book, *The Command Is Forward* (1919).

The *Stars and Stripes* was then an eight-page weekly which reached a peak of 526,000 readers, relying on the improvisational efforts of its staff to get it printed in France and distributed to U.S. troops.

World War II

On May 2, 1945, *Stars and Stripes* announced Hitler's death.

During World War II, the newspaper was printed in dozens of editions in several operating theaters. Again, both newspapermen in uniform and young soldiers, some of whom would later become important journalists, filled the staffs and showed zeal and talent in publishing and delivering the paper on time. Some of the editions were assembled and printed very close to the front in order to get the latest information to the most troops. Also, during the war, the newspaper published the 53-book series *G.I. Stories*.

After Bill Mauldin did his popular "Willie and Joe" cartoons for the WWII *Stars and Stripes*, he returned home to a successful career as an editorial cartoonist and two-time winner of the Pulitzer Prize. Former *Stars and Stripes* staffers also include *60 Minutes'* Andy Rooney and Steve Kroft, songwriter and author Shel Silverstein, comic book illustrator Tom Sutton, author Ralph G. Martin, painter and cartoonist Paul Fontaine, author and television news correspondent Tony Zappone, cartoonist Vernon Grant (*A Monster Is Loose in Tokyo*), Hollywood photographer Phil Stern and the late stock market reporter and host of public television's *Wall Street Week*, Louis Rukeyser.

A photograph in *Stars and Stripes* loosely inspired the exploits of PFC Jack Agnew in the 1965 novel and the 1967 film, *The Dirty Dozen*.

The newspaper has been published continuously in Europe since 1942 and in the Pacific since 1945.

American comic strips have been presented in a 15-page section, *Stripes' Sunday Comics*.

HARVEY: Oh yes. And in the process of getting from England to France, we received orders to transport the Stars and Stripes—which was the name of the army newspaper—to transport it from London to Paris. That's when we actually went across the channel. We went to London and picked up the Stars and Stripes, and we had all of that on our trucks. And we rolled the trucks off onto the beach, and we drove from there to Paris. And from Paris, we were assigned to Le Mans, France, south of France. We were still in the business of transporting supplies, ammunition, food, gasoline, but then we received an assignment after the Bulge, in Belgium, Bastogne. The call went out for volunteers, and our company was assigned to the 11th Armored Division. Our first assignment was to go down and pick them up as they came onto beach, transport them north of Paris, where the war was going on.

The Battle of the Bulge had already started.

Then we were ordered to deliver fresh troops to the front. These troops came directly from the United States, and they had not really had the kind of basic training we'd had, in many cases, and we sensed that they were just terrified, because they knew what was ahead—the Battle of the Bulge was underway, and they were going to be a big part of that, with General Patton's army. I could see the fear in their eyes: And the way they talked. They're nervous, and we spent a lot of time trying to calm them down. And in the time it took us to get them from the beach in France up to north of Paris in France, I think they had resigned themselves to the fact that they were going into combat. When you go into combat, any day could be your last day, and I think they were thinking about that.

Leaving the depot, or leaving a base when everything is peaceful and driving closer and closer to a battle. You knew that death could come to you at any time, particularly when you were in combat. And so, any day could be your last day. After a while, you didn't think about those things too much. You became immune to the fact that you were a soldier in combat, in the midst of killing of people, and so you could be killed at any time. The scenery changed as I came closer to the battle?

It was quite a different world, actually. We had a lot of destruction where the Germans had bombed cities, and in some cases, they destroyed churches because sometimes they didn't have the area targeted very well, or the steeples had to be destroyed They were almost indiscriminately dropping bombs. So, a lot of civilians were killed, a lot of people were out in the streets without any place to live, or any food. In many cases, we would see people eating out of trash cans. That's the nature of the devastation that occurred. As we approached the battle, there were there less civilians and more soldiers on the sides of the road? We had driven the civilians out of the places we were going, so they were out on their own in many cases.

Author's note: Some of the stories I've read, some of the Red Ball Express drivers were talking about seeing scenes of dead horses and dead soldiers on the sides of the road, and did you run into that?

In the photo? Were they working on the truck or cooking their dinner on the manifold?

HARVEY: Well, now for myself, you're talking about the area around Bastogne. There were piles of dead horses, and we learned that those horses had been used to transport the tanks used by the Germans to pull their tanks up to the line. And that's how they managed to get up to place where the Bulge was formed without being able to detect them, that was a story we had. Not a mountain, but a large pile of dead horses, and in many cases dead soldiers.

While driving the trucks, you had all your supplies in your pack. You carried a pack all the time, and the two things you always had with you; you had your M1 rifle because you were trained in infantry, you might have had a carbine which was a smaller weapon. On your back, you had your pack which carried your sleeping gear, which means the sleeping bag and your personal supplies, and your food—your c-rations and so forth. Many times, we slept on the ground. We slept north of Paris on the ground, the first night we were up there.

We cooked our food when we were out in the combat zone. In our case, we learned to heat a can of gasoline, making a fire there, and then set the c-ration can on top and heated it. That was the way we got hot food.

And you could also use the manifold on your truck?

Some soldiers did that, I did not. I don't remember doing that, I should say.

I remember the deuce-and-a-half, the ten wheeled trucks. If my memory serves me well, we called them six-by-sixes. And you always had six wheels pulling, I don't know why it was six-by-six, but they were large trucks with double wheels in the back, and no place to sleep in the truck. You just had the cab for the driver, and in my case, for the passenger, I had four trucks. I was a Corporal, and I was assigned four trucks. And they were good General Motors trucks, as I recall.

General Patton had a strategy of moving very fast. In doing that, he would sometimes encircle the Germans. He left pockets of German soldiers as he moved on, so, a lot of times in moving supplies, you had to deal with pockets of Germans. Sometimes it'd be snipers—it was a business of mobilizing, having a mobile supply dock, I guess. That's the best way to describe it: General Patton had a mobile supply dock, that's what our company was, because he carried his gasoline with him. He would take air strips as we went along, and we'd try to transfer fuel from the depot. To be honest, I don't remember precisely where we picked up the fuel by this time, because we were assigned to the 11th Armored Division. But we went to the depot, got the gas, got the ammunition, which meant that we were supplying the people that they needed to keep moving, and the ammunition. Sometimes food. But the highest priority was the gasoline, because Patton wanted those tanks moving, and in some of the areas where the pockets had been left, we had to have small tanks—what they called light tanks—accompany, so we wouldn't be attacked by the Germans.

We had protection in front, back, and all around the convoy. All of the tanks had 50 caliber machine guns, even the light ones. The problem with that was a tank didn't last very long when you traveled a long distance, so the problem was keeping those light tanks supplied when we were traveling long distance.

Crossings

We went across the channel from England to France on LST, or LCTs, landing crafts, and the trucks simply rolled onto them, stacked on there, along with the drivers, and when we got to the beach when the tide went in, we rolled in on those trucks, drove them off onto the beach. In the case of small rivers, we used bridges built by the engineers, temporary bridges. Pontoon bridges were what I think they were called, and we drove across on them.

In that case, you're right on the water in those things, so you're driving along a bridge which is just a few inches above the water.

One of my assignments was to go into this concentration camp—we only did this once—and remove the people who were confined there, the relocation places. So, we actually had to go in the places—these camps, where the people lived, and have them loaded on the back of these trucks. That's the way they rode. They were just stacked on the trucks, and it was horrible. It was the most horrible experience I've had. There was nothing in the war that dispirited me as much as that, to see the conditions of those people, and what human beings could do to other human beings.

We came with empty trucks, and we had the trucks loaded in with refugees. We saw the places where they had been put to death in these camps, and many of them had been starved because they just attacked the food we provided. That was devastation—that's the ugly side of war to deal with that sort of thing.

We took them to relocation camps. Took them to a different place. I don't remember precisely how often we did it, but we did it until we cleared that camp out, that was the assignment, to remove all of those people where they were to relocation places.

Right after I had gone into the combat zone, and we had been in this house that had been taken over, and spending the night. I got a message from the Red Cross from my father, and it said my mother had passed. They said that she'd passed on Friday, it was Monday, and he said in this telegram, "the Red Cross will get you here, if you can come." And I decided not to try to go, because the timing was too close. I couldn't be assured of being in Paris in time to get on that plane they had I assigned to. It was all problematic, and I decided, sitting on my bed, thinking about it, "the best thing you can do is try to accomplish those things your mother wanted you to accomplish, and your mother told you that you would be known as Dr. Harvey. Your Aunt convinced you to be a mathematician. So, I sort of set my mind then on getting my degree, and teaching mathematics.

This is during the war, during December 1944. The war is raging all around us, artillery is being fired over you, you know, it's hard. It's hard towards the lines, and you between the artillery and the lines. So, you're in the middle of a war.

That sort of set my position, because I think my parents had convinced me by that time, long before that, that I was going to get an education—a college education. I was not meant to be a cotton picker

Came back, discharged in November of 1945, and reentered Knoxville College, and now I've got the GI bill. I'd been working, I had scholarships, I had work assignments, and I had no money. Had no money when I went to Camden, no money when I went to Knoxville College, but I had people who believed I had potential as an athlete, and as a student—good grades—so I got scholarships and work opportunities. So now, I'm discharged from the Army, and I've got the GI bill, which means I can go to any university in the country. And that's how I finished Knoxville College, I didn't do any work as I had done before I went off to war.

When I finished Knoxville College, I went to the University of Rochester, in Rochester, New York?

When you're that young, you don't think about those things too much. I'd been in Rochester working with students with dinner foods, so I knew someone in the area, and when I finished teaching, the University of Rochester had a waiting list. I had been accepted to University of Rochester before I had decided to teach. And now, I go down and teach, and then I'm ready to do my graduate studies, so I said to my wife, "well, I know a little about Rochester, I think I know the University of Rochester there. So I'll take a bus and go up there, and establish residency, which means I'll live in the city." So, I did, and when I got off the bus I had no idea where I'd stay that night. I ended up staying on the porch of a man to whom I'd put the question: did you know of a place where I could get a fresh room? He said he did, but he said it was that time of night, said it'd be too late to go down and talk to her. So, actually, the first night in Rochester I slept out on a screened-in porch of a man who'd never seen me before. Just the kindness of another man.

Then I left Rochester, and went to Columbia University?

HARVEY: Went to Columbia, stayed out at Camp Shanks which is the veteran's housing place, this Camp Shanks. The same Camp where I had shipped out to England is now a place where veterans stayed. Columbia accepted me, and I stayed out there. I moved Edwina, my wife down there, not sure if she came directly with me to New York, she may have come back to Knoxville and then come up to Shanks. But we lived there until I finished my residency at Columbia, and then I came back to Knoxville.

Started teaching at Knoxville College, and as I say, I started as a full time teacher. In the course of my time at Knoxville College, I took leave four times. I went to the National Science Foundation as program administrator three of those times. The other time, I went to the University of Kansas to do some postdoctoral work in mathematics, but I never gave up my residency in Knoxville. Knoxville's a good place to live. I've been interim president, let me just say, more than once.

I became Dean—the president of the college convinced me to become Dean in 1965. The Dean essentially oversees the mathematic program. By this time, I'm a professor of mathematics, and the president's right hand man. He'd do a lot of the assignments the president needs done, but he doesn't get involved in those details. The next year, the president gets offered a position as president of Bronx Community College in New York. So here I am, less than a year as dean, and I'm—I'm not going into all the background, but I ended up being asked and agreeing to serve as interim. And that's how it's happened each time: the president has left, I've been there, almost every time. One time, I was at the National Science Foundation in Washington, and I came down for two weeks, and in those two weeks I helped them find an interim, I went back to my job. But that counts as an interim assignment, because we only had one president at a time. And the president there had left of his own will, but he was gone, and there's no president, and there's no dean—because the dean was also fired. And I'm in Washington. So, my wife gets a call from the chairman of the board that they need some help from me, and that's how I ended up coming down to spend two weeks. That was the first time… no, that wasn't the first time, because I knew that I was going to be doing my job. I was dean, and I was full-time. But later on, that was a two week assignment. And I had a couple of those, and last time I became interim president, I agreed to be interim president for 90 days. Well, that was August of 2005. I finally walked out of that office in January of 2010.

Well, we just had a celebration of my college and the alumni, of which they established a hall of fame in my name, and they named the college Center in my name, and they established a scholarship in my name. They had a dinner-dance down at the convention center, which was full of people, and we got a lot of accolades, and now I'm back to full time retirement.

Author's note: Okay, there you go. World War II didn't stop you from setting your goals and accomplishing what you wanted to do. Dr. Harvey, what advice do you have for returning veterans right now?

HARVEY: Well, first of all, from my own experience, I would say set your mind on what you want to accomplish, and let the service in the military be an interruption to that. Don't let the service in the military destroy your dreams, whatever they may be. And it's very difficult to readjust to civilian life when you've been in the military, particularly if you've been in a combat. It was very traumatic for me—there were nights where I didn't sleep very well, for example. But I kept my mind focused on one thing, and I wouldn't let the military service and the military take me away from that.

The GI Bill: What a blessing. You didn't think too much of military service when you were in there—it's a hard life, you'd rather be back home with your family doing whatever you were doing, doing your job. But it turned out to be a blessing for me because it provided the resources for me to go to graduate school, and I got support and allowance, which was sufficient for me and my family. Got all of my bills paid, all of my books, and it was a great blessing.

HARVEY: Every soldier is entitled to that. It's not sufficient to repay all that you should be repaid for your service, because it's taken a block out of your life, and there's no way to repay that. It's the great sacrifice for people that serve in the military that do a great service to this country.

General Patton had a job to do. He couldn't do it without supplies, reinforcements, and replacements. The Germans had destroyed the railroads. The almost-6,000 trucks moved 24/7. The drivers carried M1 rifles and hauled anti-aircraft guns to protect themselves. They were subject to sniper fire, rage from hungry citizens, and Allied soldiers needing supplies. They were targeted by the German military because they knew how important the mission was. Driving those trucks, were men from all over America, mostly black Americans. Four of those trucks were commanded by Corporal Robert Harvey, soon to be Sergeant. He returned to Knoxville to complete his college education, and to his bride, who had waited for him after getting married and coming home the next day, while her husband went to war against the Nazis, almost a year and a half.

He never saw his mother again. She died while he was away. One of his sisters passed away, too. His father's house had burned. His family didn't tell him those things until he returned. He went to Rochester, New York and started his further education, sleeping on a back porch of a friend. He got his doctorate at Columbia University, and eventually returned to Knoxville College and became dean of academics, and the interim president twice.

In November of this year (2012) Congressman John Duncan entered the life of Robert Harvey in the Congressional Record. In October of 2012, Knoxville College honored Dr. Robert Harvey by naming the alumni hall of fame after him. Before all these things happened, something else happened. It was called World War II. He had to survive as a member of the Red Ball Express. Not even World War II could stop Dr. Harvey from realizing his life's ambition, to be Dr. Robert Harvey. But first, he was one of the original delivery experts under fire.

While Doctor Harvey was delivering supplies to the soldiers at the Front, John Shell was marching into a town called St. Vith. Into a line of battle about to meet the initial onslaught of the German Army that became known as "THE BATTLE of the BULGE.

His story is next.

CHAPTER EIGHT

CAPTURED THE FIRST DAY OF THE BATTLE OF THE BULGE

We all know about Hogan's Heroes, the fun they had destroying the Germans while they were in the prisoner of war camps. That's really not what happened that's not what happened at all.

A note to the German military in World War II, "beware the Ides of March." It was the Ides of March in 1943, and the 106th Infantry Division was activated. They were trained to be replacements. They were trained in South Carolina and Tennessee. The Tennessee terrain in over 20 counties of Middle Tennessee around Lebanon, and Murfreesboro resembled the cold Ardennes Forest. In mid-October, the 106th spent several weeks in England, and then raced into Belgium. And on December 5th through the 10th, they began a march—a 5-day march in the cold rain, and ahead of them were the snowy woods and snowy mountains of the Ardennes Forest, near St. Vith, near the German border, in Belgium.

They started with about 12,000 men, and when they got to the mountains they were wet, mostly untested in battle, and they were sent to relieve a division that had been under fire for a long time and needed to rest. A division the size of the 106th was designed to defend a five mile line. It was assigned 28 miles of the front.

They expected German patrols. But they did not expect the German military, the Panzers, the German Storm Troopers, and the paratroopers that were heading right for them. It was the first hours of the Battle of the Bulge.

John Shell's company was volunteered to go forward to report what was happening, what was occurring. Portions of the 106th Infantry Division were isolated by the German onslaught. They were left with no orders to retreat, or to advance in the confusion. These Americans followed orders, as they were trained, and stayed put. They were captured by paratroopers, Panzer tanks, Storm Troopers. The paratroopers landed right where John Shell and his men were waiting. It was 35 Americans versus 1500 German paratroopers. They were not alone—two-thirds of the Division were overwhelmed, but not before exacting such a toll from the German military, that the German military was unable to complete its mission.

Lt. General Hodges, 1st Army Commander, said this of the 106th's stand:

> *"No troops in the world, disposed as your division had to be, could have withstood the impact of the German attack which had its greatest weight in your sector. Please tell these men for me what a grand job they did."*

Well, what did they do? They definitely upset the whole German timetable. But there was a second letter—a letter from Western Union. It was addressed to Wilma Shell, and it said:

> *"The Secretary of War desires me to express his deep regret that your husband, Pvt. 1st Class John Shell Jr., has been reported missing in action since 19 December in Belgium. If further details or other information are received, you will be promptly notified."*

She had a 3 month old daughter named Margie.

Having to surrender is hardly anything but a humiliating experience. Each soldier had the fear that they would be looked down on for surrendering. It has been said in mid-1944, Germany had nine million prisoners. The drain on the economy was enormous.

Captured in battle, despised by the German citizens, afraid of being executed, forced to march, malnourished, in unsanitary conditions, as pawns on the international stage, Hitler wanted to use them as a bargaining chip. Hitler was willing to kill them to accomplish his goals. If they were marching, they did not have to be sheltered.

John Shell entered service on February 27th, 1941. He left service on December 5th, 1945. The story you're about to read today is his experience as a prisoner of war in World War II.

SHELL: Before the war I was a plant manager for Knoxville Iron Company. Mercy, when I went to work, I was 13-14 years old. My uncle was superintendent down there and he thought I was a big boy, I grew up early, and my uncle worked to get me a job. Everybody needed a job back then, and I got a job working down there in the mill. Later on, they needed a crane operator, and I trained to become a crane operator.

I was not drafted! I volunteered!!!! "I wanted to go. Our country was getting involved, and I talked to a lot of adults back then, and they said we'd be in a war, and I wanted to get in there and do my part. It's a good story. Mr. King, one of the office managers down at Knoxville Iron Company went up there and told the draft board he needed me as a crane operator. It was a steel mill, and the government needed it, and he went up there and got me deferred. I had just gone up there that day and volunteered. And he came up and he was so proud, bless his heart, and he told me he got me deferred. I said, "Deferred?" I went up today and volunteered!" I remember that day. I got kind of put out at it, but we got over it. He was a sweet old man, and I went right back that same day and volunteered again. I told him I went through the draft order—maybe that's why they did it that way—but I did not get drafted. I was a volunteer!!!!!!!: When I went into the army as one of these things you read in my discharge papers, it's scout and sniper, and I like to use scout—I don't like that word "sniper."

SHELL: What was the role of a scout? It tells you on one of those pages there open that up and get one of those—oh, wait a minute, you can get...

Mr. Shell handed me his discharge papers, he was very proud of them.

SHELL: That yellow thing. Hand it over here right there. Read that to me, down at the bottom.

Author's note: "You were ordered to obtain the information concerning strength, disposition, and probable intention of enemy forces. You were in the 106th in ETO (European Theater of Operation) for eleven months, and you would knock out stray tanks with bazookas on front lines. You operated a .50 caliber machine gun, and you were a prisoner of war from 19 December 44 to 17 April 45." My gosh! You were busy!

SHELL: I made Corporal before basic training was over. 'Course, back then, they needed men, and they knew who was a good soldier—and I was a good soldier. And I went to special training and I was in Army headquarters. I tested a lot of different outfits. I even went into civilian life while I was in service, I was discharged out in Salt Lake City, Utah, and they had a copper mine out there that they couldn't get anybody to work, and the government needed it, so they let us have an opportunity to discharge and go out there and work in civilian life.

Author's note: I changed the subject, "Mr. Shell, how'd you get captured?"

SHELL: They dropped a bunch of paratroopers in on top of us while we were on patrol. I was on a mission. I looked up, and a bunch of paratroopers were coming down? Yep! Our officers ordered us to rest. What did he call that thing where you go rest after you've been on a mission of some kind, you go rest? R&R. Rest and recuperation. I was in rest and recuperation in a little town, I can't remember the name. (It was St Vith) and an Officer comes through there, and he gives some information and he asks for volunteers. Of course, most of us had been there before, and we didn't volunteer. And he says, "I hate to do it, but I'll volunteer for you." I didn't hear all this, but that's what the captain said. And he volunteered for us, and we went back. We just got in, I think maybe one day, maybe two in R&R, I don't remember. And he was needing some information. Something about clanking sounds over the next hill. We went up to get it, and we got captured. They dropped a bunch of paratroopers on us. It was 1500 of them and 32 of us.

There was no surrendering, we just stayed where we were. Some of their troops came and got us and took us down for interrogation. They were rough on us. Oh yeah. They were not nice. They didn't have anything nice about them.

When we captured them, we never took an undue advantage. You know, we did a job, and we did it good, but we didn't like it.

What would you think if you had a bunch of guys out here, and your job was to go out and kill them? We didn't like that. I can't say all of us—some of us might have liked it, I didn't like it, and most of us didn't.

I don't remember any names of my fellow prisoners except John Lux, one or two.

Most of them were my friends

Most of the soldiers that I have talked to called it "taking care of business", and some called it "we did what we had to do". That's exactly right. Now, I was driving a truck when the troops came down, and I had this—John Lux. I just found out recently that he died, and John Lux was there, and we saw Germans come up out of a bunch of bushes out there, with guns pointed at us, and our officers told us before we left that they didn't want any shooting until we got our information and got on the way back. No unnecessary killing. And John started shooting. I told him, "No, no, John, they told us not to." It would have been unfair to that German soldier.

No POW camp at first. We got on that death march first.

Captured American Soldiers

In the last German offensive of World War II, three German Armies conducted a surprise attack along a 50 mile front in the Ardennes beginning on Dec. 16, 1944, and quickly overtook thin U.S. lines.

On the second day of the 'Battle of the Bulge,' a truck convoy of Battery B of the 285th Field Artillery Observation Battalion was intercepted southeast of Malmedy by a regiment of the 1st SS Panzer Division of the Leibstandarte-SS, under the command of 29 year old SS Lt. Col. Jochen Peiper. His troops had earned the nickname "Blowtorch Battalion" after burning their way across Russia and had also been responsible for slaughtering civilians in two separate villages.

Upon sighting the trucks, the Panzer tanks opened fire and destroyed the lead vehicles. This brought the convoy to a halt while the deadly accurate tank fire continued. The outgunned Americans abandoned their vehicles and surrendered.

The captured U.S. soldiers were herded into a nearby field. An SS tank commander then ordered an SS private to shoot into the prisoners, setting off a wild killing spree as the SS opened fire with machine guns and pistols on the unarmed, terrified POWs.

Survivors were killed by a pistol shot to the head, in some cases by English speaking SS who walked among the victims asking if anyone was injured or needed help. Those who responded were shot. A total of 81 Americans were killed in the single worst atrocity against U.S. troops during World War II in Europe.

After the SS troops moved on, three survivors encountered a U.S. Army Colonel stationed at Malmedy and reported the massacre. News quickly spread among U.S. troops that "Germans are shooting POWs." As a result, the troops became determined to hold the lines against the German advance until reinforcements could arrive. Gen. Eisenhower was informed of the massacre. War correspondents in the area also spread the news.

By January of 1945, the combined efforts of the Allied armies drove the Germans back to their original starting positions in the Battle of the Bulge. U.S. troops then reached the sight of the massacre, now buried under two feet of winter snow.

Mine detectors were used to locate the 81 bodies, which had rested undisturbed since the day of the shootings and by now had frozen into grotesque positions. Forty one of the bodies were found to have been shot in the head. As each body was uncovered it was numbered.

While the U.S. medical teams performed this grim task, columns of German POWs being led by Americans passed by, with the bodies in plain view, however, no act of vengeance was taken.

Following the defeat of Nazi Germany, 74 former SS men, including Jochen Peiper and SS Gen. Sepp Dietrich, were tried by a U.S. Military Tribunal for War Crimes concerning the massacre.

I asked Mr. Shell: Did you hear that they had killed soldiers at Malmedy

SHELL: No, that's the first time I've heard about that.

The Germans, they killed our soldiers? I didn't know about that.

Author's note: *(I found this to be so interesting that John Shell would not know about Malmedy, but then he was captured at the time!)*

Really? They had killed 81 prisoners of war in Malmedy, but were you afraid they might execute you all?

SHELL: You know, for some reason or another, I was never really afraid. A lot of things happened that I didn't like or was really unpleasant, but I don't remember ever being afraid. Most of my life at that prisoner camp was pretty vivid to me, but I don't remember ever really being scared. Oh yeah, we went to a camp. We went to a headquarters, and I forget the name of the big army general, but a big German officer interrogated us, separated the Jews from the gentile.

Author's surprise: Even the American soldiers? They separated the American Jewish soldiers? Authors note: As you remember, they were doing this in Holland in 1940, now it was 1944.

SHELL: Oh, yeah. I forget this boy's name, I can't remember his name, but he and I were together at the headquarters when they interrogated us, and when he asked this Jewish buddy of mine if he was Jewish, he said "yes, and proud of it." And he asked me if I was Jewish, and I said, "no." And the German soldier that took us down there, he said something in German, and he was disagreeing with me since I was with him all the time.

I was captured December 16th, so it was already cold. We had big snow there. The Battle of the Bulge had started: Yeah, and the paratroopers were part of the Battle of the Bulge.

So they captured us, and they started moving us in towards inland Germany?

That march lasted all over the country for 90 days. They marched us all over Germany. I don't think they had enough POW Camps, so they just kept marching us every day for a long time.

Author's note: Marching POWs did not need facilities. So, they'd march you, and you'd stop at a barn, or how would you sleep?

At this time, Mr. Shell was in a hospital bed in his living room. It later proved to be his death bed.

He looked at me, raised himself up on his right arm, and looked at me with a surprised look on his face.

To be honest my interview took two weeks because the first time I met him, he would hardly talk to me. I did not know how or what to ask, so at the end of my first interview, I asked him if I could come back and talk some more. He said I could if he was still alive.

I went home and read all I could about the German Death March history during the Battle of the Bulge. I had learned that many nights, the German guards would let the prisoners sleep in old barns on the path. When I asked about the barns, John Shell, looked at me and raised up on his death bed, and supported himself with his right arm, and looked me right in the eyes.

It was like I had finally hit a spot that he was impressed that I knew about.

SHELL: How'd you know even about them barns? he said raspily, with energy.

RANDY: How'd I know about them barns? I read about it. This past week so we could talk.

SHELL: Yeah, we stopped in the barns.

The Soldiers would take turns in the barns trying to get warm, huddling together and trying to share the time evenly in and out of the barns. Yeah, we slept in the barns. Our planes would come over—we'd always be afraid they didn't know we were there, and drop a bomb on us: Occasionally, that happened.

Depending on the situation we marched eight hours a day, or twelve hours a day. We didn't have a regular schedule. Sometimes we would walk through a German town that had just been bombed by American planes. They would march us, and take us out around, and sometimes they'd take us back through the town, aggravating them. And the citizens didn't like us. But the guards wouldn't let the citizens bother us. The mood of the German troops through the winter? They kept changing. You know, they keep them in their territory. We kept getting passed off to different guards. Eventually they were older men and children.

Some of us were in groups of two hundred, or three hundred men at a time. Sometimes like in my group, five hundred. There was also a group of fifteen hundred. We had to share space time in the barns.

John Shell's face looked as if he had gone back in time and he was shivering.

"We stayed cold all the time. Stayed cold all the time, oh it was cold. We never had a warm moment on that march, we didn't have a decent minute.

I had a pair of almost-new boots when I was captured, and they took them away from me.

And they gave me an old pair of shoes. At one time, I had wooden shoes. I wore wooden shoes, didn't walk in them, but at one time I had wooden shoes, and I finally got a halfway decent pair of shoes when I went to work.

SHELL: What did we have to eat? Thirty-five pounds of potatoes made soup enough for two hundred men. Maybe. two hundred and fifty men. Each day, and there was a sweet old lady who would cook for us, and cook in our logger. Logger is a camp. They cooked in our logger. She would get dog meat, anything with red meat and put it in our soup. We got one meal a day. We had one slice of, I believe, made with sawdust, bread. It was better than on the march, they did not feed us at all. They never served us a meal. We ate cabbage roots and stuff. That we saw along the way. We would have eaten cats that we saw along the way, but, well, we didn't have no way to prepare 'em, and at the time we hadn't accustomed ourselves to the kind of living we had to do.

Sometimes we would walk through a German town that had just been bombed by American planes.: Yeah, and they would march us, and take us out around, and sometimes they'd take us back through the town, aggravating them, but they wouldn't let the citizens bother us.

Once we finally got placed in a camp they put us to work.

We were in a town, I think it was Dachau, and a railroad went through there and we were tearing up this railroad. The way I understood it, we were tearing this railroad up and taking the ties in the rail, and the spikes and everything, and putting them and mounting them at a dock house in a Jewish extermination camp.

I didn't see any Jewish prisoners. but we went through Dachau one time, I don't remember what the occasion was, but they put us on a train. Fifty men in one little 40-foot boxcar. Fifty men.

Yeah, we stayed in there four days, and there was human waste in there. Human waste was awful. You went to the bathroom in the boxcar. No, you didn't have no chance to go the bathroom.

Now, the German soldiers switched from just regular soldiers to SS at the end. They were bad, they were mean.

One day we realized we were going to make it. We were going to survive. We were in the camp, we could hear fighting. We could hear small arms, and when we would hear the big arms, we knew the firing order. And—I didn't know that, some of the boys trained in there—we knew our troops were getting close. And we knew the reaction to that was that they hadn't taken us out to work. ". I was liberated after the war was over."

I believe I was in camp11-A. I don't remember... I was in a camp that I thought was in Dachau, I thought that was the name of that little town. I don't know, I don't think we were very far from Dachau.

Authors Note:
According to Wikipedia

POW camps run by the Germans during World War II. There were around 1,000 Prisoner-of-War camps in Germany during World War II.[6]

Germany was a signatory at the Third Geneva Convention, which established the provisions relative to the treatment of Prisoners of War.

- Article 10 required that POWs should be lodged in adequately heated and lighted buildings where conditions were the same as German troops.

- Articles 27-32 detailed the conditions of labor. Enlisted ranks were required to perform whatever labor they were asked and able to do, so long as it was not dangerous and did not support the German war effort. Senior Non-commissioned officers (sergeants and above) were required to work only in a supervisory role. Commissioned officers were not required to work, although they could volunteer. The work performed was largely agricultural or industrial, ranging from coal or potash mining, stone quarrying, or work in saw mills, breweries, factories, railroad yards, and forests. POWs hired out to military and civilian contractors were supposed to receive pay. The workers were also supposed to get at least one day a week of rest.

Article 76 ensured that POWs who died in captivity were honorably buried in marked graves. Types of Camps

- **Dulag** or *Durchgangslager* (transit camp) – These camps served as a collection point for POWs prior to reassignment. These camps were intelligence collection centers.

- **Dulag Luft** or *Durchgangslager der Luftwaffe* (transit camp of the Luftwaffe) – These were transit camps for Air Force POWs. The main Dulag Luft camp at Frankfurt was the principal collecting point for intelligence derived from Allied POW interrogation

- **Heilag** or *Heimkehrerlager* (repatriation camps) - Camps for the return of prisoners. Quite often these men had suffered disabling injuries.

- **Ilag/Jlag** or *Internierungslager* ("Internment camp") – These were civilian internment camps.

- **Marlag** or *Marine-Lager* ("Marine camp") – These were Navy personnel POW camps.

- **Milag** or *Marine-Internierten-Lager* ("Marine internment camp") – These were merchant seamen internment camps.

- **Oflag** or *Offizier-Lager* ("Officer Camp") – These were POW camps for officers.

Photograph of 4 sept.1944 drawing representing the Administration Barrack III in Oflag XD, by officer PWO Léon Gossens (Tilleur, Belgium) 1908-1993

- **Stalag** or *Stammlager* ("Base camp") – These were enlisted personnel POW camps.

- **Stalag Luft** or *Luftwaffe-Stammlager* ("Luftwaffe base camp") – These were POW camps administered by the German Air Force for Allied aircrews.

RANDY: What happened to the soldiers that got too sick?

SHELL: They just died.

RANDY: What about the ones that just could not or would not march?

SHELL: Oh, they didn't. I didn't know of anybody that wouldn't march. Now, this John Lux I told about at the beginning. He was older… He didn't need to be in service, he was old! I mean, he had some age on him! And he had this great big old heavy Army coat, and he was wore out completely, and I carried it for him all I could, and I told him, "John, I can't carry this no longer." And he took it. And he carried it a while, and we went on down, kept on marching, and he stayed back. And we heard a couple of shots. And I was just sure John got killed. I was sure they killed him. I wanted to get in touch with his family and tell them how we served—how he and I served together. And in doing so, I found out he wasn't killed! He got home, and died about two or three years ago.

The American Army liberated us, and the first day out we got out we took the town over. I could barely walk. I weighed 93, 94, 95 pounds, somewhere along in there, and I was just weak. We did walk around, and some of the boys had managed better than I did, and some of them did and they got out, and one of them was just awful to the German children.

You know, some people, even today have animosity towards the German people because they lost a brother or a family member, and it's just heartbreak. Heartbreak expressing itself.

Author's note: I have a personal friend, who wanted to marry a German girl a few years ago. His mother cried and blocked the wedding because her brother had been killed by German Soldiers.35-40 years earlier.

SHELL: And I'm thankful that I don't have hatred against the whole German people. Some of 'em, I wish I had thrown in front of a firing squad.

You know, the night before the Germans knew—our guards knew we were fixing to be liberated, and all of them left. Every one of them left. Where they went, I don't know, but there were two or three in there that it was a good thing that they did. They wouldn't have made it.

Author's note: Did you all know that there were possible orders to execute you all?

SHELL: Well, we thought there might be. I remember talking to somebody about it.

When help arrived we were fed and showered. OH that felt good! It was a long time before I got home. They sent us to Wales, England, to a hospital in Wales, and we stayed in there, then they sent us to London. I never will forget the sports center, playing machines in there, and there a guy who came up and gave me a bunch of change to play it. There were some good ones in there... what was the name of that big square? Piccadilly?

John's daughter Margie had been listening during the whole second interview. She finally spoke up. She was sixty five years old when I met her... She was three months old when John first met her.

MARGIE: He was in the hospital for a long time in Florida after they got back here.

Suffering from malnutrition, and all kinds of problems, I guess?

SHELL: At the time, I was still mad at the Germans... And that didn't help any at all.

MARGIE: He was frostbitten from the knees down, and he's had trouble with that through the years. He's had heart surgery, and he had a tumor on the inside of his heart, and they said that was from complications from being beaten. He's had intestinal problems his whole life ever since he came home, and they said that's from bacteria from eating all the rotten food and stuff.

SHELL: We'd find all kinds of stuff in our soup.

We'd all been dead—all of us, if it hadn't been for that lady who cooked our soups. I never knew her name, but my wife and I, when we got back over here, we spent a lot of money trying to find her, I was gonna bring her over here. She was the cook, I was gonna bring her over here.

After the war and after recuperating, it was about three years before I could do anything. Two or three years, I wasn't able to physically and mentally do anything. But that finally got straightened out. I guess first thing I did was spend a lot of time with Jewish friends on Gay Street, talking to them, I'd go up there and they'd treat me like royalty.

They knew my story. Because I was over there, and they gave me credit for a lot I didn't do! *chuckles* Oh, they were sweet people. I started out, I guess, the first meaningful thing I did was I got to fool with antiques. I made a little money that way, got to making a little money. And then I got in with a cousin of mine, Rufus Smith—and he's dead—and Tommy, his wife, my cousin, and I got in with them and managed property, managed apartments. I made a good recovery.

And I managed West Town Manor, and two other apartments I forgot the name of. Hundred and fifty, one was two-fifty, and one was hundred, managed these apartments for him. And I got a good name in there, won apartment manager of the year several times.

I married my wife while in service. A Colonel married us down in Columbia, South Carolina, and after he married us, the very next day, he made General. Pointing at her picture, that's her, right there. We realized my health wasn't good.

We talked about it, my wife and I did. I was married 65 years.

All the time to the same woman. We realized my health wasn't good, and we weren't gonna have any more children. Margie's got twin boys. My Grandsons.

MARGIE: I was born while dad was gone.

SHELL: And I... He raised his hand waiving to Margie, "Go ahead and tell him, you'll tell him before it's over with.

MARGIE: Mom got a telegram, dad knew she was pregnant before she left, and he got a telegram from her, and it said something about how he was all right, has the boy arrived?

MARGIE: A boy has arrived.

SHELL: That's what I put there on the telegram. Hope boy has arrived.

MARGIE: Well, I was already here, I was about three months old. And dad said, "Hope boy has arrived!" *laughs*

SHELL: Yeah, hope boy. And it was a girl! And I live with that now, I hear that a lot. Have all 65 years. After I quit managing apartments, I got deep into the antiques business. I learned a lot about it, and Charlie Changas and I bought this building down here where the mattress factory is. But it was in Charlie's name, I helped him buy it. We bought it, and opened up a flea market, and my wife ran all the booths—we had 27 booths in there. And we had an auction house in the back. We all had an auction, and we did, oh we did…

RANDY: What was the name, did you have a name for your business?

SHELL: Flea market.

RANDY: Okay. So you got home, and you took a couple years to cure, to heal, and you went into the antique business and the real estate business and here it is sixty five years later. And here you are………

At this point John smiled,

SHELL: Yeah.

RANDY: What advice do you have for soldiers coming home that are wounded, or hurt?

SHELL: That I love them, and I pray for them.

Keep your chin up, I appreciate what they did, and what they're doing now. I wish we could get it straightened up a lot more than it is, but...

RANDY: Wars are a lot different now, aren't they?

SHELL: Yeah.

RANDY: The enemy is not always in uniform, and there is not always a battle line drawn.

SHELL: We fought a real war back then.

Author's note: The 106th Division was green when it went into the Battle of the Bulge. In three days after its first big fight, it was reduced to one third of its size. Two thirds of its unit had been captured. They were sent back to join another division because they didn't have enough men to make a full division anymore. And then, they realized what damage they had done to the German troops, and the German mission, and they realized it was the 106th that stopped most of it.

They got the opportunity to go back to St. Vith, and challenge the same German soldiers that had run them out. They took the point, and pushed the Germans into Germany. All that time, the rest of their comrades and friends were marching across Germany in -17 degree weather. Their shoes had been taken from them, they were being beaten regularly, starved, and shot if they couldn't go forward any longer.

John Shell weighed 93 pounds when he got home. He had seen many, many, many things that he just didn't want to talk about for a while. But he talked to a doctor that told him that when life throws an obstacle in your path, you can't keep going around it. You have to clean it up, and get through it. And if you do that, your life will be easier.

For John Shell's service, he got the American Campaign medal, the American Defense medal, the Good Conduct medal, the European-African-Middle East Campaign medal, two Bronze Stars, World War II Victory medal, the Purple Heart, and the POW medal. He will be 93 years old this year. He's got a good sense of humor, he loves to tell stories and talk, he loves to share his experiences.

The 106th? Well, they fought across Germany. At the end of the war, they were put in charge of the German POWs.

John Shell passed away not long after our interview.

Thank you, John Shell.

While John Shell was being captured, the 76th Infantry Division was starting preparations for battle soon to begin. The push for Berlin was about to begin.

In that Division was a young man named Charles Beal. My mother, Juanita Belle Kinzalow Baxter/Haun taught his children at Robert Huff Elementary School. His story is next!

CHAPTER NINE

"WHAT AM I GONNA DO?!"

Charles Beal and his Experience in World War II

Have you ever wondered why soldiers don't talk about their experiences after they've returned from war? We're going to be talking about that in a little bit. But first, our topic today is the 76th Infantry Division of the United States Army.

It was activated in 1942, and after training it went overseas on December 10th, 1944. They left right about the same time as the Battle of the Bulge was getting ready to start. Their campaigns were in the Ardennes-Alsace, the Rhineland, and Central Europe. The soldiers in the division were in combat for 107 days. They had two distinguished unit citations. Their training and activation began in April 1943, in Virginia, but their winter training in 1943 was in Wisconsin. They used skis, snowshoes, toboggans, snow tractors, snow goggles, winter camouflage suits, Eskimo parkas. They knew they weren't going to the South Pacific.

The 76th Infantry Division arrived in England on the 20th of December after 10 days at sea and a brief stop in Plymouth, where it received additional training, then off to France and a long two week march into battle. They proceeded to a place called the Limesy concentration area, then to Beine, east of Reims, then to Champlon, Belgium. The preparation for combat began. The relief of the 87th Division was the initial goal, and they were placed in defensive positions along the Sauer and Moselle Rivers in the vicinity of Echternach, Luxembourg. On the 25th of January, in the middle of winter, they had to cross the Echternach River. Then, they ran into the Siegfried Line—if you know about that, that's when the Germans had been chased out of France and they were fighting on their own soil, and they became tougher and meaner.

The advance continued across two more rivers, and in mid-February, the 76th Division conquered two fortresses and pushed on to a town called Trier, where they had to charge across a bridge with German soldiers shooting at them on the other side. They crossed another river. They took three more towns, and then they swung south and cleared the area north of the Moselle on March 18th.

Moving to the Rhine, the 76th took over defenses from Boppard to St. Goar and crossed the Rhine at Boppard, on March 27. It drove east and took Kamberg in a house-to-house struggle on the 29th of March. A new attack was launched April 4th, and they crossed another river. The attack continued in conjunction with the 6th Armored Division. Some more towns fell, another river was crossed. April 14th and 14th a town called Zeitz was captured after a violent struggle. The 76th reached another river on 16 April, and went into defensive positions to hold a bridgehead across the Mulde near Chemnitz until Victory in Europe Day.

Well, that was a lot, wasn't it? 105 days in battle, and all this happened while Charles Beal was in his 19th year of life.

Charles Beal of Knoxville, TN was with the 76th Infantry Division of the United States Army.

Fresh out of high school, Private Beal had just taken a long trip across the Atlantic Ocean and had landed in France, and for two weeks, had been traveling across France until he had gotten to Luxembourg. And then, they were unloaded, and handed their gear, and their leader pointed at a mountain!

BEAL: "And the officers said, "You are going have to carry everything you've got to the top of that mountain up there. And we had a pack of everything we had on our back, plus we had all of our clothes, food, ammunition, Everything.": "We had to go all the way through the town and turn around on that big, steep hill, and on top it started snowing on us. We were told "it won't be long; the truck will come and get you. It was a day and a half before they came there and got us. We were in deep snow, and we thought about sleeping in the hay that we had."

There was a buddy system when it came time to rest.

"It was always two-for-two—you would sleep for two hours, then your buddy would come and swap with you.": "Yeah. We always stayed together. You always knew where your buddy was, and he always knew where I was.: If one of us was not there, the other had to go report them." anyhow, they'd get you a new buddy.

It was so cold at night, but we went out to the schools and got the wooden desks to make a fire." We were from all over. Most of them were Yankees... We all accepted each other. They treated us pretty good, but, it got pretty rough sometimes. We finally got a ride on a truck. We put our gear in the back of the truck, and sat on top of the gear.

And, driving up to the front, tree limbs were hitting us—we couldn't get down in there, we had it loaded and we were on top.

Author's note: Sometimes I wonder if maybe Private Beal possibly could have been hauled in by Robert Harvey, another soldier in this book, but that's an earlier story.

"Yeah. We had to walk a while, and ride a while. But, no, we didn't really get into any fighting until we got close to Germany, and that's where we got serious. We had one time where we had the Germans across the river. You'd see a gentleman walking over there and he'd look at you, and he'd wave at you, and you'd wave back and, *pew-pew!* The bullets would start flying, we knew on both sides we had come here to fight. So, the civilians, they'd go out in the woods and find a tree, and hang a white-something over it, and make a place in there to stay while we were fightin' the Germans. And when the fighting was over, they'd go back to their house. That's why they'd put that white stuff up there so we could see they were there. And the Germans honored it, so they stayed away from it, so they wouldn't be shooting at them in the city. That's what we did, we destroyed cities, too.: We went to one city over there that had an old man and an old woman—the only house left standing. The rest of them were up in the mountains underneath that white stuff. They were too old to go hide. I asked the captain in charge, to let me go in there and look around. The captain said, "Take another man in there and search the house. I did, and I said "captain, there's an old man and an old woman in there. They're real old. They need to stay in that basement"

"No! "Said the Captain. "Get them out of here!" It was still snowing. They made me do it—I told them they had to leave, and I helped them get a baby buggy and something to keep warm—a hat, a jacket, and I helped them on the road. Those poor old people, they could barely push that buggy.: And they didn't take any food with them." Maybe they lived maybe they did not. We did not know, because we moved on."

BEAL: Coming in there, the soldiers who had come ahead of us had killed Germans all up and down the two roads. We had to kill them too, you know.: Anyhow, we invaded Germany. We had to paddle across a river, and the Germans were in there shooting everything at us. I mean, they were just letting us have it, right and left. And we got across—lost a lot of good men. Trouble was, we had six hand grenades—two, here, two here, and two here, and about everyone else did, too. And then you've got all your other paraphernalia on you and you can't swim with all that stuff on you.

When the soldiers crossing the river had their boat shot up they went straight down. The little boats we had—it was made out of a little wood, and canvas, so they went straight down when shot up, and the soldiers sank, too. When they got hit, the people in the boat had so much weight and equipment that they drowned?

But, we got across there. Trouble was, my outfit didn't know a thing about paddling the boat. We got over there and started paddling, got out, and it was dark. You couldn't see your hand in front of you. So, I've got two hands full of machine gun ammunition, plus my rifle over here, and all my other stuff. So, I got out there, and fell in a hole. It must have been a big shell hole. It was so dark, you couldn't see nothing. When I started to fall, I just turned loose and hit the ground.

I could see it was dark. I had to find my helmet, my rifle was upside-down, and my gear was everywhere. Anyhow, I got up and got to searching for my stuff. Finally, I felt around and found my helmet and found my ammunition. I got up and got everything ready and looked around, and everyone was already gone. "Silence was your friend, you don't talk to nobody." It was so dark; I didn't know where they went! But I looked up in the side of the mountain, and there was a fork of trees up there, and I said that must be the way they'd go. And I got on it. And sure enough, that was it.: It was winter, I was wet and muddy.

And I went on up there, I got to the first man, who was the last man in the company. Now I was the last man. I began to call my name, and every time I'd pass a man I'd call out my name. And somehow or another, I missed my buddy or he missed me. I went all the way to the first man leading the whole thing. He was almost to the top of the mountain. I started calling for my buddy as the soldiers walked by me. Anyhow, we got to fighting; oh we had the most hellish battle. And we lost a lot of men. We'd run, and run, and run, and they had us surrounded. But, anyhow, we managed to get away from them, finally got enough men between the Germans and us and that scared them, and they ran and left us up there. But first of all, they got around us, but we couldn't get out. No food or nothing. They dropped the food to us by plane. But it landed nearby and all went to the Germans.

That happened a lot. *chuckles*

But we went to the city of Trier; I have some pictures of it.

Author's note: If you remember the song, His war was in color, too. The photos were black and white. Trier, T-R-I-E-R? That is the oldest city in Germany founded in about 16 BC. Trier lies in a valley in West Germany near the border of Luxemburg in the wine region.

BEAL: Yeah, and we had to run across the bridge to get to the houses, the buildings, and they were shooting at us. We had to get over there, and we lost a lot of men. But we took the city of Trier. We went to this side of the city, where there wasn't much houses or nothing, and we were standing over there talking. And a shell, a bullet, came up from up on the top of the mountain over there. And my buddy next to me got it through the neck—it killed him. And another buddy was right downhill, we grabbed him, but he was wounded. He grabbed his leg and said, "They got my leg," so we got around a building where they couldn't shoot at us. It had gone through his leg sideways. So, we got out of that. We just got scattered here and there and everywhere.

The Germans got us one time up on a hill, we were here, and the Germans right here, we'd run them over here, and over here, all of a sudden, we were ordered to "halt! So stop it, and dig in!" The Germans would come back on us. Me and my buddy dug a hole, oh, it was a nice one. Best hole we ever had. You could stand up in it and you couldn't be seen, and you could stand up and shoot out the top. But then you'd put a cover on top of the thing, and then you'd put dirt on top of that, and it'd look like part of the country.

My buddy says, "Tell you what, I'm gonna lay down." Everything was two-for-two.

He'd go to sleep for two hours, then he'd take over and I'd go to sleep for two hours. And it didn't work, because they called and said, "Get out of here, the Germans are coming back on us." And we didn't get to sleep at all!

We worked all night long on the best hole we'd ever had and got run out of it before we had time to sleep in it?

One of our men was told to take three German prisoners back to trade them to somebody over behind us.

He wasn't gone long, we heard three shots.

He said they tried to run away. I think he just killed 'em.

I don't know what was in his mind, you don't know if somebody in his family had been killed by a German soldier, or, you know, the guy probably never intended to be a murderer. He was just a young man, a soldier, scared, hurt, and mad, and didn't know what was going to come on, and when you say that you heard three shots, I'm not saying that was a good thing to do, but I guess I'm saying you wouldn't know what you would do.

No you don't, no sir. No sir, you had no idea. We got pinned in. We took three pillboxes. One night, I was in this one here, and another was in this one, and another was in this one, and the next one up there was for the Germans. So, they had so many of 'em, we couldn't do nothing, we had to stay in our pillboxes. And after a while, we would run out of water, and there was a hole out there by our pillbox that had a German soldier's head in it. And one of our sergeant's was out there, dead. And they began to swell, the bodies. We'd go out there where that German was in the hole and get some water and take it back inside there, because if we stayed for two minutes, they'd kill us.

And we'd run back in our pillboxes and put pills in it, and let the mud settle in the bottom of it, and we could drink it. We had two guys in there that had been fighting the whole time and hadn't been hit or nothing, and they said that they got there and found a bucket. There was a spring out there, we all knew where the spring was, but it was wide open.

Everybody could see you. So, we kept trying to tell them to stay, "no, no, no, no, don't go," but they went any way, into the street. One shell, from an 88, got 'em.

They were so thirsty, that they were willing to risk their lives for a drink of water.

We told them they were going to get killed! "Oh, no," they said, "they've been shooting at us for days, weeks now, they can't hit us!"

Then it came time that we had to move up, so, we came out of our pillboxes, and a young boy next to us—he got shot. I forgot where it hit him, but he fell down, and the road was about that far below the cloud level. And this guy that got shot—his buddy came to help him, so he took his helmet off and got down on his hands and knees and was trying to doctor him, and another shell came and took the top of his head off right here.

Just like he took a knife and took it off, and then his brains poured out. And he was on his knees and hands—his body stayed that way, froze that way.

Yeah. Well, to make a short story about him, we came back to our sergeant who got wounded in the hip and the leg, and we were taking care of him. And this boy, his body was still there, on his hands and knees, where he got shot, where they took the top of his head off.

Yeah, we were fighting so much, nobody tried to move the bodies. We went on from there up to the pillbox the Germans were in. They came out with their hands over their heads, four of 'em then. And we all lowered our guns. We were right there with them, we were a little bit farther behind them but we saw those Germans with their hands down and they lowered their guns. But that last man behind them, they didn't see him; the other man came out with fully automatic guns.

So the other German in there came out from behind his buddies?

He started shooting. And all of our men, they started—well, he killed them, the best man we had. He killed the first, best men we had in our outfit. And then the others opened fired and killed all five of 'em.

I never saw an American soldier pull a trick like that? Doesn't that make you think, and wonder, you know, if American soldiers—I don't think they'd ever use the bodies of their buddies as a shield?

No, no. Later, my lieutenant and I, somehow or another, got separated from the whole outfit. There was a big field up here, and our men were all around in the woods. You know, the Germans were in those woods, too. They started shooting at us, because we were in the middle of it. And we found a pillbox—not really a pillbox, but a place where they had a dugout. You could get in there and get below ground level. So, me and the lieutenant got in there, didn't say a word, and started shooting at everything around us. Finally, they kind of slowed up on their shooting, and lieutenant said, "Let's get out of here." He stood up on the bank, I came up over here, and a shell busted. It was an 88. His body fell down, and I knew he was dead. And I'm alive in there, right in the middle of a big open field. And I stood there for a minute, and they're shooting at me. What am I gonna do? What am I gonna do?

Author's note: Mr. Beal had tears in his eyes when he said, What am I gonna do?

WHAT AM I GONNA TO DO???!!!!!!

Author's note: What would you have done, if you were Charles Beal? You are about to find out!

BEAL: And I stood there for a minute, and they were shooting at me. "What am I gonna do?" So, I thought,'" gotta run". I didn't run towards the Americans, I ran towards the Germans, 'cause they were closer to a place I could hide. So, I started running, and they started shooting at me. I ran down there and zig zagged with my steps. And when I ran out of my second breath, I started praying. You can pray when bullets are hitting around you.

And I just quit running and walking, and the bullets are going *pew-pew-pew-pew*, but I made it to the woods. So I went over in the woods, and there's one of my buddies out there in field, and he's got a whole butt cheek cut off. And the medic is out there, he's lying on his belly cussing the Germans out in the middle of the field.

They literally shot his butt off! So, I knew if I stayed there—I had a gun in my hand, see. And I knew if I stayed there, they would kill me. And I don't know why I ran there, but I ran up and down this way, and left him there—of course, he had a medic with him, and most Germans wouldn't shoot a wounded man with a medic. So, I went on down there and there's one of our men out there in the field. The BAR, that's a Browning Automatic Rifle, that's a whole lot heavier than him, so, he's out there with it, cocked in his hand, and he's got a hand grenade in his hand with his trigger pulled. *chuckle* Yelling at the Germans. And he said, "come out of there," at the pillbox in there, and there's a hole in the ground where they get in there. And it's about five stories down that you went into. No one came out.

So, we started that way, and I realized there were two German pillboxes behind us, and why they didn't shoot at us, I didn't know. We went in there and some of the other fellows went in there— no light or electricity in there because as the Germans retreated, they cut the electric wires. The Pillbox Inside had a tunnel, it's all of 300-feet from there from where you've gotta turn, then you've got steps going down five stories with the pillbox on top.

But we got in the middle of there, and people kept lighting matches and paper. It wasn't long until the paper would wear out, and we couldn't get a match to light. We used up the whole box in there.

But one of our men went down in there in one room and found a light, it had electricity all through it, but the Germans turned it off. But anyhow, we went through there, and five stories up, and we met our boys up there in it, in the pillbox. We did not know they were American, but we knew they were shooting at us.

So my buddy went down, and I got up and stayed on the second floor. And after a while, I heard something, bang-bang-bang-bang calling down through the place where you had fresh air coming in.

And it was a grenade. It went off—that room wasn't very big—

Yeah. But Germans had it set up to protect themselves, there were two tubes in there that hand grenade would fall down through, where it would stop down here. It had a way of stopping the shrapnel. And I never saw anything, but it was that close to me.

It was an American hand grenade!

They call it the THE FOG of WAR!

That's exactly what it was, yeah!

We never found out who it was.

We had come in the back door and the Americans were coming down the chimney?

It was a terrible thing, the whole ordeal. One of the villages we were fighting, the Germans and all the families had got out of 'em. And they had left everything just like it was, in the kitchen and everywhere else. So we had enough men standing around out there, that some of us would take a nap on the floor. We'd get in the bed on the floor, and then, anyhow, they said, "move out, we're gonna get hit." So, I picked up everything but one grenade, I had it in there somewhere, but I was in a hurry. So, I got up with the rest of us, and we were gone for a few hours, then we pushed it to Germany. And where we had been, the woman had a little boy and a little girl. And she'd come back while we was gone. And they found out that little boy had found the hand grenade and pulled the pin on it and killed both of 'em. And the fighting went on.

But, so many things like that happened every day, it was terrible.

RANDY: When did you find you were able to start talking about that? When did you—did you talk about it when you came home?

BEAL: No.

RANDY: Well, why? Why not?

BEAL: I didn't want to. I kept it hid in my mind.

RANDY: Blocked it out?

BEAL: And I started drinking. And I drank pretty heavy, you didn't find me out here drinking, but I found other things to keep my mind on, and the preacher at the VA, told me one time, he said, "do you ever talk about what you've been into?" And I said, "No, I don't tell nobody about all that old stuff." And he said, "You need to talk to somebody about it." And he kept telling me that, and finally I got to talk to somebody, and it helped me.

RANDY: Yes, it did.

BEAL: I got to talking about it, and then my drinking left me.

RANDY: Your drinking left you?

BEAL: Well, I left it! *laughs*

RANDY: Yeah? It's hard to hold things in like that, and during World War II, they didn't offer you guys a lot of treatment. They would say you were shell-shocked, or they would say different things, but they didn't actually treat the soldiers, or debrief them, or help them.

BEAL: Our captain first went into combat, first day, got shot straight through his hand. A million dollar wound.: He was in charge of the whole company.: We had nine different company commanders in a short period of time. Most had been wounded or killed.

We had to adjust to getting these new commanders all the time? The commanders didn't know you, so they were just there to get the job done and give you orders: You showed up, and you knew who they were, and you did what they said.

But I want to talk some more about what we first talked about that a while ago, about the Germans coming out of that pillbox, we shot them all, but, anyhow, from there, we went walking farther and we didn't see any Germans. And when we got in the field, it was a bald knob kind of humped like this, and there weren't hardly any trees or bushes or nothing on it. And all around it was trees. And we still went along the trees, well, then there was no trees hardly, and we got way over in it, and there were machine guns on both sides of us, and down in there, began shooting at us. And they really let us have it.

And my buddy, I showed you his picture right over there... Him and his sergeant.

He had the leg wound? His lieutenant got killed and fell on his body. He couldn't move. I didn't move his body off to protect him. That's when that German came and found him, and got him out of there. He became a prisoner of war.: And we lost men in there because we were surrounded on three sides by Germans.

After it was all cleared, and we were told get out of there. We ran out in the open, and we ran zigzags. They were so good with those guns, they were shooting at us, and bullets were hitting us from far away. They were shells—the shells weren't bullets, really. And, one went off behind us, and the man with me, he got shot in the leg right here. That one shot picked up a rock, and it hit me on my pack and knocked me on the face. But, I got up right quick, threw my pack away. OH, I had a fine Christmas cake in there! *laughs* I had to leave it!

My buddy up there, he's down on one leg, but we got out of there!

Author's note: There was a box on a table that had my curiosity. Mr. Beal, can we take a look at what's in that box?

BEAL: Yeah, you'd have to fight with a rifle to get one of those.

It was a bronze star, those are my dog tags. And my unit pin for the 76th Infantry? Or 76th Division?

RANDY: And you've got a bronze star that you've won three times?

BEAL: No, no, there's just one. That's special. This one is where you're fighting three battles.

BEAL: And they gave me this bronze star because they say, I was brave, or something, you know.

Charles Beal was 19 years old. He carried his gear across the mountains and rivers of Germany. He crossed rivers he could drown in, fell in a large hole and got left by his company, was engaged in several firefights, witnessed several deaths of friends and comrades as they occurred heard the escape and gunning down of three German soldiers. Following his captain's order, sent an elderly couple out into the cold. He may have left a grenade in a house that killed a mother and her child. He went through nine company commanders. He got trapped in machine gun crossfire, was almost killed by an American grenade, and could have suffocated. He also lost his Christmas cake. He came home, got married, had children, and now he's a grandfather of many, many grandchildren.

The World War II Generation has been called the "Greatest Generation." When I first met Charles Beal, he was the father of many of my friends I went to school with. My mother was a school teacher. Two of his sons, Mark and Paul, became best friends with my little brother, Rusty. Rusty died early at age 17 in a car accident. I know that accident hurt Mr. Beal and his sons. I knew him as a father of my brother's best friends, a neighbor, long before I ever knew him as a soldier. He passed away on January 3, 2012. He was an old man before I ever called him a friend. That was my loss.

Thank you, Charles Beal, for your service in the US Army, 76th Infantry Division, 1945.

I sent this chapter to a friend of mine for review. A Vietnam Veteran. Someone I respect as a friend and a business colleague. This is what he had to say.

Randy, Thank you for allowing me to review the chapter. Some thoughts:

- The account was of 105 days, or 15 weeks of combat. There are periods of cold, hunger, thirst, sleeplessness, horror and irony (like American troops rolling hand grenades down onto Beal and his squad).

- The title of the chapter which is a question of what to do when a young, inexperienced low ranking infantry soldier is left alone after the death of his lieutenant is answered in his description of continuing the mission (army slang is Charlie Mike), where he takes the initiative without orders from a superior.

- Particularly valuable are Beal's accounts of the dark side of war, such as the German head in the waterhole, soldiers drowning under the weight of their gear, the death of innocent civilians, and seeing his comrades obliterated by the antiaircraft German 88. To understand war as a brutal unforgiving scourge there is no viewpoint more appropriate than that of a participant at ground level….the American infantryman. While today with the technology of drones, satellite surveillance, night vision devices, armored up soldiers and vehicles, and amazing air assets from attack helicopters and fighter bombers with their bunker busting smart bombs, it may seem that war is just a more realistic video game, the reality remains that for the individual on the ground it is most certainly no game.

Raymond Wells
Medicare Guide

WWW.RAYWELLSMEDICAREGUIDE.COM

His review brought me to tears…

I did not realize how brave Charles Beal was until after I had read the review from Mr. Wells.

Charlie Mike i.e. Continue the mission. SALUTE!

So far, we have discussed land and sea battles, but the skies were busy, too! In 2012 while I was helping families with the Aid and Attendance Benefits for many of our veterans, I met a man named Harold Johnson. He was a B-17 pilot over Germany. I had to hear his stories.

CHAPTER TEN

THE GERMANS HAVE JETS?

The B-17 was a bomber airplane manufactured by Boeing in the United States of America. We manufactured 12,732 of these planes, and we lost 4,750 in combat. Approximately 46,500 pilots, co-pilots, navigators, engineers, bombardiers, back gunners, tail gunners, ball gunners, side gunners, were killed in action. Several models were manufactured. E-models were used for training. Our guest today flew mostly in the F and G-models that were used for combat missions. Later on, some of the B-17s were called pathfinders, and they were equipped with radar, originally for bad weather, but later for all missions. The B-17 was a big part of the Eighth Air Force, and the Eighth Air Force was used for strategic operations. Strategic bombing doctrine was embodied in Air War Plans Department One, which called for a sustained air offense against the Axis power to destroy their will and capacity to wage war. It was hoped that air ascendency would make an invasion of the continent unnecessary. Strategic operations were different from tactical operations, in that tactical operations were used when you needed to move troops forward a few hundred yards, or a few miles, or if you needed to knock out a position, you would use the tactical air command. This would be the Ninth Air Force. When you wanted to destroy your opponent and knock down their buildings and blow up their factories and stop their will, you would use the Eighth Air Force for strategic operations. The groups were broken down into what was called bombardment groups, and today, we're going to discuss the 388th Bombardment Group. The air offense they operated in Normandy, Northern France, Rhineland, Ardennes-Alsace, and Central Germany. They got the Distinguished Unit Citations, and we're going to concentrate our time today on one particular pilot: Hal Johnson, of Knoxville, Tennessee.

Mr. Harold (Hal) Johnson, formerly Lt. Johnson of the US Army Air Corp Eighth Air Force 388th Bombardment Group. Mr. Johnson lives in Knoxville, Tennessee, he will be in his 90's by the time you read this book. He flew somewhere between 22 and 24 missions, and we're going to start by letting him tell us a bit about taking his plane to England.

HAROLD: In those days, there were several different routes to get there. Some of them would go through the Azores or Iceland, or Alaska, or wherever it was and go to Scotland. We went from Gander, Newfoundland, and then the next day we had to fly from Raleigh, Wales to Liverpool, England, which was kind of fun, because, you know, those aircraft in those days always have a Jeep that said "follow me" when you landed. Well, the damn thing left the airfield! It was out in the city streets, and we were going through the streets and the traffic was all stopped and I was afraid the wings would hit the lamp post or something, but they didn't. So, we climbed up a big hill, and then there was a vast hill—a vast space for airplanes where hundreds of B-17s, B-24s, fighter planes, cargo planes, as far as the eye could see, and we had to leave our airplane there. This was 1944-45.

Many think the air battle over England was over by then. No, no way. The V1 and V2 rockets were still being launched. Hell yes. Well, excuse me, there were, but not as many as there were earlier. 42, 43, 44. By 1945, very few—some did come. 1945 was the high point of the American Eighth Air Force. We flew literally every day. A couple of thousand B-24s and B-17s were flying over Germany or different targets. That happened until war's end, which was in early May 1945.

The number of missions a pilot flew depended on circumstances beyond the pilot's control… It would change around—I had about 24 or 25 missions between some parts of March and all of April. Then sometimes I'd get three day passes, we'd go down to London or something like that. So, that would happen. It'd take a little time. It's hard to tell how long it took. But that's why I did not get more missions than I did, and I didn't even want anymore. The Eighth Air Force was a strategic air command. I was in the 388th Bomb Group. There were many, many bomb groups, but they were all Eighth Air Force. There were two Air Forces in World War II. There was the strategic air force, then there was the tactical. I was in with a bomber group. Of course, there were fighter groups, and B-17 and B-24 groups. We were strictly a B-17 group in Knettishall, England. I was the commander of the whole plane?

Early in the war there were ten men in a crew, because they had two in the waist gunner position. After a while, the fighters were less and less from the Germans, and they made it just one guy in the waist. All the rest were the same—tail gunners, ball turret gunners, and waist gunners. So, there were four officers and five enlisted men, ready to operate.

When we went on a mission with friends in other planes who didn't come back. We were all emotionally upset. Well, I was very upset, you know, because I didn't know anything at all about if he was alive or dead or anything. This happened to lots of folks. You really couldn't tell, and even though this was not as bad or tough for us in 1945 as it had been earlier, it was still tough. Some people came to our barracks, two or three of them, the first time ever, and the next day, they were gone. They were shot down. You got kind of used to it—you didn't like it, but you kind of got used to it. You have to feel, you know, not too worried about things. You have to close your mind on doing what you're supposed to do. [

Author's note: The Luftwaffe came to know the Boeing B-17 Flying Fortress intimately. In the air they credited it with speed, load carrying, ruggedness and bristling defensive firepower. Based upon the principle that shooting down a single engine fighter gained the victor one point, the downing of a four-engine bomber was scored as three points. Two points were awarded for damaging a heavy bomber sufficient to force it to leave the safety of the combat box, what the Luftwaffe called "herausschuss", literally meaning "shooting out." Only one point was awarded for a bomber that had become separated, because this task was considered less hazardous. In the end, the Germans shot down over 4000 Flying Fortresses in combat. At first, American heavy bombers flew in combat boxes of 18 aircraft with succeeding boxes following one and a half miles behind. To improve the defensive formation, this was replaced by the wing formation that combined three 18-plane groups. Also, instead of flying behind each other, the groups were positioned at high, medium and low level. The medium altitude group would fly slight ahead in the lead with the high squadron above and to the right while the low squadron beneath and on the left. The resulting 54 plane formation occupied a stretch of sky 600 yards long, a mile or so wide and half a mile deep. Other wings might fly identical formations to the target at six-mile intervals.

"Fips" Phillips, a 200+ Eastern Front Ace wrote the following while in command defending against American Bombers over Northern Germany:

> *"Against 20 Russians trying to shoot you down or even 20 Spitfires, it can be exciting, even fun. But curve in towards 40 fortresses and all your past sins flash before your eyes."*

Lt Franz Stigler, a 500 mission veteran describes a 1944 attack against American bombers like this:

> *"It was early 1944 and an unescorted formation of about 100 B-17's came up from the Mediterranean to bomb Germany. Our group of 36 aircraft was ordered off to intercept with my squadron flying high cover to ward off any escorting fighters, while the other two went after the bombers. We made contact just north of the Alps, a few miles from Munich We had a good chance to inflict maximum damage to the Fortresses below us and I led my 12-plane squadron down in a screaming dive. We flashed past the high combat box in an overhead pass, continuing through in a breakaway before climbing back up for another attack. With high speed built up in a dive, my*

aircraft made a very fleeting target and the more vertical my descent, the more difficult it was for the top turret gunner to get an angle on me. I targeted the pilot's cabin, the engines and wing's oil and fuel tanks. On this type of approach, the firing time was extremely limited. I could get in only one short burst. But I was going so fast that I was also harder to hit and the real danger was that I might collide with my quarry. I was through the formation before he even saw me and climbing back for another pass."

Later in the war, the Germans introduced the Mk 108 30mm heavy cannon capable of firing 600 11-ounce high explosive rounds per minute. Three hits with this weapon were usually sufficient to bring down a Flying Fortress. On the other hand it was a low velocity weapon and its effective range was shorter than the 20-mm cannon forcing German pilots to fly even closer to get hits.

HAROLD: We used to call some trips milk runs, or not, and a milk run would be nothing bad happening at all, very little or no flak. Only a couple of times did we see fighter planes. The worst one was really late, when the Germans had these Me 262s, and our tail gunner said, "bogey at 6 o'clock," and I looked out my left wing and this damn thing was coming 400 miles an hour, versus our 150, and just as it got to the wing, it stuttered, and under the belly came a missile, and it went right past us and hit a B-17 six or seven ahead of us, just blew it to bits. That was late in the war, and I thought, "my God, if they had used that thing like I saw today, we would have never been able to send all those bombers over there." But, Hitler, in his stupidity, instead of using those as fighters against our bombers, he was trying to make bombers out of those planes. It was dumb. Thank God for his dumbness.

HAROLD: We would be woken up 4 AM or 5AM, something like that.

They simply said, "Up and at 'em!" We had to get something to eat before briefing, so, they said, "you're flying today!" That's about all we knew. So we went to the mess hall and got breakfast, and then we were in trucks all the time. Either we were on the trucks, or we were on our bicycles. We knew where the briefing was going to be, so we'd go there, and I can't recall whether it was just pilots or other crew members there, I just don't remember. But then we would learn to map charts, where we were going to go, and there needed to be a fight plan. Then when we finished the mission, we got another debriefing, and we had to describe what and so forth had happened. So, the wakeup time was early, and when you're young like that, you didn't need that much sleep.

This is an interesting part about it, too. The first thing you had to do was get in formation with this big bomber stream, and you'd climb to an altitude of maybe eight or nine thousand feet. At that time, the weather in England is terrible, so we get some of these absolute peak fog days, and our bomb group had a yellow flare or a green flare or whatever it was, and every airplane—they were all over the place—that's how you'd get in position. We missed mid-air collisions by inches. Well, this great flight engineer we had, Mac O'Connell, said, "Don't do that anymore, that's too damn dangerous. If it's one of those kinds of days, we know where the groups, the whole stream of planes is going to go. We know where we fit in, what position we have, whether upper, middle, or lower level. We know exactly where we're going, the navigator can get us there, and we can join over the English Channel or something. We don't have to go through all this dangerous stuff. So, we did that. A number of flights, we didn't have to go through that crazy stuff after that first experience. So, that's where a good crew member came in handy, we never had any more problems. Another funny thing was when the war was over, you know, Jimmy Doolittle was head of the Air Force then. The war was over, and somebody declared there was going to be an air parade over London for Jimmy Doolittle, and they wanted all the B-24 and B-17 groups to fly low over the streets of London, and turned out to be one of those pea soup days! So, we got up, we were on the way, and we said, "hell no, we're not going to get in this nonsense!" So, we took off and flew around other places and went back to land, and there were four to five mid-air collisions on that thing. Doolittle had a fit, he said, "who the hell would—who was stupid enough to do that!" Because it was all unnecessary. But that happened.

RANDY: So, you go on our mission, and does the crew know when you've taken off? Does the crew know if it's going to be a rough mission, or not a rough mission, and did you tell them, or, you know, would they know in advance that it was going to be a milk run, or not a milk run?

HAROLD: Randy, I don't exactly remember. I don't think so. I think the guys, the officers in national briefing would know where you were going, and I just don't recall that the gunners and radio operators and all that knew exactly where we were going. That's my recollection.

I WAS ON A FIRST NAME BASIS WITH MY CREW!

As a child, I attended the McCalla Avenue Baptist Church. One of the fathers in our church owned a gas station in Burlington. A neighborhood I grew up in, in East Knoxville. Mr. Moulton was in an air crew in a plane that got shot down and he became a prisoner of war. We called him Corky Moulton.

HAROLD: I was on a first name basis with all my crew members. Yeah. Corky—something was a ball turret gunner.

HAROLD: Corky. *chuckles*

RANDY: Corky? I thought for a minute. Is the world that small?

HAROLD: Yeah, C-O-R-K-Y. Corky.

RANDY: He was on your plane?

HAROLD: He was a ball turret gunner. A little short guy.

RANDY: I knew a guy named Corky Moulton that was a crew member in an airplane. He became a prisoner of war.

HAROLD: That was definitely his first name. I didn't hold protocol on any officer over enlisted men. Enlisted men were a lot smarter than a lot of the officers were!

RANDY: Okay, so, there you've taken off into the pea soup, rendezvous with the group?

HAROLD: With the group.

RANDY: Okay, you knew each member personally. Did that affect anything when you had to give an order?

HAROLD: No. If I gave an order, they would obey.

Messerschmitt Me 262

From Wikipedia, the free encyclopedia

Messerschmitt Me 262 A-1a late production model

Role	Fighter aircraft and fighter-bomber
Manufacturer	Messerschmitt
First flight	18 April 1941 with piston engine(Junkers Jumo 210) 18 July 1942 with jet engines[1]
Introduction	April 1944[2][3]
Retired	1945, Germany 1951, Czechoslovakia[4]
Primary users	Luftwaffe Czechoslovak Air Force (S-92)
Number built	1,430

The **Messerschmitt Me 262**, nicknamed Schwalbe (German: "Swallow") in fighter versions, or Sturmvogel (German: "Storm Bird") in fighter-bomber versions, was the world's first operational jet-powered fighter aircraft. Design work started before World War II began, but problems with engines, metallurgy and top-level interference kept the aircraft from operational status with the Luftwaffe until mid-1944. The Me 262 was faster and more heavily armed than any Allied fighter, including the British jet-powered Gloster Meteor.[5] One of the most advanced aviation designs in operational use during World War II,[6] the Me 262's roles included light bomber, reconnaissance and experimental night fighter versions.

Me 262 pilots claimed a total of 542 Allied aircraft shot down,[7] although higher claims are sometimes made.[Note 1] The Allies countered its effectiveness in the air by attacking the aircraft on the ground and during takeoff and landing. Strategic materials shortages and design compromises on the Junkers Jumo 004 axial-flow turbojet engines led to reliability problems. Attacks by Allied forces on fuel supplies during the deteriorating late-war situation also reduced the effectiveness of the aircraft as a fighting force. Armament production within Germany was focused on more easily manufactured aircraft.[9] In the end, the Me 262 had a negligible impact on the course of the war as a result of its late introduction and the consequently small numbers put in operational service.[10]

HAROLD: Let's get back to that German jet. I was in flight when the ME 262 came up and took out one of the planes ahead of me It was horrible. We flew through the plane coming apart.

Yeah, well, I was worried about pieces that could hurt our plane, so I went this way, other planes are going this way to get out of the way. That was just—the thing was just totally blown up. Boom!

And I thought, "oh my God," you know, it happened so fast. I was the only guy that really saw it, because it was right out the wing I was looking at. I had a window on the side.

I could get word from the crew members what was around us, and they'd warn about getting close to other airplanes, avoiding midair collisions.

We got along very well. We really had a great crew, we really were very together, and very aware of everybody's needs, so. Yes. As I said, we didn't see that many fighter planes. We'd rarely see one, and when you saw one, we'd see about fifteen P-51s on their tail.

As soon as they showed up? Yeah, they were really keeping them away from us! That was great! The P-51s were everywhere. But the fighter planes were just all over those guys, and they were all looking for shots, to become aces and shoot their planes down. So, that part was great. It was better being in the air in 1945 than it had been earlier, no question about that: When the war was over, we took a lot of the ground personnel that had never been flying, you know, and took them through a low flight over prison camps and such. We went low enough to see some of those horror camps where they killed so many people. Piles of dead bodies. So, when Iran or other organizations says there's no such thing as the Holocaust, you know, I got a personal view of the damn thing. Those trips were milk runs. They took most of our crew space, but we left room for the loads we needed to return. Once we delivered a lot of those French guys… But that was all after the war ended.

We flew over so much damage. You couldn't really tell what it was, just incredible damage. Obliterated, this had been going on for years, this bombing. All these buildings were down, it's a miracle they could ever be rebuilt. It was total devastation, looking down at it.

Those post war flights were really for the benefit of the ground guys at our base, who had spent all this work fixing the airplanes and gassing it and all that, first time for them to actually get out and see something. I enjoyed doing that, they got a great kick out of that.

Once we dropped our bombs, we stayed in formation, pretty much. Sometimes, something happened to make you separate, I'm trying to think of what caused it. Could have been some airplanes had some major damage, so they had to get out of formation. But, we stayed in formation, most of the time coming back.

The tower determined landing order. You know, people would radio in. Lot of radio stuff going on. Let me tell you a little about something on the way home, this might interest you. When it came time to fly home, we went first back to a place in Wales again, then we had to go to one of the Azore Island airports, Terceira Island was what it was. And there were hundreds of bombers there, all on the way home to America. So, our turn came, we were fully gassed, and we had a lot of ground personnel along with our crew. We were very heavy, totally filled up with gas and totally filled up with people. We took off, and we were out about twenty minutes to a half an hour when a light came on in the instrument panels. One of the engines had an oil problem. We weren't about to fly across the Atlantic Ocean with that light on, so we radioed that we were going back to where we came from. Of course, first of all, all we could get were the people in the tower that talk Portuguese. We finally got some English speaking people, and I heard them announce that they had told all the other aircraft to stop where they were, because there was a plane coming in with trouble. So, we come back to the airport, and we came down on three engines. We stopped one engine, and as we were coming down, just as we were there, some damn B-17 pulled out and got right on the runway. If we hadn't pulled up, we would have landed right on top of them. So, God, that was a scary moment, we were pushing those throttles to get airspeed to lift. Ahead of us was a mountain, just straight ahead. To the right was a smaller mountain. So, obviously not to stall out, we kept slowly climbing. I just did manage to get over this hill, and we actually had some tree branches between the engines and the side of the airplane. So, we got around, and we landed without incident, and then we had to go taxi over to where the repair guys were. We just sat there, and then, what came back was there was plenty of oil, the only thing that was wrong was the damn reading on that flight panel. That was the problem. So, they said, "you're ready to go again!" I thought, "how ****ing close it was after all we had been through in combat in all that. How close we came to getting wiped out doing that crazy thing. But, flying back was a piece of cake. We navigated it just right, we went back to the same place in Newfoundland, and flew to an airport near Hartford, Connecticut. That's where we saw our last of the B-17.

That was the last I ever flew again. Well, that's not true. As I said, the wheels didn't stop right away, so when we flew through South Dakota, we went to Colorado Springs to take that training, but we did some flying there, but it was all B-17s. No B-52s, just B-17s. It was mainly to get our flight pay. So, that was our last B-17 flight. Two low flights there. I haven't flown since, myself.

Author's Note: Life and death at 20,000 feet.

You know, it's pretty hard for large groups of bombers to maintain formation as they flew through flak over German targets. The B-17 and B-24 heavy bombers were on the cutting edge of technology. However, they were not pressurized, waist windows were open, and the turrets were not sealed. Temperatures inside the plane often fell to 20 to 40 degrees below zero.

Heavy losses suffered by US bombers showed they needed fighter support. The deployment of P-51 Mustangs in 1944 allowed a huge bomber formation to challenge the Luftwaffe over Germany.

What did the US and British strategic bombing achieve? German war production increased in tandem with the tonnage of Allied bombs dropped in Germany. The shortcomings of Allied strategic bombing campaigns were attributed to poor coordination, an impossibility until late in the war, relentless attacks on key priority targets, and technological shortcomings that continued to make precision bombing difficult. However, the bombing was more effective than the Allied realized, and prevented German war production from increasing faster than it actually did.

Well, we've been talking about the life of a B-17 fighter crew today. We've talked about them taking their planes over to England, how sometimes they would go on missions and the crews that left that morning after eating breakfast with them at the end of the day, not all of those crews would come home. Sometimes, you wouldn't know what happened to those crews. They may have been exploded in air, they may have been shot down and crashed into the sea, or on the land in France or Germany, maybe even taken prisoner.

You know, we didn't have time to talk about, sometimes, fifty years later, there'd be a reunion and you'd get to go to that reunion and see the face of a friend that you had not seen in a long, long time. Maybe he'd grown to love and protect, and you didn't see him because you had to go to college, and you had to work, and get married, and have babies, and time went by, and fifty years later, there they were in a reunion.

Sometimes, you even got the chance to fly again in the B-17 years later, when one would land at an airport, and you could get to go for a ride. Of the 12,732 B-17s that were manufactured, right now, I believe Mr. Johnson said there may be ten still flying today in the United States.

We even learned about the crews, and how this one particular crew with Mr. Johnson was very informal—they were all on a first name basis, and the officers and enlisted men, they just acted as a crew. There wasn't any real official officer non-com relationship, they were all a team. And then, we've learned the respect the German pilots had for flying into the formations, and how they needed to do that with such precision, that they had to attack so quick, get in, and get their shots off and fly through the formation before they got gunned down, and to do that, they were going to have to fly through a formation of B-17s that was a half mile long and maybe a mile and a half deep. A typical B-17 crew started out with ten members, and as the war wore down a little bit, it went down to nine. And Hal Johnson's particular crew, he was the pilot. The co-pilot was Dan Hahn. Navigator, E. P. Silverman. The other navigator, E. A. Vincent. Radio operator, C. E. Gardella. Engineers were J. R. Clauson and Buckle Connell. The bombardiers were H. M. Hill, C. T. Turback, and A. E. Isaac. The waist gunner, O. A. Jones. The tail gunner, R. R. Watts, and the ball turret was little Corky Linwick.

Author's note: Not the Corky I knew by the way.

As Mr. Johnson told us in his interview, he believes that he is the only surviving member of that crew. A Page of history with one remaining storyteller.

But there is more:

There was a B-17 called: The City of Savannah. Not the city, but a B-17 bomber. It's actually a tale of two cities. The Mighty 8th Air Force Museum welcomed the B-17, serial number 44-83814 to Savannah on January 15th, 2009. Today, the airplane occupies a place of honor in the museum's Combat Gallery. It also has a new name—the *City of Savannah*. The story of how the airplane arrived at its permanent home in the gallery, and how it got its name is really two stories.

The first story starts in late 1944, at the height of World War II, when the residents of Chatham County, Georgia, the home of the Mighty Eighth Air Force Museum, raised $500,000 to pay for the production of one B-17 bomber and the training of the 10 men who would make up its crew. In late November 1944, new B-17s and recently graduated air crews were brought together at Hunter Field in Savannah, Ga., then sent to overseas units. Shortly after Thanksgiving, the U.S. Army Air Corps matched the crew piloted by Lt. Ralph Kittle with a B-17 bomber, serial number 43-39049, which happened to be the 5,000th airplane to be processed through Hunter Field destined to support Allied forces in Europe. The airplane was painted with the name *City of Savannah* to honor the Chatham County fundraisers. Lt. Kittle and his crew were photographed with the airplane. The citizens of Chatham County were honored for their generosity and support at a ceremony, and a special blessing was bestowed on the crew for its safety. And then the crew and the airplane departed for England. Not long after they arrived in England, Lt. Kittle and his crew were separated from the City of Savannah. They were assigned to the 388th Bomb Group, and were shot down by anti-aircraft fire on March 5, 1945 while on their 13th mission. They were flying an older "F" model B-17 with the Tail Number 42-97642. One crew member, tail gunner Robert H. Warren was killed. The remaining crewmen became prisoners of war until they were repatriated in May of 1945. The B-17 bomber they flew to England, S/N 43-39049, and the original *City of Savannah* returned to the United States in July 1945 and was eventually scrapped.

Story number two begins 64 years later. Historians conducting research on the present B-17 *City of Savannah* discovered that S/N 44-83814 was produced in May 1945 at an aircraft-assembly plant in Long Beach, Calif. Unfortunately, it was built too late to take part in the war. By the time it rolled out of the hangar, the war in Europe was drawing to a close, so the Army Air Force simply dropped the airplane from its rolls. 44-83814 managed to avoid the scrap yards after the war. It passed through a series of civilian owners who used it to perform a variety of tasks. It spent 20 years taking photographs around the world for a mapmaking company in Canada. Part of its duties involved charting the Distant Early Warning Line. The DEW Line was a series of radar stations situated primarily in the far northern reaches of the Canadian Arctic. They were established to provide advanced notice of an airborne or land-based invasion by Soviet aircraft or troops during the Cold War. Later, from 1974 to 1984, the airplane served as a slurry bomber fighting forest fires. It operated out of a base in Arizona. In 1984, the airplane was traded to the Smithsonian

Institution and placed in long-term storage. It remained in storage until the Smithsonian presented it to the Mighty Eighth Air Force Museum in 2009.

Mr. Harold Johnson who just finished telling us his story (HISTORY?) was a B-17 pilot and a member of the 388 Bombardment Group H Association, and the "H" meant heavy. He was part of the 8th Air Force, which was a strategic air command set up to knock out factories or to accomplish political goals, or major strategies like taking out ball-bearing factories and things like that. It was the 45th Combat Wing Station 136 in Knettishall, England, and the time frame where it was a major air base was from 1943 to 1945. So, let's get back with Mr. Harold Johnson.

HAROLD: A few weeks ago, Jim Morrow. Last year's president of this association here. This year's president, Henry Krivatz, in an e-mail, invited me to come to this year's reunion to talk about a Savannah hero, Ralph Kittle.

RANDY: How did you get to be a friend of Ralph Kittle?

HAROLD: We were buddies in B-17 training at Avon Park, Florida, We left about the same time to fly to Savannah, where we got so far apart was he left earlier and had.

RANDY: Mr. Johnson, or should I say, Lt. Johnson, tell us about what you know of the B-17 bomber known as the City of Savannah, and it's original pilot, Mr. Ralph Kittle.

HAROLD: As Ralph thundered down the runway, a few weeks later, our time came. Jim Morrow has told me the City of Savannah had engine troubles, so Ralph and crew had to fly another B-17. It was news to me all these years. This happened: the City of Savannah, the original one, was in 1944, when we all were over there in late 1944. And the pilot they picked for it was Ralph Kittle because he was a native Georgian. That was the original City of Savannah, where this all started. Then, when he left, they had those grandstands full of people who bought war bonds, including us—me, I was in the grandstand watching him go.

RANDY: 1st Lieutenant Ralph Wade Kittle Sr. was born on was born on 19 July 1920 in Ringgold, GA., where his father was a partner in a lumber mill and cotton gin and the owner of several houses. After his father died in 1924, Kittle helped his mother and sisters by raising chickens and collecting rent from their tenants during the depression. He graduated from Catoosa County High School, attended Mercer University in Georgia and graduated from the University of Chattanooga in 1941. He worked briefly for the Tennessee Valley Authority while attending Chattanooga College of Law at night. He enlisted as a private in the U.S. Army Air Corps in 1942 and attended flight school and officer training school in Colorado Springs. On 3 December 1944, Lt. Kittle was selected to fly the famous "City of Savannah", the 5,000th airplane to be processed through Hunter Field, GA. The gleaming new B-17 bomber (seen at left) was paid for by Savannah's citizens and schoolchildren. After a concert of military tunes, a prayer by the base chaplain for the blessings on the bomber, Kittle and his crew took off for England.

HAROLD: He got to our base much sooner than I did, that's why he had ten missions. When I got there, we didn't have any. So the mission where he got shot down was his thirteenth and my third.

RANDY: March 5th, 1945. Mission #272. A total of 38 B-17s were dispatched to bomb marshalling yards in Eastern Germany. They were airborne between 5:40 AM and 6:37 AM. The Flying Fortress' had little difficulty making formation over the continent. But because of cloud cover over the primary target, the lead and high group attacked the marshalling yards at Plauen, Germany. Bombing was done by squadrons with bombs away at 11:06 hours from 25,500 feet. 1st Lt. Ralph W. Kittle was the pilot of the B-17G 42-97542, "City of Savannah" of the 563rd Bomb Squadron. Kittle and his crew were on their twelfth mission and in the Hi-1-2 position. This was to be the second and last time Kittle flew the "City of Savannah. On the way to the target area, Kittle and his nine man crew were hit by flak and suffered mechanical failure of their aircraft. Two engines were feathered. Kittle jettisoned his bombs to lighten the load but number 3 engine failed. Kittle was able to keep the aircraft under control and contacted the command pilot, stating he was going to try and land in Russian territory. He ordered the crew to bail out while maintaining level flight before bailing out himself. Kittle was wounded and captured by German soldiers. The aircraft crashed near Friedland, Germany. Four crew members were killed. Missing Air Crew Report 12926 was filed after the crew failed to return to base. Several of the squadron aircraft had to land in France for more gas before returning home to Knettishall, England.

HAROLD: He landed in a heavily wooded area… The townsfolk, of course, found these guys, and they were beating them with clubs and sticks and he was about to pass out. He saw three guys coming with axes on their shoulders, so Ralph thought, "wow, this is it!" Well, it was just the opposite, these guys with the axes had common sense, and they stopped the people from beating them, and they took them down to prison camp. So, he served from March 6th I think it was, until after the war. And after the war, all of those bomber groups were sending troops over to Europe to find guys that were in POW camps. So, fairly quickly after the war was over, they found Ralph Kittle. So, Ralph came back to the infirmary, and we went to see him, and God, he looked awful. He was very pale, he'd lost about 50 or 60 pounds, had big scars across his cheeks. He started to tell me how all this happened. When the war wasn't quite over, maybe a week before it really ended, these Russians were advancing so fast coming westward, they were overrunning these prison camps. Well, the Germans were trying to prevent that, so they were evacuating the prison camps. So, they would put all these guys, the prisoners and guards and everything, on the road hiking and marching. **Remember the John Shell Story?** In doing this, after a day or so, a flock of fighter planes came over, and Ralph didn't know if they were American or English or German or French or Russian or whatever, but they began strafing them, thinking they were German soldiers. Ralph had made a friend when he was in camp of a British RAF pilot, had been there a long time and really knew the ropes in that camp—what to try to do, what not to try to do. He was great help to Ralph. He was marching right next to Ralph, and a bullet hit him right in the skull and killed him outright, and one wounded Ralph across his cheek. And first thing- he said to me -he looked terrible, like I said. He looked at me and had tears in his cheek, and he says, "I lost the Spirit of Savannah." I was trying to cheer him up and I said, "Ralph, that plane was just a piece of equipment. You and most of your men are safely back, thank God."

RANDY: You just heard a little story about a B-17 that got shot down. But you know, so many B-17s got shot up on their flights into Germany. Sometimes, they would have holes in the side when they landed that might be six or seven feet wide, it may be five or six feet wide. Sometimes, the covers off the wings would be shot off, and it would just be a skeleton craft landing. Those planes were so powerful and so well built, that I saw a picture of even one landing that had no cockpit. It was just wings and the front end of a plane, and somehow, they got it landed.

When a World War II air crew failed to return home, and the eyewitnesses provided convincing evidence that they had been shot down, little time was wasted in clearing out their personal belongings. Early that morning, they were there, full of life, cocky and confident. Then gone.

Someone would slip in and pick up their things. Those who did return, would go about rearranging their quarters. A move from a drafty door, or to a cot with a desk made by its former occupant. But, another mission tomorrow. The crew was remembered as just missing, but not all forgot.

HAROLD: All I could do now was listen. Hearing on the radio that he lost two engines. He got permission to drop his bombs early to lighten the load of the airplane. And next thing we heard was, "I have to bail out." I don't know any more than that.

RANDY: So, you heard he was given permission to fly to the Russian lines.

HAROLD: Yeah, exactly, to where the Russians were advancing, and they were doing that big time in 1945.

RANDY: Yeah. They were coming on strong, weren't they?

HAROLD: Yeah.

RANDY: They were mad!

HAROLD: They were. *laughs* Still are.

RANDY: *laughs* so, he bailed out, and he got captured?

HAROLD: Yes.

RANDY: Do you know anything about that? I've talked to a couple of other pilots that have been captured before, and they were told that if they escaped and got captured again, they would be treated as spies. Did you all ever go over that, or:

HAROLD: I think Ralph did. I mentioned before one of his best buddies in that prison camp was an RAF pilot who had been there a long time and knew the ropes, and he told Ralph what to try and what not to try, because he said basically that in some cases, when they caught these Americans trying to escape, they shot them. So, he didn't want to do that. He didn't make any real attempt to escape when he was in the prison camp. Because they had taken aerial photos. If they escaped and had time to look at the land and everything, then I think the Germans believed that they were a real military risk, because now they had seen the sky and seen the land, and they had told them they would treat them as spies if they escaped. We all carried with us at all times maps of all sorts, and I'm sure when they got to prison camp they were all taken away from them.

All POWs lost a lot of weight? He really did. That was after that shooting business on the march. He was alright before that, but when we did see him again, in the 1990s, he was healthy as a horse.

Author's note: After returning from World War II, Lt. Ralph Kittle enrolled in the University of Virginia law school on the G.I. Bill, and lived close to the university grounds due to his wounds. He served on the managing board of the Virginia Law Review and was editor-in-chief of *The Virginia Spectator* magazine, as well as student assistant to the dean of the law school. He married Cornelia Ely and shortly after his graduation from law school in 1948, moved to New York City, where they lived for 25 years and raised their three children. Kittle joined the New York law firm Davis, Polk & Wardwelol, where he specialized in labor law. In 1953, he became counsel to the Senate Labor Committee and Sen. Robert A. Taft, and worked on the drafting of the Taft-Hartley Act. For the next 32 years, Kittle worked for International Paper Company, first as a labor lawyer and later as vice president in charge of government relations. He opened its Washington office in 1970. In response to growing government regulation of the paper industry, he created and managed the largest corporate government relations program in the country, through coordinated constituent "grassroots lobbying" by company employees in 36 states and 127 Congressional districts. He logged more than 2 million air miles, much of it on the shuttle, and was a familiar figure on Capitol Hill. Kittle served as an advisor to numerous Congressional committees and advisory boards on legislative policy. In 1966, he was a participant in the National Conference on Air Pollution and, starting in 1968, he served three years as a member of the President's Advisory Board on Water Pollution Control. In the 1970's, Kittle became active in issues relating to education and employment opportunities for women and minorities. He was chairman of the Board of Trustees of Mary Baldwin College, a member of the Board of Directors of the Hispanic Women's Center, a member of the Advisory Council of the Women's Institute at American University, a trustee of Lee's College in Jackson, KY and a member of the Education Task Force of the New York Urban Coalition. He also served as a special consultant on equal employment opportunity for the U.S. Department of Labor and a member of the Advisory Committee on Women to the secretary of labor. He retired from International Paper in 1985, and became a counsel to the McNair Law Firm in Washington on government and legislation, and a member of the District Export Council of the U.S. Department of Commerce. He was a member of the Folger Shakespeare Library Council and the Capitol Hill Club in Washington, and the Keswick Hunt Club. All that happened after he saw the three Germans coming at him with an axe.

HAROLD: Yeah, well it took probably, let's see… This was '45 to '94. 50 years before I saw him again. I didn't know where he lived, or: No Google searches available at the time. No. Didn't know anything, but how the hell did I know how we found him! What we found out was that my flight engineer, he had flown all these missions early with North Africa and Italy, went to just all kinds of reunions. He knew where all our crew were, and he knew where a lot of other crews were. He also knew Ralph Kittle. So, we had three great reunions with our crew members and their wives, and Ralph gave me his phone number and all that stuff. So, I phoned him, this would be about 1994. So, Ralph said "oh my God, you and your wife get in the car and come drive up here and see us!"

I did not attend the reunions. I was too busy. First thing when I got back, I had to go back to college. Two years. I went back with my wife, we had a baby girl then, too. So then, I had to get a job and start making an income. So I did very quickly, worked with a textile company. And all the years I was there, the government was doing less and less American textiles. They were trying to lower the price of textiles using foreign things. But the president of the company, Roger Milliken, put in an incredibly great research corporation building. So, I just got something in an e-mail the other day, that just last year, this year, Milliken had made more money than they ever had before, because of that research facility. They have 60,000 patents, and they own mills, textile mills in Europe, France, Germany, and recently, one in China. So, I still got my pension from them, all the other ones must have gone south.

RANDY: Okay, so, 45 and 50 years went by, and you get an invitation to go and have a reunion with the people in your crew, or just the whole squadron, or the whole battalion.

HAROLD: No, the only invitations I've ever gotten were this bomb group thing in Savannah. The funny thing is, at one point, they got mail, one of these type things I've showed you, and from Washington—the state of Washington, where I had to pay ten bucks to something to do something, make a contribution. So, that made me think, I don't know if they're the same groups or how—I don't know anything about all the organization of these alumni groups. All I really know something about is the ones that are in Savannah, Georgia, and that—the name of it's on that piece of paper I gave you.

RANDY: You used a word in here, when you got the invitation, you were thrilled.

HAROLD: I was thrilled when I found Ralph. And to hear his voice again, he was inviting us to come up there. That's why I was thrilled. I had no idea what happened to him when he came home.

I called him, and he said, "Wow! Come on up here!" So, we did it, we drove up there. He fixed us up, put us in a very classy placed called Keswick, which was a super nice place. And then he told me all about what he had done after the war, which law school. He then had a very prestigious job in a law firm in Washington D.C., and do you remember the Taft-Hartley Act?

Taft called that law firm and said, "could you send us a lawyer," because they wanted to get some things straightened out for the legislation. So, they sent Ralph. So, they were so impressed—Taft was so impressed with Ralph, he said, "why don't you leave that company and come on my staff?" Which, he did. So, they had a lot of years living high on the hog in Washington, going out with all these top-notch, top people here, you know, before he retired. That's when he moved to Charlottesville. About the same time I retired, he retired.

HAROLD: My friend looked good, that scar was gone, and he was very active at that time. There was always something going on in Savannah, Georgia, which I presume is this thing we're talking about. At that time, in 1994, it might have been something a little different, but that was before—they had this thing going on, putting the B-17 in there now is something 20 years later. This was 1994, and now, they're boating that thing in. It's got all the parts—it'll never fly again, but it's got all the parts, the guns—they're all rusted, but it's on display there. That all happened now, so at the time, I don't know what the connection was. I got word living here from the newspaper, about an airplane coming in. A B-17 called "Aluminum Overcast." It was coming to airports all around and it came to Knoxville. This was three or four, five years ago, and offering rides to anybody that wanted a half-hour flight for about six hundred dollars or something. But being an ex-pilot and everything, I got a free ride, and I could take friends with me—not in the airplane, but they could tour the plane on the ground. So, I got two of those rides. There was this friend of mine—a Navy guy—he sent me a magazine that listed how many B-17s there still are, which was ten. And then it had an article in there about the one that's being put into Savannah, and one was that Overcast thing. Overcast isn't doing it anymore because it was too costly to keep up all the stuff, so they're gone. The other one.

RANDY: You're talking about the Aluminum Overcast?

HAROLD: The Aluminum Overcast is a thing of the past. The other one is the one going on in Savannah, this B-17 that's in the museum. That's not counted as one of the ten B-17s in existence—flying B-17s.

RANDY: Original B-17s.

HAROLD: Original B-17s, yeah.

RANDY: So, you think you're the only surviving member of your crew?

HAROLD: Yeah, I think I am, except after Kittle—excuse me, the navigator, we got a replacement whose name I can't remember now, and he was with us till the very end. Helped fly us home and all that stuff. He went to Brown University, I remember that, and he was in the retail business in some way, lived in Dayton, Ohio. He came to one of our reunions—matter of fact, Kittle set us up for these reunions in Jacksonville, and he and his wife came to one of those. So, I know that he's still alive is because I got a Christmas card from him recently.

RANDY: How did you feel when you learned Ralph had passed away?

HAROLD: Very sad. What happened was after we made that trip, we kept in touch quite often with telephone calls. This was before I was sending e-mails or anything. So, one day I call him and he answered the phone, and he was crying. I said, "Ralph!" He said, whatever his wife's name is, so-and-so has died. I said, "Oh my God, I'm sorry, I called at a bad time." I didn't know what to say. He said, "Well, okay, thank you, goodbye" and hung up. Well, he died probably about three months after that. I never spoke to him again, but that was a shock when he said that.

Author's note: We've been talking about the B-17 bombers and the "City of Savannah" and Lt. Ralph Kittle, and Lt. Harold Johnson today. On June 13th, 2011, one of eleven B-17 bombers crashed near Chicago, Illinois. One spectator said flames were coming off the left side. During World War II, the immediate need for the flying fortress, the B-17 bomber, was met with the mass production of thousands of units. I've read reports that over 12 to 14,000 B-17 bombers were manufactured. Somewhere, around 80% of these planes were shot down during combat missions. And after World War II ended, the remaining planes were not in very big demand. Many of the remaining planes in the B-17 fleets were retired, and after that, they were melted down and sold for scrap. But a few planes stayed in service for alternate uses after the war. The military air transport service operated these planes as Dumbo air sea rescue planes. Some B-17s were disarmed, having their heavy machine guns removed, while others remained outfitted due to the fact they would be flying in areas where active combat was under way. In present day, only about fifty-one B-17 bombers remain in whole or in part. Nineteen of the fifty-one are only partial hulks and frames, not a complete unit at all. There remain about ten B-17 bombers that still fly actively. In addition, there are nine B-17 units on display in museums, two being restored to be flown in the future, three being restored for display purposes, the "City of Savannah" is one of those planes. Five units are in storage. In 1945, sixteen flying fortress B-17 planes were transferred to the Coast Guard for use in sea-air rescues. Some of these planes were outfitted with droppable lifeboats, so they could have effective sea rescue capabilities. Flying over the ocean could provide a full picture of the situation, and at that point, the plane could come in lower and easily drop a lifeboat where needed. Another important use of the B-17 was iceberg spotting. The early warning to ships in the area of existence of dangerous icebergs was extremely important. Everyone knows the history of ships and icebergs, and the service of iceberg spotting saved a lot of lives. Photo mapping was yet another great service provided by the B-17 bombers. The planes were stripped of guns and war time machinery. The plexiglass of the ball turret was the best place to mount a camera for recording the places flown over. Some of the planes were used as "drones", meaning they were flown remotely without a crew through mushroom clouds during the testing of nuclear weapons. The purpose of such tests was to determine if a live crew would be able to survive this kind of exposure. They were also used to conduct atmospheric testing, and for target testing on surface to air missiles. When World War II was over, the B-17 bombers were dispersed all over the world, and went on to other things. So did the B-17 pilots. When they came home from the war, most of them were 19 or 20 years old. They went to school on the G.I. Bill, they went to college, they got jobs, they worked in factories, they became lawyers, they became doctors, they became leaders of what we know today as the free world and the roaring 1950's. And what we've learned today, that of all the travails that the B-17 plane went through and the problems of being captured and coming back to your base with your buddy's bed empty and all the things they had to deal with. All those things are disappearing now. I just finished telling you where maybe ten complete B-17s and maybe forty other pieces and parts. Let me ask you a question: how many B-17 pilots and crew members do you know?

For my 2012 Christmas present to myself this year I went to Hobby Lobby and bought a Model B-17 and built it. It is in my living room today. What an honor it is to know Lt. Harold Johnson.

He has a model in his office, too!

Author's note: After talking to Harold Johnson Santa Clause brought me a B-17 model to build. I kept it for about 10 years until July of 2019. I had never taken the time to install the decals. I recently sold an office building and was cleaning out, and reducing inventory, and the model reappeared. The new owners of the building brought his young son with him and the B-17 was sitting next to a German FE109 model and a British Spitfire. His eyes lit up and he asked his dad if he had bought the model, too. His disappointment was evident. I knew what had to happen, I gave him the B-17, and told him he could take it home. Again, a big smile appeared and he decide I could keep the FE and the Spitfire. He was so happy with the B-17. I hope it sparks an interest, and I hope he learns more about this wonderful airplane.

Let's go back to the Pacific, and sail the high seas! A mountain boy sailed the Pacific, on the USS Pittsburg. His name is Clyde Beeler.

CHAPTER ELEVEN

"THE USS PITTSBURGH HAS JUST LOST ITS BOW!"

We're going to spend most of our time in this chapter out in the Pacific Ocean in World War II. First of all, we're going to talk about what was going on out there in the early part of World War II. We were basically getting our fannies kicked around on the water and on land. We had to learn how to fight the way the Japanese were fighting. The cost of that came in large numbers of men and equipment, which we sort of measured our progress in the Pacific Ocean by losses that were announced with our aircraft carriers. One of the first sinking that broke all of our hearts was the USS Lexington. And it went down early in the war. Not long after that, it was followed by the USS Yorktown. The Japanese had thought they had sunk it, until it miraculously reappeared at the Battle of Midway. The USS Wasp struck by torpedoes out in the Pacific. It took us six weeks to report it, because we really didn't want the Japanese to know that they had done so much damage to one of our aircraft carriers. Then in 1944, although we had won the Battle of Midway before that, things began to change a little bit. We were winning the Pacific Sea Battles. On February 22nd, 1944, the US Navy launched a ship called the USS Pittsburgh. In October of that same year, on October 10th, the Pittsburgh was commissioned. The training had been done, and it was ready to go to war. On that ship, was one 19-year-old man from East Tennessee—actually, he was from Grainger County. The USS Pittsburgh went through the Panama Canal and headed deep into the war, and wound up as part of the fleet at Iwo Jima. That fleet consisted of over 800, almost 900 ships, and they were constantly bombarded and attacked by kamikazes.

We've all heard the stories of the Marines at Iwo Jima, and most of us don't know that out in the ocean where our aircraft carriers were, and all the cruisers, there were some ships out there whose job was to protect those aircraft carriers from these Japanese flying bombs. The USS Pittsburgh was one of those ships. When the Battle of Iwo Jima was over, they started heading towards Okinawa. A Japanese airplane slipped through our defenses, and let two of its bombs go, and they both exploded on one of our aircraft carriers called the USS Franklin. Hundreds of men burned to death on that crippled ship, as the magazine was hit, and there were sympathetic explosions everywhere. Seaman First Class Clyde Beeler was on the USS Pittsburgh. He saw those bombs hit USS Franklin. It was a direct hit, and another one of our aircraft carriers was in trouble. Not only did he see the bombs hit, but he also participated in towing that ship back to port. Not long after that, the USS Pittsburgh went to Okinawa. 1300 ships or more were at that battle. When that battle was over, they were out to sea, and the USS Navy reported there was a storm brewing in the Philippine Sea, heading for the American fleet. That storm became known as Typhoon Viper, and our story today is the ordeal of the USS Pittsburgh and that typhoon.

You see two photos right now. They're old black and white photos, 1944, of Clyde Beeler standing in his front yard in Grainger County and one of him standing on his ship at sea. For those of you that know about Grainger County, there's a mountain that runs right up the middle of it, and the county's kind of split to a North side and a South side. Clyde lived up on Liberty Hill on the North side of Clinch Mountain, and that old house he's standing in front of was his father's home. It was an old mountain home. There he stands, in his new Navy uniform, standing at attention. You know, later on in this interview, we're going to talk about how I got to own that uniform recently, had some stains on it. But anyway, he's standing there at attention, and he's got his Navy white sailor hat on, like Popeye used to wear. The other picture of Clyde while he's at sea out in the Pacific, and he's not standing at attention. He's got his foot up on a rope spool, and his hand on a railing, another hand on his hip. He's got one of those blue Navy shirts on that's not buttoned up, it's tied in the middle, and tied in a knot. But he's still wearing that white hat. I have that shirt, too. **The war really was in color.**

BEELER: Right here's the cap that went through the war with me. The same cap in that picture. It's got my name stapled in it. It's made out of

214

cotton. That went through the war! Not all the way through the war, but, 'course I was in there 24 months, and I was at sea 21 months. I started on the East Coast, went through the Panama Canal, and up through Hawaii and right into the battle.

That is not what I expected why I enlisted!

I was Seaman First Class. I was just thinking, I could tell you stories here for a week. We didn't do no bombarding. We protected our aircraft carriers. We had AA guns that shot a 300 pound shell, and then we had six-inch guns that shot a 52-inch shell, and we had 40 millimeters that shot a. I don't know, a shell about 16 inches long. I was a loader on a 40 millimeter gun.

Author's Note: We discussed loading the 40mm in the chapter about Mr. Julian. If you remember, a loader was making a mistake and almost got everyone killed.

BEELER: We had 20 millimeters on there, too. When the planes was coming in, when it was out of range of the smaller guns, like when they come in on the radar and pick them up, the five-inch guns shot at them. Then if they got in the range of the 40s, they took over. And if the 40s missed them, the 20s took over shooting at 'em.

Author's note Wow. I had never thought about the fighting order. Earlier we read about James Julian and he was on a 20mm, so the planes he was fighting must have been close!

BEELER: Sometimes, some of our planes, they get messed up and had to get out of the range of them enemy planes, and they'd come over our ships, and we'd fire at them cause we didn't have time to look, you just fired.

Author's note: More fog of war.

BEELER: You had to protect yourself. Yeah, I could tell you stories. I was in Iwo Jima in February, and when that battle was over, we headed up to Okinawa?

Author's note: Something else had happened between Iwo Jima and Okinawa. Iwo Jima was a battle that was fought primarily in February, and Okinawa, started on Easter Sunday, on April 1, 1945. On March 19th, 1945, the USS Franklin, an aircraft carrier, had maneuvered closer to the Japanese homeland than any other US carrier, and had launched a pre-dawn strike against the island of Honshu, as well as a later strike against shipping in Kobe Harbor. Suddenly, a single Japanese plane came through the cloud cover, made a low level run on the ship, and dropped two armor-piercing bombs. One struck the flight deck, centerline, penetrating to the hangar deck, which it devastated. The bomb also ignited fires to the second and third decks, and knocked out the combat information center and air plot. The second bomb hit aft and fore through two decks, fanning fires which detonated ammunition, bombs and rockets. I had learned earlier that that was called sympathetic explosions. Many of the crew were either blown overboard, or driven off by fire, or killed, or wounded. Remaining were 106 officers, and 604 enlisted men, who by sheer valor and tenacity, saved the ship. Casualties during those two explosions totaled 724 killed, and 265 wounded. That's a thousand sailors with two dropped bombs, in just a matter of minutes. The USS Franklin, the most heavily damaged aircraft carrier during the war, to remain afloat, and after a tow from the USS Pittsburgh, proceeded under her own power to Pearl Harbor for repairs. So, the jet plane which injured the USS Franklin was not a suicider, but a bomber which carefully placed two bombs where they would do the greatest damage? So, he was way up high and dropped those bombs on the USS Franklin?

BEELER: I seen it, yeah, I seen it hit it. I was on the deck of our ship, getting breakfast in the breakfast line, and we were going to breakfast, and I seen that plane come in, and we were attacking that plane, and they passed word over to the speakers to quit attacking, it was a friendly plane. In a few minutes, the bomb hit. I seen 'em hit. It was not far away.

USS FRANKLIN GUTTED BY FLAMES, INLAND SEA 253-1

Author's note: Seaman First Class Clyde Beeler had some photos that he had been saving over time of that day with the USS Franklin. I was lucky enough for him to let me make copies of a couple of them. The first one that I'm looking at is a picture of the USS Franklin, full aircraft carrier, gutted with flames. And that means, when I say gutted, when you take the left-hand side looking at the ship, from the left to the right, the flames started on the left side, left-front of the boat, went all the way past the operation tower, where the captains and everybody were giving orders, and halfway to the other end of the ship, and it was all one big flame, with smoke probably a half a mile high. Then he showed me another picture of the USS Pittsburgh—his ship—and it's got the front of it heading toward the USS Franklin to save the crew, the crew members in the water. They pulled about 30 of them out themselves. And in that picture, you can see the different levels of guns that Clyde was talking about, the big eight-inch guns, and the 40 millimeters and the 20 millimeters, and they're heading straight for the USS Franklin as it smokes. And, there's another picture, after most of the flames have been put out, and the USS Franklin is leaning over at about a 40 degree angle. You can tell it's just a wounded, devastated ship. In the last picture he showed me, was the rear of the USS Pittsburgh, with a big steel cable tied to it. And the Captain, Captain Gingrich, Captain of the USS Pittsburgh, looking at that cable, and he sat at that end of the ship for 37 hours while the USS Pittsburgh towed the USS Franklin back to port for repairs. In the background, about a quarter of a mile away, you can see the wounded, huge aircraft carrier, being towed down like a broken down car across the Pacific Ocean. That's not all of it! After the destruction of the USS Franklin, the USS Pittsburgh went to Okinawa. If you were sitting in Okinawa, maybe on the island, looking out and saw the American fleet, this is probably what you would have seen. You would have seen a bunch of assorted patrol boats, some landing ships, some carrying infantry, maybe 75 to 100 of them. Then there were some net layers and mine sweepers, and destroyer mine craft, and four ocean tugs, and seaplane tenders, and repair ships, and cargo ships, and more landing ships—some ships that could bring tanks in. Forty-four—maybe fifty depending on who's counting—transports full of troops. Destroyer transports, destroyer escorts. And you know, you're still barely out to the horizon, because out and beyond the horizon, you'd probably see 44 more destroyers protecting our aircraft carriers, maybe close to 20 cruisers, and the Pittsburgh was one of those cruisers. The Pittsburgh was a heavy cruiser, and you probably wouldn't have seen it from Okinawa. It was out there, beyond the horizon, in the ocean, in front of the aircraft carriers, waiting on the Japanese kamikaze to come. Then there were the battleships, and the aircraft carriers. As those kamikaze came, they could come into the range, according to Seaman First Class Clyde Beeler, of the eight-inch guns with the 300 pound shells. The guns with the 52-inch shells would start firing next, and if the kamikazes made it past the 52-inch shells, they'd go into the 40 millimeter range, and that's where Seaman First Class Clyde Beeler was—he was loading the 40 millimeter guns as the kamikazes came after him. And if they got underneath that, they had to run into the 20 millimeter guns that were shooting the smaller bullets all frantically, some of them on the ship, there were groups of four, and some, there were groups of two, and the sailors were like Seaman First Class Clyde Beeler said, you've got to protect yourself. Of the 193 kamikaze attacks coming at the aircraft carriers in Okinawa, 169 were destroyed. But 24 got through. When they did, they hit the American aircraft carriers and the battleships.

The American aircraft carriers didn't have the metal floors and metal walls that the British aircraft carriers had, so when they hit, there was a lot of destruction. The destruction, however, of so many kamikaze flights, did a great deal to undermine the potential for damage that the kamikazes could have inflicted. Before the actual invasion, America had gathered together 300 warships, and almost 1200 other ships. The first landing of Marines took place in April, and they met little opposition. By the end of the day, 60,000 American military personnel had landed in Hagushi Bay. They wouldn't have been able to do that if the aircraft carriers hadn't have been protected by the ships that were manned by people like Seaman First Class Clyde Beeler.: So far in our conversation with Seaman First Class Clyde Beeler of the USS Pittsburgh in World War II, we went through training and through the Panama Canal and up to Pearl Harbor and into the battle of Iwo Jima. Then, we left Iwo Jima and went in to save the USS Franklin, an aircraft carrier that had been bombed and almost half its crew died or wounded. After that, they sailed into the Battle of Okinawa on April 1, 1945—boy, there were lots of things going on then. About a month later, everybody around the world got the news Germany had surrendered. It was May 1945. And the soldiers that are in Europe, they're going, "oh boy, we're going home." But some of those soldiers knew that, "oh my gosh!" they may be going to the Pacific for the invasion of Japan. The Army Air Corps, the pilots like Lt. Harold Johnson, knew what they were doing. They were being shipped back to the states almost immediately, and they were going to Minnesota and other training places. Their planes were being refitted and prepared for the attack on Japan. So, a lot of folks in our military, they didn't think the war was over, and they just thought they were going to be exchanging theaters.

Everybody in early June was celebrating the one year anniversary of the D-Day invasion in 1944. Out in the Pacific Ocean, the US Navy had made an announcement that there was a storm brewing a little bit northeast of the Philippines. It was heading right for the US fleet. On June 4th, 1945, the USS Pittsburgh began to fight that typhoon. It would intensify into the next day. Smaller ships would describe the storm as producing mountainous seas. Shortly after her starboard scout plane had been lifted off its catapult and dashed onto the deck by the wind, USS Pittsburgh's second deck buckled, her bow structure thrust upward, and took over 100 feet of the 600 foot long ship, and broke it off, and wretched it free. Remarkably, the ships internal bulk catcher remained intact, and watertight doors kept the sea back. Engineers on the ship had told the captain that the ship was going to break, and they had prepared for that—they moved the sailors back, and battened down the hatches and sealed the doors. To save the ship, 20 sailors, led by Executive Officer Horacio Rivero and Damage Control Officer John Kircher, manually reinforced the ship's bow with wood shoring to withstand the continued pounding of the sea.

The storm was so great, all the sailors were underneath or down below deck, and there was half of a ship somewhere floating next to their ship, and occasionally, the fear was that it would crash into the mother ship.

The ship's commanding officer, Capt. John Gingrich, was forced to reverse the ship's engines, maneuvering to avoid being rammed by the drifting bow and further lessen the stress on the forward part of the ship. That's the same Captain Gingrich that you heard earlier that was watching the steel cables pull the USS Franklin to safety. Bowless, the ship would pass through the eye of the hurricane and back again into the brunt of the storm. The crew feared the ship would also lose its stern as it pushed backwards into the storm. What a great seaman that captain must have been! Unable to use its rudder to maneuver, the Pittsburgh negotiated sea and wind entirely by engine manipulations for seven hours until the storm subsided. It would eventually make it back to forward operating bases in Guam on June 10th.

The shorn bow would continue to have a life of its own. A Navy tug reported back having found the still floating bow with the radio message "sighted the suburb of USS Pittsburgh and have taken it in tow." The bow would be nicknamed the "USS McKeesport", which is a suburb of Pittsburgh, and be towed into Guam to be salvaged. A false bow would eventually be fit onto the Pittsburgh for her return trip to the states.

BEELER: Well, yeah, we got in a bad storm once, and they asked everybody to get below deck. And everybody didn't, and some got knocked overboard, and of course we couldn't turn around and get 'em, we just went on and left 'em.

Author's question: So what was going on in your mind when you found out the ship might break?

BEELER: Well, I was a lot younger then. I was scared to death. But, you know, you had to hold onto something, you'd take a 45 degree roll and it'd throw you into a wall, you had to hold onto something! Just to walk around. And the plates, and knives, and forks, and everything, was on the deck, just every time the ship would rock, they'd just go from one side, it was the messiest thing you've ever seen. I did not see many sick sailors? I never did get seasick. No. The captain announced it.

He said, "The USS Pittsburgh just lost its bow."

BEELER: Yep. And there wasn't a man in or on it. The captain knew it could break in two.

T the crew? They were maybe in one room, they may just be four or five or six or seven or eight or ten, you know, and that's scattered all over the ship. We were scared to death. If we went down, there wouldn't of been no chance. Would have been gone. That typhoon was in June. June the 5th, 1945.

Author's note: Okay, all right. So, the Indianapolis hadn't been sunk yet? The bomb had not been dropped.

BEELER: I don't think so. We were coming back from an attack on an island in Japan? We was still fighting. 'course, we tried—the captain tried to miss it, but he got right in the middle of it. He tried to miss that typhoon, he knew it was coming.

Halsey was the captain, I mean, was the... Admiral? Admiral Halsey?

Yeah, I remember a lot about it, but a lot of it I don't.

Well, of course, we was all together out there, they spread out as wide as they could, you know, keep them from hitting each other. We were worried about that bow hitting us, that broken bow. Yep. They, actually, after that typhoon was over, they came out there and got that bow.

And they got it out, wouldn't even sink, it just sunk down level with the water. We had battened all the hatches, I guess.

RANDY: Did your family know you were on that ship?

BEELER: Yeah.

Author's note: I'm looking at some more photos that Seaman First Class Clyde Beeler let me get copies of, and the first one is of the USS Pittsburgh. It was a beautiful ship, and we talked a little bit about the guns in the center of the ship, and in front of the center of the ship was the big 300 pound eight inch guns, and there were six of them on the front, looks like three on the back. Then, after that, came those six inch guns that shot those 52 inch shells, and then in front of that is a little bunker, looks like it's got the 40 millimeters in it, and then about fifty feet in front of that, are the 20 millimeter guns. And then there's the 20 millimeter guns on the sides, and on the rear. The next picture I'm looking at is a picture of the USS Pittsburgh in a typhoon, with a 600-foot long ship, with 104 feet breaking off of the front. The bow is completely breaking off, and it looks like its breaking off right there, about 15 feet in front of those big eight inch guns, so the 40 millimeters and the 20 millimeters broke away, started floating in the Pacific Ocean, banging against the side of the ship.

And then I've got three other pictures here, there's one of the USS Pittsburgh sailing into the Pacific Ocean, with the front end of the ship totally gone. Then I have another picture of it being towed into port at Guam, and the crews repairing it and putting a fake bow on it, so they can send it home to the United States.

You've been reading about the ordeal, or the experience that Seaman First Class Clyde Beeler had and his experience in the Navy, he was in there for 24 months, 21 months of that at sea.

After 21 months at sea, Clyde Beeler came home. He married his childhood sweetheart—she was the daughter of the doctor in Grainger County on that side of the mountain. He also had two children, and now he lives in North Knoxville. And, you know, of all the people I have interviewed in this show. I've learned that you can't always tell what other people have been through, and what they've done, and what their experiences are. And this small framed gentleman in Knoxville went to hell and back in the Pacific Ocean in World War II. I first met Clyde Beeler when he was a guest on a radio show that came on right before mine on Sunday mornings. It was a local yard sale type radio show and Clyde called in every week trying to sell a large black skillet.

He would name his price and mention a few times he was in the US Navy in World War II.

I would go in early to get ready for my show, and one day he was a guest on the prior radio program. I got to meet him and asked him a few questions about his experiences in World War II.

When I learned he was a young East Tennessee mountain man on a ship that broke in half in the Pacific Typhoon during World War II I became one of his fans. He was just a country farm boy, with a fascinating story. I attended his last birthday party. When he saw how many from the radio station showed up and all the gifts and cake he was showered with he cried. When his family was liquidating his estate, I bought his navy outfits, and his World War II photos, and all his medals, and memorabilia from the war. It seemed to have little value to his family. It became a treasure trove for me as a collector.

If you look around and check your neighborhood out, you might meet somebody just like him. Another Veteran Next Door.

There is one more ship I want to tell you about. It was called the USS Indianapolis.

I have a friend whose father was on that ship. I attended the 65th anniversary of the sinking of that ship in August of 2012. I got to meet several of the surviving crew members.

My friend's name is Earl Henry, Jr. His father was an outdoorsman, a taxidermist, and an artist.

He was also a Lt. Commander on the ship you are about to learn about.

CHAPTER TWELVE

AN OUTDOORSMAN, A TAXIDERMIST, AND ARTIST, AND A DENTIST ON A SHIP AT SEA

That's my Dad!

We all know that story, the bombing of Pearl Harbor on December 7, 1941. We all know the first ship that everybody learns about—the USS Arizona. That was our first great ship sunk as far as what everybody knows. Let's discuss one of the last ships to be sunk in World War II in the Pacific, the USS Indianapolis. We're also going to be talking about one of the sailors on board, a young man from Knoxville, Tennessee: Lt. Commander Earl Henry.*The USS Indianapolis was a heavy cruiser built in 1930 by the New York Shipbuilding Corporation in Camden, New Jersey. Followed by launching and a shakedown voyage to Guantanamo in 1931 and 1932. President Roosevelt went on a two-day cruise with his cabinet on the USS Indianapolis and in 1936, he took his third cruise on the same ship to South America. As tension grew, the crew was trained to be a fighting machine. One of the sailors on the USS Indianapolis was born in 1911. His name was Earl Henry. 14 years later, he lived in Knoxville, Tennessee, but he was born Clinton, TN just east of Oak Ridge and north of Knoxville. He had learned to work with birds and had become a taxidermist. His birds were displayed on Gay Street in downtown Knoxville in a sporting goods store in the 1930's. In 1939, he started painting. And then one day, he decided he had to give up his taxidermy to become a dentist in 1935. In 1941, he joined the Navy Reserve.

Our story is told mostly by Earl Henry's son His father is the man I described in the earlier segment. He was six weeks old when his father died at sea. An officer on the ship that delivered the main components of the Atom Bombs to the Island of Tinian just before they were taken to their final destinations of Hiroshima, and Nagasaki. Earl Henry Sr. was quite a birdwatcher and a bird artist and a bird whistler, I have a copy of one of his prints in my office. I wondered how he ever got interested in birds. So I asked his son.

EARL: He got interested in birds from collecting Arm & Hammer bird cards, and I know that seems strange to people today, but back then—and that would have been about 1923, at age 12, my father collected Arm & Hammer bird cards. They were very high quality prints on cards very much like baseball cards that I collected, with the image of the bird on one side and information about the bird on the other side. And my father and two of his friends started collecting those cards. A young teenager in North Knoxville up on Scott Street, he's got radio to listen to, didn't have TV, didn't have a lot of other things we have today, so he got interested in birds, and he turned that interest in birds into becoming a taxidermist. That was after having joined the Knoxville Bird Club that is the Knoxville chapter of the Tennessee Ornithological Society and being mentored by members of that club. And apparently, he had the natural talents to become a really good birder, and I'm aware of them because they're skills that I don't have. One of them, he must have had excellent eyesight, and he must have had excellent hearing, because one of the things he quickly learned to do was to do imitations of bird calls. Ultimately, he learned to do about 60 different bird call imitations.

Author's Note: I have a copy of this man's bird calls in my computer, they are perfect imitations of several local birds. So he was interested in birds, taxidermy, and he was leaving some of his work at a local sporting goods store?

EARL: Yes, and this was in the late 1930s. He loaned every year, every fall, some of the mounted ducks for the store display of a sporting goods store owned by Bob Burch. Mr. Burch sold a lot of hunting paraphernalia: you know: guns, shells, hunting jackets, that type of equipment—to hunters. In his store display, he would put corn shucks, and the hunting equipment, and he would borrow some of my father's mounted ducks to put in the store display. One day, some of the displays came back, and they were a little tattered and worn?: I imagine those were some of the things my father noticed that nobody would have noticed, except the person who had done the birds, but noticing that feathers were bent, or missing, so he decided he wasn't going to let Mr. Burch borrow the mounted ducks anymore. Mr. Burch was such a good friend, he didn't really know how to tell him no, and the way my grandfather told it to me, he said, "one day, I know what I'll do: I'll paint him some ducks." And, so, very quickly, he started painting ducks for Bob Burch.

Author's note: So, the taxidermist bird caller became an artist to protect his previous work: And then he was just painting some ducks, but as time went on he became very good at painting birds, didn't he?

EARL: Well, that was later. That was after my mother and father had married, they married in 1941, and it was right after they married that Pearl Harbor was bombed. My father was already in the Navy Reserve. He was given orders to report to Parris Island, South Carolina. My Mother and Father lived there for a year, and that's where the serious bird painting started. My mother deserved a lot of the credit for that, because she encouraged him to paint. She said, "Why don't you paint more than just ducks?" As it turned out, he never painted any more ducks. I'm sure he would have had he lived, but he started painting beautiful songbirds, shorebirds, birds of prey, marsh birds, and she also encouraged him to put as much emphasis in the background as he did in the birds, because his interest was in the birds, after all, and that tended to be his focus.

Author's note: In December 1941, the Indianapolis had left one day early to go on a bombing practice run. In February, 1942 the Indianapolis fought its first action near Rabaul in the South Pacific, a Japanese base that was standing in the way of MacArthur and his desire to cut off supplies to the Japanese nation by cutting off all their trade routes. Battle number two in March of 42, the Indianapolis assisted the Yorktown to attack New Guinea. They also right after that went back to San Francisco to be refitted, and went on a trip to Alaska, and in the Aleutian Islands, to resist the Japanese who had taken over the islands up there.

In February of 1943, they sunk a Japanese ship up near the Aleutian Islands that exploded when it was hit, so it was assumed that it was full of ammunition. The Indianapolis also served as a flagship for Admiral Spruance and his invasion of the Gilbert Islands. Battle number seven is a very famous battle called Kwajalein. I met a sailor one day in Lenoir City who rode into the islands at Kwajalein shooting a 30 caliber gun. His ship dropped the marines off and went back for more. Early in the battle, on the 2nd and third trips in, he said the marines he had dropped off earlier were already dead. He was 19 years older than his sister. When I told her about his experience, she said she did not know what he had done. All she knew as a child was brother went to war, but back to our story, then the USS Indianapolis was in the Western Carolines, and then on to Saipan. So, the USS Indianapolis, while Earl Henry had learned to be a taxidermist and artist after he started painting his birds, and had become an officer in the US Navy, had already fought in nine battles before he ever became a member of its crew.

To get to know Earl Henry the sailor, who was on the USS Indianapolis. Let's go back a bit to his younger days. He learned to be a taxidermist, didn't he?

EARL: He learned to be a taxidermist while he was in high school, and this would maybe surprise people, but he learned to do taxidermy through a correspondence course. It's hard for me to imagine people learning or being able to learn that through taxidermy, but I knew he had a natural gift to do detail with his hands. He may have been mentored by Mr. H. P. Ijams of the Knoxville Chapter of the Bird Club.

Well, Mr. Ijams, as I understand, was quite a naturalist. He was also an artist himself, and my father became a very close friend of his. One of the things my mother told me about—and this was shortly after they got married in the fall of 1941, or maybe right before my father went on duty with the Navy in early '42, that they had dinner at the home of Mr. and Mrs. Ijams. One of the things that my father especially wanted to make sure my mother saw was a passenger pigeon that was in the in the possession of Mr. Ijams. Passenger pigeons were long extinct by that time, but this one that he had purchased, one that had been shot by someone around 1850 in the area of Nashville.

Author's note: As my friend Chip Mahood jokingly says, "Let's kill it and look at it." So, it was stuffed?

EARL: It was stuffed. Mr. Ijams left his property, which is a lovely sight for birding near where the Tennessee River is formed. It's just right below where the French Broad River and the Holston River come together. It's a bird sanctuary, and he left this property to the city of Knoxville. Since then, they have built a really state-of-the-art nature center, a large building there, and they have all kinds of programs, especially for youth. It is a very highly regarded institution in Knoxville. People can go there and see my father's work? because when they built the new center in the late 1990's, we donated our father's mounted bird collection. There are 87 of my father's mounted birds, the rarest one being a peregrine falcon. My father's prints are also there, they sell them in the gift shop in the form of a box of note cards, and as matted and unmatted prints.

To get copies of these prints go to: www.earlhenrybirdprints.com

Author's Note: Okay, now, we have a taxidermist who has his artwork and his taxidermy work at Ijams Park, who, at some point in his life, decided he wanted to be a dentist?

EARL: Yes, and he had graduated from the University of Tennessee in Knoxville in undergraduate school, and he went on to the College of Dentistry in Memphis in 1935, and came back to Knoxville that year to begin his practice in dentistry. Isn't it amazing, that a man that could work with his hands stuffing birds and worked with his hands to paint birds would also work with his hands to fill the teeth and cavities in people's mouths, and that would be an artist's work, too.

I it's interesting the way that I have learned information about my father, and the taxidermy of course, I never saw him do, but it was just a few years ago that my uncle in Kentucky found a newspaper article from the Knoxville Sunday Journal in 1933 that tells about my father and his taxidermy, and it tells more detail than I previously knew about it, but if there was one important message in that article, it was that my father planned to give up taxidermy after he started practicing dentistry, because he thought a patient would not go to a dentist who has had his hands involved in doing taxidermy of a bird. It's messy, there was arsenic involved, at least at that time mounting birds.

I think in that article it said he had to give up his taxidermy for forceps. That was in 1943, so he was a 21 year old man who had already graduated from the University of Tennessee, and had been regionally known as a taxidermist. He would have been 24 by the time he graduated from dental school.

He was a taxidermist, he was an artist, and he was a dentist. All of those involved the skill of doing detail with your hands, and that was a natural God-given gift which apparently he had.

I don't know a lot of detail, but sometime in 1941, he joined the Naval Reserve. I know he had to go to Nashville to officially become an officer in the Naval Reserve, and that would have been less than a year before the bombing of Pearl Harbor.

When he enlisted, he had no intention of going to Annapolis? No, he had no idea where he would be assigned. This was before the war itself started. He was commissioned in the United States Naval Dental Corp.

Annapolis was his second assignment. His first assignment that we talked a little about earlier was that he first went to Parris Island, South Carolina, and that's where he began painting birds. After being there for a year, he was given orders to report again as a dental officer, this time at the Naval

Academy in Annapolis. There were somewhere close to thirty dentists there I understand, at the Naval Academy. He was there for a little over a year, and he continued to do his painting of birds. One of the things that I'm fortunate that happened is while he was there, a foreign language professor there invited my father for dinner, and while he was there, he made recordings of my father doing imitations of bird calls, which I think I mentioned earlier he could do 60 different bird calls. So, that's how he got to Annapolis.

Author's note: I met Mr. Earl Henry Jr. at a gift show in Gatlinburg, TN. He was behind a table handing out samples of prints of birds. I looked up and saw that he had a picture of his father, who was a naval officer, and I had to ask him what those prints were all about. I ran into him again at the same show in another year. These prints are just beautiful works of art he did while he was at Annapolis.

EARL: Well, it was at Parris Island, South Carolina. That's where he began seriously painting, and he carried that on at Annapolis, and after he went to sea, he did four more paintings that I'm aware of. A couple of them were aboard his ship. We had twenty different prints so far. We hoped that there would be more that we would be able to have, but I sell more assortments with twelve different bird images in it than I do anything else, and they're all nature prints except one of them that he later painted onboard his ship, which I describe as a war poster picture. I put one of those in all the assortments, unless requests that I not include it, because it's very dramatic and it helps people remember the artist.

My Father thought he should take his turn at sea. He didn't have to go to sea, but he volunteered for sea duty, and he received an assignment that most people would have thought at the time was a choice assignment. He was assigned as the dental officer on the USS Indianapolis.

As a dental officer, he had duties. Routine dental duties were one of the things, and as well as being part of a medical team. He worked very closely with two doctors that were on the ship, and the sickbay and dentist offices were right next to each other, so they became a team. As far as the dental work, he wrote about that in his letters a lot—his letters to my mother—talking about the mission. Apparently, this was true of most dentists serving World War II, that they felt a real duty to provide dental service to the sailors and the Marines in the Navy, because those boys had grown up in the Depression. A lot of them and their families couldn't afford to send them to dentists. This was before the public water systems were treated with fluoride, the fluoridation of the water supply. So, there were a lot more cavities in a typical young person back then than you would expect to see today. So, there was a lot of work to do, and I know my father took that very seriously.

Author's note: During peacetime, the USS Indianapolis had around 625 members on its decks, but during war time it had close to 1200—I think it was 1190. So, there probably were a lot of dental problems or dental issues on that boat. Your father was probably really busy.

RANDY: Okay. When he was on that ship—I'm looking at one of the printed cards right now—when he was on that ship, he had painted a picture of what's called "An American Eagle in the Pacific." Can you take a minute and describe this card?

EARL: Yes I can. That's my favorite painting of his. Up until that time, all of my father's paintings were what you would call nature prints. They were songbirds, shorebirds, birds of prey, whatever, in nature scenes. But this one, I call a war poster picture, and it's just beautiful. It has an eagle—very detailed—and its wings are open at an angle, and behind it is the American flag, which was 48-star American flag at that time. The snake in its talons—it's gripping a serpent or snake, and it's dripping blood, and tied to the tail of a snake is a tiny, tattered Japanese army flag. So, it's just full of symbolism of the period and of the place where it was painted in the Pacific. I think my father was expressing the emotions that the American fighting men in the Pacific felt.

RANDY: When I look at this card and look at the snake, the snake has some pretty mean looking fangs on it, but those fangs are useless because he's in the claws of the American eagle.

EARL: Right, and I think that's the way most Americans felt the war was going, and I know from my father's letters, they felt like this war was going to be over before long.

Author's note: Lt. Commander Earl Henry USN joined the USS INDIANAPOLIS in Saipan. It became the first ship to enter the bay in Guam, and went into the tenth battle where they bombarded Peleliu. Some day in another book, I hope to tell you the story of the battle at Peleliu, and two brothers, one a marine and one in the army on that island at the same time. That was in September of 1944. When that battle was over, the USS INDIANAPOLIS had to return to San Francisco to Mayor Island. That was in October and November, is there anything you want to tell us about that?

EARL: Well, that's important to me. I'm really glad the ship came in, and I'm really glad my mother joined my father out there for about six weeks. If my mother had not joined my father there, I might not have showed up for this interview today.

Author's note: And maybe his story never would have been told, that's true. Go Navy! February 1945, after the ship left, they participated in attacking

Japan for the first time since Doolittle's raid, and part of that in February of 1945 was the twelfth battle for the USS Indianapolis. It was the Battle of IWO JIMA. One month later, the thirteenth battle there were in, they attacked Japan, and in battle fourteen, they attacked Okinawa. So, we've got a ship so far that has been in the South Pacific, it came back home and got refitted, and went to Alaska and fought battles there, and went back and refitted, and came back to help the Marines fight in the island hopping campaigns. It's just been everywhere—it's been in the whole war. But on March 31, 1945, the Indianapolis suffered heavy damage from bombs and a plane crashed into it. When that plane crashed, it killed nine crewmen, bent the propeller shafts on a big ship, the fuel tanks were ruptured, and the water distillery was ruined. What was your father doing during that time?

EARL: It was a very busy time between IWO JIMA and the invasion of Okinawa. I might mention that my mother's birthday was coming up, and my father wrote her how busy they were, and they didn't have time—there wasn't any way he could order her a birthday present, so he did a painting for her, his last painting on the ship that he mailed to her. But specifically, after he did that painting on March the 31st, when the kamikaze plane struck the ship. My father had to identify the nine sailors who were killed in that kamikaze attack. Using the dental records.

Author's Note: So, he wasn't always in there patching teeth up, sometimes he was a soldier of war.

EARL: Right. And there may have been other times he had to identify casualties with dental records, but that's the only specific instance that I know of.

Author's Note: Okay, and then he also wrote you a letter, didn't he?

EARL: Yes, this was later. After the invasion of Okinawa and the plane, being the kamikaze plane, damaging the ship. The ship had to come back to Mayor Island again for repairs. My father took a three week leave and came to Kentucky and visited my mother, and left right before I was born. Maybe he would have stayed a little longer had he known I was going to come early, but I was born prematurely. I was not expected for another six weeks. That was the last time anybody has accused me of being early, I might mention.

My father went back to California, and suddenly they got orders to depart, and they left San Francisco. They, of course, would not have known they were carrying the components for the first two atomic bombs, but it was a high speed mission, and they went to Tinian and delivered the components of the first atomic bombs. That was July 26th, and the ship went from there to Guam, which was very close by. And at Guam, my father received the first and only pictures he ever saw of me, and he wrote a little note to me from there, and he did it on the back of a calling card, where on one side it says "Earl O'Dell Henry, Lt. Commander of the United States Naval Dental Corp." On the back of it, he says something like, "son, if I can be just as good a father as your mother is a mother, son, you'll turn out alright. Love, Earl." And my Father had no idea that would be his last port of call and his last opportunity, but I'm so grateful he wrote that little note to me.

Author's note: Okay, so, what I have learned in this experience so far is that you have learned a lot about your father by searching and absorbing and people bringing you information, so you know your father very well, don't you?

EARL: I know my father very well, and I was flattered by overhearing a lady, a former neighbor of mine, after I had spoken to her garden club telling somebody, "Gosh, he knows his father better than I know mine." Well, actually I don't. Of course I don't. But I am so blessed that I know as much as I do, because he left so much tangible evidence in his work. The mounted birds, the beautiful bird paintings, dental jewelry he made using dental silver for my mother, and I'm able to listen to my father's voice on the bird call imitations, and I probably know more about my father's personality from his letters. His letters were so rich, and it's amazing because they were censored. He couldn't say where they were, or what they were doing, but it was full of information about people he had seen and met, or about letters that he had received from others, and he was asking questions about "how are my Mother and Father" and things like that. I've also been fortunate enough that I've come across so much in reading—accidental discoveries about my father, references, and a book by the first chief naturalist of the Smoky Mountains talking about birds. My father discovered this—I mean, my uncle discovered this newspaper article just about three years ago, and that was written in 1933 about my father and his taxidermy, and members of the family. And there was a point in time, especially when a friend would die, that I would be thinking, "I'll probably never learn anything new about my father," and then, pop, something comes up totally unexpected. I'm very blessed to know as much as I do about my father.

If anyone is interested in the prints, they can send me an e-mail, or I can tell them about the prints, and my e-mail address is simply henrybirdprints@ aol.com.

Author's note: I've got a set of these cards. I got some a couple years ago and mailed them to my friends, but if you want a really beautiful card to send to a friend or relative—it doesn't have to be Christmas, because these are just beautiful bird prints. I had a hard time mailing mine out because I didn't want to not have them anymore.

EARL: Twelve cards reasonably priced! These are beautiful cards, you cannot go into a Hallmark store and buy as good a card as these are, and I think it's something in which you might be interested. henrybirdprints@ aol.com.

Author's note: After repairs in San Francisco, the Indianapolis was ordered to go on a special mission to deliver parts—key parts—to the nuclear bombs that were going to be dropped on Japan. They took those parts to Tinian. After that, they were on the way to the Philippines to another battle. Once they had delivered the parts and left for the Philippines, the Indianapolis was hit by two torpedoes on the starboard side. She sank in twelve minutes. The survivors were picked up at the end, there were 316 survivors of the crew of 1199. The captain was later court martialed for his actions—he failed to zig-zag. He was ordered to get there as fast as he could, but he failed to zig-zag. So, the first ship to be sunk was the USS Arizona. The last ship, the USS Indianapolis. If you had to die connected to the USS Indianapolis, these were your options: you could have been killed by a Japanese kamikaze pilot. You could have been killed in any of the many battles the Indianapolis participated in. If you died when the ship was hit by two submarine torpedo blasts, you may have been killed when the front of the ship on the starboard side was hit and broke off from the rest of the ship. You may have died in the second torpedo blast that hit the ship in the middle. You may have drowned when the ship went down. If, when you manned battle stations were below deck, and you could not jump. If you survived the sinking of the ship, which sank in twelve minutes when it was hit, and you were a survivor in the ocean, there were originally 800 survivors floating in the ocean. Very few had lifeboats, most just had life jackets. But you had more tribulations. Some were mercilessly burned, so soaked in oil that caused their eyes to swell in the salt water, so they could not shut their eyes for days in the heat. Many of the survivors died of dehydration in the Pacific. No food or water, and relentlessly trying to stay afloat for five days took its toll. Many went insane and just swam away. Some bled to death from their wounds, and many suffered the worst death of all—being dragged down underwater by the hundreds of sharks that surrounded the survivors and feasted on the helpless survivors until they were found and rescued. Of the 800 floating when the ship went down, a little over 317 or so were rescued. You may have committed suicide like Captain McVeigh, who could no longer bear the burdens associated with the sinking of the Indianapolis.

In August of 2012 Mr. Edgar Harrell emailed me and invited me to attend the 65th anniversary of the sinking of the USS Indianapolis, in Indianapolis, Indiana. Of course I went.

I had the opportunity to meet 22 of the 45 surviving sailors from that most famous of ships in World War II. Mr. Harrell was a Marine on the ship guarding the precious cargo, and I attended his speaking engagement and heard him tell his story of survival in the Pacific Ocean for 5 days,

Surrounded by wounded, and burned sailors, trying to stay afloat, while being circled by sharks.

But that is another story in my next volume of stories coming soon. Four days after the rescue, they floated in the Pacific Ocean for four or five days, and then four days after that, the first atomic bomb was dropped from Tinian. Bombs with parts that were delivered to Tinian by the USS Indianapolis. Lt. Commander Earl Henry was in the medical area when the torpedoes hit, and he went down with the ship. No one knows exactly how he died. He left behind a wife and a newborn child, and a series of bird paintings that could last forever.

Think about this for a minute: The ship is sinking, here is oil burning in the water. You dive in to save yourself. You dive through the burning oil, when you come up for air, you come up through the oil. It gets in your eyes, you swallow some. You float all night with sharks bumping you. As the sun rises, the heat also rises. The heat burns the oil in your eyes. You are almost totally blind, and another shark bumps you.

Think about this also, you are a marine, and your tough SGT. orders you not to dive into the water, but to calmly walk off the ship and keep your head above water. The sharks are still bumping you, but you can see, and the heat does not do as much damage. That same Sgt. Orders you to not swallow any water. Will you do what he says?

Not long after that the war was over, and the soldiers began coming home, many to a little town in East Tennessee called Athens. My parents are from Athens and close by Riceville, Tn.

When the veterans came home they did not like what they found in the county courthouse.

They used their Second Amendment rights to correct the situation as you are about to learn.

It's time to learn about: "The Battle of Athens, Tennessee 1946."

CHAPTER THIRTEEN

THE BATTLE OF ATHENS, TENNESSEE 1946

It started before the Revolutionary War. Most revolutions are internal revolts intent on overthrowing a national government, ours was different. We did not seek the overthrow of England, just the separation. We needed to prove to the world that we were capable of that status. The American experiment was underway. The notion that people would govern themselves was unprecedented. There were no models, no examples to choose from. For the first time, man had acted into law, human rights. Not just government given rights. The authors deemed those rights so important, they made a provision to protect those rights so they could never be taken away.

When added to the Constitution, we called them the Bill of rights.

Here is a list of the Bill of Rights:

- **First Amendment**: Congress shall make no law respecting an establishment of religion, or prohibiting the free exercise thereof; or abridging the freedom of speech, or of the press; or the right of the people peaceably to assemble, and to petition the Government for a redress of grievances.

- **Second Amendment**: A well-regulated Militia, being necessary to the security of a Free State, the right of the people to keep and bear Arms, shall not be infringed.

- **Third Amendment**: No Soldier shall, in time of peace be quartered in any house, without the consent of the Owner, nor in time of war, but in a manner to be prescribed by law.

- **Fourth Amendment**: The right of the people to be secure in their persons, houses, papers, and effects, against unreasonable searches and seizures, shall not be violated, and no Warrants shall issue, but upon probable cause, supported by Oath or affirmation, and particularly describing the place to be searched, and the persons or things to be seized.

- **Fifth Amendment**: No person shall be held to answer for a capital, or otherwise infamous crime, unless on a presentment or indictment of a Grand Jury, except in cases arising in the land or naval forces, or in the Militia, when in actual service in time of War or public danger; nor shall any person be subject for the same offence to be twice put in jeopardy of life or limb; nor shall be compelled in any criminal case to be a witness against himself, nor be deprived of life, liberty, or property, without due process of law; nor shall private property be taken for public use, without just compensation.

- **Sixth Amendment**: In all criminal prosecutions, the accused shall enjoy the right to a speedy and public trial, by an impartial jury of the State and district wherein the crime shall have been committed, which district shall have been previously ascertained by law, and to be informed of the nature and cause of the accusation; to be confronted with the witnesses against him; to have compulsory process for obtaining witnesses in his favor, and to have the Assistance of Counsel for his defense.

- **Seventh Amendment**: In suits at common law, where the value in controversy shall exceed twenty dollars, the right of trial by jury shall be preserved, and no fact tried by a jury, shall be otherwise reexamined in any Court of the United States, than according to the rules of the common law.

- **Eighth Amendment**: Excessive bail shall not be required, nor excessive fines imposed, nor cruel and unusual punishments inflicted.

- **Ninth Amendment**: The enumeration in the Constitution, of certain rights, shall not be construed to deny or disparage others retained by the people.

- **Tenth Amendment**: The powers not delegated to the United States by the Constitution, nor prohibited by it to the States, are reserved to the States respectively, or to the people.

So what does the Second Amendment have to do with our story and this book? There is a little town in East Tennessee, the time line of this report on events is 1946, and our soldiers were returning home from World War II. The town is known as Athens, Tennessee. It's about halfway from Knoxville, Tennessee heading south towards Chattanooga. The last military related event that happened in Athens occurred in 1863 when Confederate General Longstreet passed through.

After World War II, as our soldiers were coming home after being in Europe, Africa, and Asia, in the Atlantic, or in the Pacific, they realized that they weren't going to be held down on the farm anymore. They had seen too much, and done too much. Athens was surrounded by farmland. My parents were from this area of East Tennessee. My father was born and raised in Athens, Tennessee during that time. My mother was born and raised in a little town right outside of Athens, called Riceville, Tennessee. I had no idea, as a child, exactly what had happened. I had heard stories about the Battle of Athens and didn't think much about it, didn't know what it was. A little bit north of Athens was Knoxville, Tennessee. A little bit, same distance South was Chattanooga, Tennessee. Today, if you travel from Knoxville to Chattanooga, it's all interstate, with little communities all along the way. But back then, 11-E twirled around a little bit and Athens was in the middle, and it was just a little country town. A lot of the roads were dirt and gravel. Knoxville had not reached out to Athens, and Chattanooga had not reached out to Athens. It was surrounded by farmland. When the soldiers came home—these farm boys—found a situation they didn't like.

1946: McMinn County, Tennessee. A wealthy family, the Cantrell's, had taken control of the county political scene. Paul Cantrell was elected county sheriff in 1936, 38, and 40, and in 42 and 44 he was elected to the state Senate while his chief deputy, Pat Mansfield, was elected county sheriff. US Department of Justice received complaints from county citizens of electoral fraud in 1940, 42, and 44. These complaints went unanswered.

Deputies commonly accepted bribes, intimidated voters, tampered with ballot boxes, and began beating those who spoke out. The sheriff's department falsely ticketed and arrested individuals to obtain finances for personal and political purposes. Local political bosses were just as corrupt.

World War II veterans returning to their home county were outraged by the tyrannical establishment. During 1946 elections, veterans fielded their own non-partisan candidates and attempted to have a fraud-free election. Paul Cantrell was again running for sheriff. On August 1st, Election Day, Pat Mansfield brought in two hundred deputies from surrounding counties to detain and beat ex-GI poll watchers, in addition to taking the ballot boxes back to the jailhouses for an "official count." Taking the ballot boxes was against the law. Enraged veterans armed themselves and sought to obtain the ballot boxes to stop electoral fraud, and it became known as "the Battle of Athens." There was a radio report from a Knoxville reporter during the event: This is how it was reported.

STOUT: Ladies and gentlemen, this is Allen Stout, at WORL in Knoxville. On August 1st, 1946, Frank Lark, a WORL news editor and myself had the—as we felt at the time—unenviable opportunity of reporting on one of the nation's most tumultuous elections in its long history. I'm speaking of the GI uprising at Athens' county seat of McMinn County, Tennessee. In this quiet, sleepy little town of about 6,000 people, a political powder keg exploded when the GIs returned bullets for ballots, stormed the county jail to recover some ballot boxes, stolen by the Paul Cantrell political machine then in power, and proceeded to see that a fair count was made of the ballot, and no stuffing of the boxes was to be the order of this particular election day. Most of you are familiar with the story, since it generated nationwide interest and comment. However, just to refresh your memory, here is the man who covered the entire uprising, got caught in crossfire between the two battling factions, and who provided the information for me to broadcast throughout the long hours of the night of August 1st, and into the wee, small hours of the morning of the second. He is Frank Lark, WORL news bureau chief. Frank, tell us briefly the background of the Athens situation, and the election night action as you saw it.

LARK: How do you do, ladies and gentlemen? I will attempt to give you a little background of the events leading up to the Election Day violence of Athens, Tennessee, and the overthrow of the Paul Cantrell political machine by enraged ex-servicemen. This spring, former GIs banded together and placed a non-partisan ticket in the field, in an attempt to defeat the political machine in McMinn County. This was the first opposition the machine had faced in ten years. It was a generally accepted fact that the Cantrell machine would not stand for a fair count of ballots, and this meant the law, controlled by the machine, would begin to steal ballot boxes if necessary. On the other hand, the former servicemen were just as determined to make sure the ballots were counted as cast. These two stands could only mean one thing: violence, explosive violence! That was the picture that faced veteran newsmen, and this picture reeked with news. The people were aroused, and determined to overthrow machine rule at the polls. As a former newspaper man, I had kept my eyes on the McMinn County political machine for the past six years, and during that period, I had written stories about ballot box stealing, and had watched Representative John Jennings, in his life; try to put an end to the wretched political practices. The congressman had failed. And I point out the political machine was the Democratic Party, and the county is considered Republican. Getting up to the day of action, August 1st, Allen Stout and I arrived in Athens, about one hour before the polls closed at 4 o'clock. The arrangements for our equipment for our broadcast from Athens had been made six days before. Just as soon as we arrived, we made a tour of the voting precinct and learned one GI judge had been removed from the first precinct.

Author's note: Let's get you up to date on what you're reading. The corruption was so bad in McMinn County, that August 1st day in 1946, it had been reported that the deputies got a per-diem fee every time they pulled somebody out of traffic or any time they arrested somebody and put them in the courthouse—when the victim paid a fee, then they would let them go. So, a lot of the income in the courthouse was based on how many people they could arrest during the day. If you were traveling from Knoxville to Chattanooga, you'd better watch out. And again, the income was so good, that the regime didn't care to steal a ballot box if they needed to.

Here is one of the time lines of events that were reported:

Election Day, August 1, 1946, nine a.m. The voting polls opened. The voter turnout was heavy. And the first flare up was ready to occur in precinct one, at the jailhouse. The jailing of Walter Ellis. This occurred very shortly after 10 a.m. conflicting reports as to when Walter Ellis, the GI election judge was arrested, one account was 9:30, another says shortly after 10, but the overall details are consistent. Ellis was summarily arrested and hauled off to the county jail. He was replaced by Fred West. A dispute over who exactly Fred West was immediately erupted. The sheriff office described West as another GI. The GI ticket manager, described him as a deputy sheriff, and local bartender. But he could have been a GI too, but he was obviously on the sheriff's side. Ellis was held incommunicado in the county jail, and Sheriff Mansfield's men flatly declined to permit reporters or anyone else to see him. Magistrate Herman Moses, when asked what charges had been placed, declared Ellis had attempted to perpetuate a fraud by marking ballots in precinct one at the courthouse. He was probably marking them so he could identify them later in the count, but that is purely speculation. The ticket manager admitted, frankly, he did not know what happened in the voting precinct prior to Ellis's arrest, but said Sheriff Mansfield's men had refused to permit him to make bond for Ellis, or to tell him what charges had been placed against the ex-GI.

The corridor at the courthouse was crowded with voters, both men and women. Ellis already had been removed, but evidently, in fear of some disorder, some twenty deputies—hands on pistols and blackjacks ready—pushed through the crowd to the voting precinct. This overgrown combat squad was reinforced by several uniformed and armed city policemen, a state highway patrolman with his hand fingering a heavy revolver. The deputies arranged themselves around the voting precinct, and one, dressed like a character from a Western movie, placed themselves on the steps where they could watch the entire corridor. Ex-servicemen regarded today's proceedings with varying attitudes, but most of them displayed a bitterness seldom displayed in the fighting lines. Watching the guarded vote counting before it was moved to the county jail, one ex-soldier said, "Over there, we had something to fight back with." Another remarked, "We just aren't well enough organized, and we haven't got guns. We haven't got a chance with this Gestapo." "This is causing a lot of bitterness, and a lot of it will come later today," another man remarked.

LARK: There's two hundred and fifty special deputies, some of them imported from outside the county and the state, were patrolling the streets with their pistols and shiny badges. Small groups of citizens, talking softly, moved up and down the streets. We went to the jail to interview the sheriff. While we were there, a deputy, Wendy Wise, led an elderly Negro, Tom Gillispie, to the jail. The deputy announced, and I quote, "I've just shot him, what do you want me to do with him?" Another deputy was instructed to take the Negro to the hospital. He had been shot in the side.

Author's note: Yes you read that right! All morning, tensions had been building at the courthouse, and then at 2:45 p.m. Tom Gillispie, a black farmer from around Athens, went into the Athens Water Company building—which was serving as the eleventh precinct to vote—it is not clear which of Cantrell's men positioned themselves behind Gillispie to observe his vote, but when he was observed to be preparing to vote the wrong way, the Cantrell man told Gillispie, "you have to get out of here, you're voting in the wrong precinct!" Gillispie protested to Deputy Wendy Wise, "I've always voted here before!" For this monumental impertinence, Wise slugged Gillispie with brass knuckles, and shot him with what was said to be a U.S.

Army .45 as he stumbled out the door. Gillispie suffered a flesh wound in the small of his back, and was taken off by deputy sheriffs for what they said would be treatment. Just to show that the racial question didn't enter into this travesty of an election; the deputies directed their attention to the GI election clerks and women who were witnessing the count. Apparently, their presence was embarrassing to the potential election thieves. Election judge and deputy sheriff Carl Neil, pistol on his hip, ordered Mrs. H. A. Vestel and five other women to lead the polls. "Get out!" said Neil. The women stood their ground, "we have a right to watch you count the ballots!" "Go on, get out of here!" shouted Neil, and the women filed out, protesting. This wasn't enough, four GIs remained to keep the ballot thieves in line. The Cantrell machine had six of its bigger muscled boys there, three wearing side arms. Deputy Neil then ordered Cartwright and Hyde, the GI judges, to go up into the front and sit down. They said they couldn't see the count from there. "Go on up front and sit down, you don't have to see us count. "The GI judge said he wouldn't stay if he couldn't witness the counts, so he and his buddy left. This left Vestel and Scott as the only GI watchers for precinct eleven. When Cartwright and Hyde emerged, a roar of anger went up from the hundreds of citizens across the street. The eight or nine deputies in front of the waterworks office fingered their weapons. Charles Scott, Sr. sent word in to his son to come on out, he didn't want his boy alone in there with those gangsters. At 3:15, GI judge Bob Harrow was beaten. Bob Harrow—GI judge—beaten by Mennis Wilburn, officer of the election, twelfth precinct, North, White Street, Athens. The first poll was closed illegally. Again the reporter did his job. This is what he said.

LARK: "When the government went back to the precinct of the courthouse, I walked in just before the polls closed. A large group of church women walked up to the door. One of the ladies requested me to ask the armed election official if he would watch the counting of the ballots. His answer was to wait until it was time to close the polls and see. A second later, a policeman standing at the door slammed at my face with these words: "The polls are closed." The door was locked. Just a short time before, the GI judge, Bob Harrow, was beaten with a blackjack by a deputy at one of the precincts. At 4:45, just one hour before our first scheduled broadcast, two GI watchers, Carl Scott Jr. and Ed Vestel, crashed through the plate glass of the precinct where they were held virtually as prisoners."

Author's note: They closed the precinct before the time was due. At 3:55 p.m. the time of the first closing of the twelfth precinct, in the back of the Dixie Cafe and next to the county jail, the legal closing time was 4:00 p.m. The door was locked and Sheriff Manfields's men lifted an automobile to the sidewalk and placed it directly in front of the precinct door. Two other cars were placed across the narrow alley to block the entrance of the voting area, and sheriff deputies, hands on their pistols, guarded the area. Fifteen minutes later, while GIs watched with a scowl, Sheriff Mansfield and a dozen of his deputies piled into two cars and drove off to the eleventh precinct, at the water commission office. There, deputies with guns ready kept all observers away from the sidewalk in front of the office, and a throng of several hundred watched silently from the street. The votes were being counted.

Inside at 4:20 p.m. according to stories told to GIs later, Carl Scott Jr. and James Howard Vestel, watchers for the GI ticket, were ordered to take seats in front of the room, while the vote was being counted by Cantrell men in the rear of the room. Vestel and Scott demanded that they either be permitted to see the ballots, or be allowed to leave the area. The sheriff's men refused, and ordered them to sit down—"you're staying right here!" They sat down. A few minutes later, Scott told the machine politicians again that they were leaving. At this, the machine men barricaded the ex-GIs behind the counter, and locked the door.

"We jumped on the counter, climbed over it, and tried to get out. The door was locked," Vestel said. Charlie hit it with his shoulder. "They were right at us, and trying to slug us with knuckles and their guns. The glass broke, and we stumbled through." Charlie was cut around his shoulders, and fell down coming through the door. The door was a plate glass, set in a wood frame. Over a thousand people witnessed a sickening sight. Vestel, who was until January this year, a 1st Lieutenant in the Army Engineer Corps, and twice wounded in the Pacific, scrambled to his feet, blood dripping from a gash in his left hand,. Scott, too, picked himself up, through the broken glass, and got immediately on their heels. Sheriff Deputy Wendy Wise, holding a shiny .38 revolver, shouted something that was lost in the moan. A shout went through the crowd, "oh God, here it comes!" From the sidewalk came gasps, then cries, "let's go get 'em!"

"No, we got no guns, stay away from them .45s!"

A bit of military wisdom from within the crowd.

Vestel and Scott, whether heeding orders or through quick instinct, threw their hands slowly above their heads and walked slowly and alone across the empty street, to the refuge of the crowd. Wise leveled his revolver at their backs, then whirled with the instinct of the gunman to one side, then the other to ensure against a potshot against himself from the crowd, then aimed again at the backs of the veterans. George Sperling, another deputy, popped up at Wise's side and slowly brought his pistol down at the direction of the retreating boys, either aiming at them or some of the jeering GIs on the sidewalk to which they were going. He and Wise, for a few seconds, gave every appearance of being trigger happy. It seemed to us, standing just across the street, that Sperling was in the act of pressing his trigger when another deputy half-grabbed his arm, gave him a half-dozen swift slaps in the ribs as a signal not to fire. Vestel and Scott had completed their long, measured march. Their GI comrades, boiling mad by now, cried to Wise and the other deputies, "throw down your guns, and come out in the street, and we'll fight you man for man!"

One man had been shot in the back, women have been told to leave, and some of the GI judges, under gunpoint, escaped.

Now back to the original reporting:

LARK: "A second later, policemen standing at the door slammed at my face with these words: "The polls are closed." The door was locked. Just a short time before, a GI judge, Bob Harrow, was beaten with a blackjack by a deputy at one of the precincts. At 4:45, just one hour before our first scheduled broadcast, two GI watchers, Carl Scott Jr. and Ed Vestel, crashed through the plate glass of the precinct where they were held virtually as prisoners. Sheriff Mansfield and his deputies arrived on the scene. The ballot box was taken from the precinct to the jail. Enraged citizens stepped forward as they might attempt to take the ballot box from the deputies. Fifteen armed officers pulled their pistols, and the motions stopped. The lead on our first broadcast was, quote, "The political powder keg of East Tennessee has exploded in balance, and violence has broken out here in Athens."

RANDY: One of the GI judges was treated in a physician's office. He had two stitches to close the gash in his ankle, and he had also suffered from a cut hand. He was a 1st Lieutenant, and a 3rd Combat Engineer, 24th Division. He was overseas 30 months, was hit by a hand grenade once and wounded by artillery fire once. "How did today compare to fighting overseas?" he was asked. Well, he was quiet for a moment, and said, "Well, today, it made you madder than it did over there, and it was closer range."

Later, at 5:10 p.m. W.O. Kennedy, the election commissioner, and a crowd of veterans, walked to Kennedy's garage and tire shop near the center of town. Two deputies, with badges and side arms, walked towards the crowd. This was a mistake, as this was most assuredly seen in the abstract as a representation of a decade of tyranny and oppression of the despotic government, the Cantrell political machine. The crowd was quickly inflamed by the arrogance of the two deputies and suddenly, there were yells of, "Kill them! Kill them!" were sounding in the streets. The deputies drew their pistols, ready to shoot down anyone who came near. It's the trained and instinctive nature of veterans of war to react offensively at such an offensive act committed by deputies. Otto Kennedy and his civilian task force accepted the challenge. They rushed across the street, and overwhelmed the two deputies before the pair could choose a target for their fire. Kennedy, his two brothers, and other furious veterans attacked the deputies with a proper assault and battery across their faces and ripping their clothes. The crowds packing the main square heard of an impending attack by the sheriff's force, and rushed to assume the best view.

Cries of, "here they come!" sent the onlookers scattering for shelter, but the garage garrison stood firm, awaiting the assault. When no more gunmen appeared, after five minutes, the crowd came out from behind the hedges, homes, and parked cars. By now, there were literally thousands of people, mostly men, strung along a three block area. They were frightened people, and people who were ashamed of their town's politics. But something in the attitude of these embattled veterans held them up.

The veterans waited. The mob huddled back against the store as soon as the shot came. Another thunderous warning, "here they come!" entered the streets. It was an anti-climax. There was no onrush of deputies. Only two deputies appeared. They had guns, of course, but the group at the garage had two guns now. Kennedy's rangers made short work of them as they had the first two. The second pair was marched into the garage to join the first pair. The Chattanooga Times reported that Richard Rogers attempted to mingle among the crowd when he was spotted as an unrecognizable intruder by a veteran, and that veteran challenged him for his business for being there. The reporter identified himself and was promptly escorted into the garage where the captured deputies were. In any act of revolt, there is the human nature to extract the same kind of punishment upon the tyrannical opponents that had been inflicted upon the city. The veteran guards, over the four deputies, and using intimidation and humiliation tactics common in any war, goaded any one or all the deputies to attempt anything to give justification in the veterans' desire to shoot them, saying, "go ahead, you sons of bitches, I'd like to fucking kill one of you." (I want to apologize for the language, but that was a direct quote!)

The reporters escort pushed them closer to the deputies, quite possibly to give the opportunity to interview the prisoners, saying to the deputies, "Here's a reporter." This interview arrangement was interrupted by another alarm outside, "here they come!" The reporter's escort spun around, and ran outside again. One guard ran after him—this left the four deputies with one veteran guard and the reporter. The lone guard threatened the prisoner, saying, "If those guys get in here and get mad at me, I'll kill you first." Another yell bellowed from the street. A veteran stuck his head through a door and shouted, "Watch out! They're going to rush us!" The reporter ducked down behind the stack of tires. Just then, there came the loudest, most frightening, skin-crawling roar of voices those people could emit. The reporter saw the lone guard waving one gun in his direction, and upon seeing its muzzle, compared it to the size of Chattanooga's Brainerd Tunnel, he jumped through the window which was behind him and the stack of tires.

Now out on the street the reporter had seen that the crowd had grown and saw one carrying a 12-gauge shotgun and another had a repeating rifle. Unexpectedly, three deputies appeared on the street. Two were overcome immediately. The third was overpowered by Otto Kennedy, throwing himself upon the larger man, shoved his own .45 against the fellow's face and the fight went out of the deputy. That was the last capture of the engagement.

The crowd remained in the streets. The veterans pleaded for volunteers to haul the deputies out of town, and one by one, citizens came forward with automobiles.

One of these was an aged gentleman who operates a hardware store in Athens… He introduced himself as Emmett Johnson. "Do you live in Athens, sir?"

"I do, and today I'm ashamed of my home. These gangsters have disgraced us. If the boys want my car, they can have it. They can have anything. They should have started cleaning up on those crooks a long time ago." As the deputies lives were in grave danger they were put into cars and driven out of town. Then the crowd was told to scatter. The crowd reluctantly dispersed.

W. O. Kennedy agreed to an interview with the Chattanooga Times. Five of the Times staff drove a mile into the country to Kennedy's home. At the Kennedy home were Otto Kennedy introducing his brothers J.P. and C.O.; J.B. Adams, his son-in-law, and Frank McCracken.

Otto Kennedy revealed the deputies were out-of-towners. One of the captured deputies claimed he got arrested that morning on a traffic charge and instead of paying the fine they made him a deputy and gave him a gun.

RANDY: "I don't believe that deputy, do you?"

By 6:35 p.m. The sheriff's men, assisted by state highway patrolmen and city policemen removed the automobile from in front of Precinct 12 and carried the ballot box into the McMinn County Bastille, where presumably, Ellis and several other GIs still were being held incommunicado. As the sheriff's men carried the box across the jailhouse lawn, they were preceded by two men armed with shotguns and followed by four more equipped with heavy-gauge shotguns and high-powered rifles. Apparently pistols, of which several hundred were on display, were no longer considered to handle the occasion. As the sun began to set, the GIs began converging on the jail. A crowd of about 500 armed with pistols and light rifles moved in on the courthouse.

Now back to the reporters!

LARK: At 7:30 p.m. the GIs began gathering at their headquarters. Fifteen minutes later, they marched on the jail and demanded the return of the ballot box the deputies took from the reporting precinct. Our second broadcast at 8:30 ended, "a crowd is converging on the county jail at this time, but no violence has been reported. Everyone here acts as if they were waiting for a time bomb to explode. That may happen. All women have just been ordered off the streets." The sheriff refused to hand over the ballot box to the GIs, and the firing on the jail started ten minutes after nine. It lasted for about six hours, when the deputies surrendered the jail. But, here's Allen Stout to tell you about the conditions under which he worked to give you one of the most vivid broadcasts heard in a long, long time:

STOUT: Yes, Frank, it might be well to explain the conditions under which we are broadcasting. As you stated, we were set up in the headquarters of the then-powerful political machine of Paul Cantrell. In view of the fact we had gained those facilities, by promising not to editorialize, or attempt to analyze the news from Athens, but just report the facts, we naturally felt it behooved us to stand by that promise, not only from the standpoint of integrity, but also from the standpoint of personal safety. We had done three reports from our location, prior to the start of the shooting, each time making sure to report only fact with no comment on our part as to what we might think about the general Athens situation. Then, shortly after 9 p.m. Athens time, the action began. It seemed as if the whole world had suddenly exploded. A barrage of gunfire that was not only startling, but terrifying, broke the silence of that August 1st night. We did not know at the time of the attack, therefore, we assumed it was gunfire in the streets between the deputies and the GIs. Immediately, we turned out the light, and got on the floor behind the brick wall, and started broadcasting the noise and a brief description of the activities. In view of the fact the gunfire seemed to only be a few feet from our window, we naturally did not want to give our location away, so all the description was done in a hushed voice. After all, a stray bullet is just as deadly as an accurately aimed one if it hits you. And as feelings were running high between both sides, we dared not antagonize any side with any comment we might make to the radio audience. So, from a crouched position on the floor, and later, from the straight back chair situated behind the brick wall, we proceeded to tell the Athens story. For approximately six hours, Frank Lark darted in and out of our broadcasting location to advise me of the activity, just outside in the inky blackness. At that time, our listeners heard something like this:

We take you to Allen Stout, somewhere in McMinn County. Come in, Allen.

STOUT: *hushed* Ladies and gentlemen, suddenly, a huddle of activity is taking place here. One of the loudest explosions we've heard since the firing started. *loud bang* There's another one. People are running, people are yelling, and we don't know what the activity is. But there has been sporadic firing (GUN FIRE!) There is another shot. It sounds very much like a grenade, or a small bomb. What it is—I don't know, (IT WAS DYNOMITE!) there are signals of activity beginning. You can hear the firing in the background. People are running, hurrying, and scurrying here and there, to find out just what it is, and there are several hundred people that are in the streets here at this hour of the morning. Of course, *loud bang* it is only fifteen minutes until 3 a.m. in Athens, in McMinn County.

RANDY: Hundreds of rounds of shots were exchanged between ex-GIs and an estimated 75 deputies barricaded in the McMinn County jail. By 3:00 a.m., August 2nd, the officers began filing out of the battered building.

They were searched, and roughly might I say, by the attackers and marched back into the building to be locked in cells under guard of the ex-GIs. When Wise came out, the crowd surged forward and mauled him with fists and elbows before he could be returned to comparative safety of the bullet scarred jail. Automobiles belonging to deputy sheriffs overturned in streets, smashed and burned. With the battle over, the veterans, armed with rifles, patrolled the streets to maintain order by sunrise.

By 7:05 in the morning, Frank Cantrell, who was the Mayor of Etowah (a nearby town), issued the following statement: "In behalf of my brother Paul Cantrell, I wish to concede the election to the G.I. candidates in order to prevent further shooting." At 10:00 a.m., the next morning, the GIs dispersed.

RANDY: I want to be sure and give special credit to Don Hamrick who wrote the information that I've been presenting to you.

There was another newspaper report from the Daily-Post Athenian, on August 7th, 1946, and it was a story by Mrs. Eleanor Roosevelt, and the title was:

McMinn: A Warning.

Mrs. Roosevelt quoted in the article, "After any war, the use of force throughout the world is almost taken for granted. Men involved in the war have been trained to use force, and they have discovered that, when you want something, you can take it. The return to peacetime methods governed by law and persuasion is usually difficult".

We in the U.S.A., who have long boasted that, in our political life, freedom in the use of the secret ballot made it possible for us to register the will of the people without the use of force, have had a rude awakening as we read of conditions in McMinn County, Tennessee, which brought about the use of force in the recent primary. If a political machine does not allow the people free expression, then freedom-loving people lose their faith in the machinery under which their government functions.

In this particular case, a group of young veterans organized to oust the local machine and elect their own slate in the primary. We may deplore the use of force but we must also recognize the lesson which this incident points for us all. When the majority of the people know what they want, they will obtain it.

When the people decide that conditions in their town, county, state or country must change, they will change them. If the leadership has been wise, they will be able to do it peacefully through a secret ballot which is honestly counted, but if the leader has become inflated and too sure of his own importance, he may bring about the kind of action which was taken in Tennessee.

If we want to continue to be a mature people who, at home and abroad, settle our difficulties peacefully and not through the use of force, then we will take to heart this lesson and we will jealously guard our rights. What goes on before an election, the threats or persuasion by political leaders may be bad but it cannot prevent the people from really registering their will if they wish to.

The decisive action which has just occurred in our midst is a warning, and one which we cannot afford to overlook."

Two weeks later, after that report in the Daily-Post Athenian, an article was written by John Peck. And he was talking about Abraham Lincoln. And Lincoln, in this article, says "The government, with its institutions, belongs to the people who inhabit it. Whenever they shall grow weary of the existing government, they can exercise their constitutional right of amending it, or their revolutionary right to dismember or overthrow it."

What Lincoln meant was just this: The government of any group of people is in the hands of the people and they must carry on an active part in maintaining their government unless they want to abide by the rule of a few unscrupulous persons who find ways and means of getting the reins of power in governmental offices. If the people as a whole do not maintain a vigilant watch over matters of government a few people, grasping for power and domination find it easy to undermine all the principles of democracy.

The people who are elected must have the knowledge that they have the backing of all the people in their community when they go to the various meetings of the Board of Directors and vote on the matters of government that come before that body.

You know, the choice is in our hands. If we take an active part in our government, and do our duty and privilege as citizens, the next time we find that our government has fallen into the hands of unscrupulous politicians, we won't have to say, "It's my fault." But if you don't vote, or you don't participate, maybe you'll have to say, "It's my own fault, I had a chance to do something about it, but slept through it."

Becoming involved with the Veterans from World War II has been an honor for me, and meeting their families and seeing the pride in their faces proved to me that the people, these children of the Depression were truly made of a fiber we seldom see in today's world events.

You have been reading about The Veteran Next Door, My name is Randy Baxter, and I hope you enjoyed this book.

CHAPTER FOURTEEN

EPILOGUE

In choosing which people and their lives to present to you in this book, there were so many I could have introduced to you. Paratroopers from Operation Market Garden, submariners, PT Boat operators, Ninth Air Force P-51 fighters, submarine hunters off the coast of the United States, Sherman Tank drivers, medics, landing craft operators, tail gunners, reporters and even people like my mother who worked at Oak Ridge, Tennessee. There are the brothers I became aware of who were both at Peilelui, and only one came home. Most of the people I have interviewed for this book are no longer with us. The others are struggling with the frailties of age.

I could have included the gentle man who would become my daughter's grandfather, I know he loved her so much. Our assisted living communities and nursing homes are filled with these warriors and their spouses. Our cemeteries are swelling from the new additions daily of the surviving heroes from another age. Those that remain want to share their stories, with their loved ones and the public who care enough to want to know. Recently a soldier from the 309th Division of the 78th Infantry contacted me and wanted to sing a few songs for me. His frost bite wounds from 1944 were giving him some trouble. But he wanted to sing for me. A few years ago a man from Lenoir City was a Trust Client. He was nearly blind from old age in his eyes. He was a troop transport driver in Kwajelein, He delivered marines to the island and when he would return with reinforcements, the marines he originally left had been killed. When he returned, he married and forgot the war. His sister was 20 years younger than he, and all she knew until he was an old man was that Brother had gone off to war. He operated a 30 caliber machine gun on the front of his landing craft.

The same things are true about Korea, FOX Company at Chosin reservoir, the spy missions, and the experiences of our prisoners of war in that "police action".

And then there are our Vietnam heroes, who are owed an apology from this nation. It was our inability to separate an unpopular war from those we sent to fight it.

Our soldiers in Iraq and Afghanistan have carried our freedoms to foreign shores once more. For now they will have service related disabilities and issues of returning home. In years to come there will be non-service related disabilities in which we have promised to consider and to provide benefits in the future.

We need to be aware we are still paying the costs of World War II, and we have many promises to keep. I wanted to share with you a broad spectrum of people affected by World War II.

We are all affected in some way.

I left the Generals and Admirals out of the choices because this was not to be a war novel or a history of great battles, and struggles. The battles and struggles of WW II are different now, but still going on.

Maybe you will learn of my friends we discussed above in Volume Two of THE VETERAN NEXT DOOR. Let me know what you think using the information on the next page.

THE END (But probably not)

US MILITARY PERSONNEL (1939-1945)

Year	Army	Navy	Marines	Coast Guard	Total
1939	189,839	125,202	19,432		334,473
1940	269,023	160,997	28,345		458,365
1941	1,462,315	284,427	54,359		1,801,101
1942	3,075,608	640,570	142,613	56,716*	3,915,507
1943	6,994,472	1,741,750	308,523	151,167	9,195,912
1944	7,994,750	2,981,365	475,604	171,749	11,623,468
1945	8,267,958	3,380,817	474,680	85,783	12,209,238

Coast Guard listed only as wartime strength

PROFILE OF US SERVICEMEN (1941-1945)

- 38.8% (6,332,000) of U.S. servicemen and all servicewomen were volunteers
- 61.2% (11,535,000) were draftees
- Average duration of service: 33 months
- Overseas service: 73% served overseas, with an average of 16 months abroad
- Combat survivability (out of 1,000): 8.6 were killed in action, 3 died from other causes, and 17.7 received non-fatal combat wounds
- Non-combat jobs: 38.8% of enlisted personnel had rear echelon assignments—administrative, support, or manual labor.
- Average base pay: enlisted—$71.33 per month; officer—$203.50 per month

MINORITY PARTICIPATION IN THE MILITARY

African American	901,896
Puerto Rican	51,438*
Japanese American	33,000
American Indian	20,000
Chinese American	13,311
Filipino American	11,506
Hawaiian	1,320

Full Latino numbers are not known because Latinos, other than Puerto Ricans, did not serve in segregated units, like African Americans.

WOMEN IN THE US MILITARY

Women's Army Corps (WAC)	150,000
Navy's Women Accepted for Voluntary Emergency Service (WAVES)	100,000
Coast Guard Women's Reserves (SPARS)	10,000
Marine Corps Women's Reserve	23,000
Army Nurse Corps	60,000
Navy Nurse Corps	14,000
Women's Airforce Service Pilots (WASP)	1,074

US MILITARY CASUALTIES IN WORLD WAR II

Branch	Killed	Wounded
Army and Air Force	318,274	565,861
Navy	62,614	37,778
Marines	24,511	68,207
Coast Guard	1,917	Unknown
TOTAL	407,316	671,278

MERCHANT MARINE CASUALTIES

Died as POWs	37
Dead	5,662
Missing/Presumed Dead	4,780
Killed at Sea	845

INVITATION TO SHARE REACTIONS

I hope you enjoyed the Veteran Next Door Stories From World War II Vol. 1, 1939-1946. I would like for you to share some of your reactions to the stories in this book.

You can contact me by email: randallbaxter@randallbaxter.com or at support@randallbaxter.com

Or you can write me at THE VETERAN NEXT DOOR RADIO PROGRAM at 5520 Crestwood Drive Knoxville, Tennessee 37914.

I have a fax number: 865-321-8384
An office phone: 865-525-2323

My website is www.theveterannextdoor.com

You can order signed copies of this book on my website or in any of the others methods above.

Let me know what you think. Have something to add? Or even a correction if you see a need.

I would love to know what you are thinking.

In fact, it's very important that I hear from you.

The greatest treasure that all Americans share is our Freedom. The veterans that paid for our Freedom are now needing our assistance. The new improved Pension Benefit is a little known program that allows our Vets to age in dignity and honor and be able to help pay for their Cost of Care. This pension can mean the difference between receiving the care they need or doing without. If you know of any veteran in need of assistance please contact your local U.S.S.V Volunteer Veteran Advocate, or use the information at the top of this page.

D-Day, Omaha Beach, Normandy, 38th Parallel, Sabre Jets, Tet of '68, these are all reminders that there is a vast assemblage of people in our society that worked to maintain our quality of life in the United States- now it is our turn to help them as payment for their sacrifices that they made in our behalf.

WHO IS RANDALL BAXTER?

My name is Randall Baxter, I am a successful sales coach and estate planner, and I also hosted The Veteran Next Door, a radio show for six years. You can hear pod casts of my show at www.theveterannextdoor.com.

I am not a veteran myself but I take a keen interest in veterans' affairs. I explain my fascination with the cause in my poem "I Never Was a Soldier," one of several pieces of poetry that has been a part of my radio show, The Veteran Next Door.

Our Mission

The Veteran Next Door's mission is to locate, communicate with and entertain Active Military Personnel and Veterans of all Services. We encourage open communication to those leaders and all veterans as we create an open forum among all veterans to communicate between Veterans and non-veterans

FOR THOSE WHOSE STORY
THAT MAY NEVER BE TOLD,
KNOW THAT YOU ARE
NEVER FORGOTTEN.

www.ingramcontent.com/pod-product-compliance
Lightning Source LLC
Chambersburg PA
CBHW071715120626
46550CB00001B/240